FOOTSTEPS INTO THE FUTURE

PREFERRED WORLDS FOR THE 1990's

Saul H. Mendlovitz, General Editor

On the Creation of a Just World Order: Preferred Worlds for the 1990's
edited by Saul H. Mendlovitz

Footsteps into the Future: Diagnosis of the Present World and a Design for an Alternative
Rajni Kothari

A World Federation of Cultures: An African Perspective
Ali A. Mazrui

A Study of Future Worlds
Richard A. Falk

The True Worlds: A Transnational Perspective
Johan Galtung

A program of the World Order Models Project.
Sponsored by The Institute for World Order, Inc.
New York, New York

FOOTSTEPS INTO THE FUTURE

Diagnosis of the Present World and a Design for an Alternative

Rajni Kothari

THE FREE PRESS
A Division of Macmillan Publishing Co., Inc.
NEW YORK

The Free Press
A Division of Macmillan Publishing Co., Inc.
866 Third Avenue, New York, N.Y. 10022

Collier–Macmillan Canada Ltd.

Library of Congress Catalog Card Number: 74–31357

Printed in the United States of America

printing number
1   2   3   4   5   6   7   8   9   10

Library of Congress Cataloging in Publication Data

Kothari, Rajni.
    Footsteps into the future.

    Includes index.
    1. Regionalism (International organization)   2. International organization.   3.   Underdeveloped areas.
I.   Title.
JX1979.K68   1975   341.2   74-31357
ISBN 0-02-917570-4
ISBN 0-02-917580-1 pbk.

The publication of this volume has been made possible by collaboration among the following publishers:

The Free Press
A Division of Macmillan Publishing Co., Inc.
New York, N. Y.

Ghana Publishing Corporation
Accra, Ghana

North-Holland Publishing Company
Amsterdam, The Netherlands

Orient Longman Limited
New Delhi, India

DEDICATION

The value of autonomy and the struggle to achieve it under conditions that violate it for a large part of the human race are central themes in this book. It also offers a perspective on building a viable structure of interdependence in the world and as means to that end, strategies for regional cooperation and a pooling of efforts and resources at various levels.

Jawaharlal Nehru's life and work were devoted to these very tasks: a struggle for the autonomy of two-thirds of humanity and, simultaneously, an effort to promote an enduring structure of peace and justice in the world. He also strove to promote regional cooperation as a basis for a more equal and in course of time a more united world. He did not quite succeed in his efforts, given the overwhelming forces at work against the values for which he stood, some of which he failed to fully perceive. But his was a mammoth effort. And he left behind a strong current of thought.

Since the passing away of Nehru, Julius Nyerere has held the torch of autonomy in a world still more subject to domination and inequity than in Nehru's time, and has striven to promote both regional and interregional solidarity in the Third World. Nyerere's, like Nehru's, is a voice of sanity in a world that has lost its moorings. And he too is struggling against heavy odds.

It is to these two stalwarts of the Third World that this book is dedicated.

CONTENTS

EDITOR'S INTRODUCTION

SCHOLARS and intellectuals need to interpret and come to grips with the crises plaguing the contemporary global political and social system. Indeed their obligation to do so may be a particularly special and important one. They are, or are supposed to be, able to discern trends, detect signals warning us of emerging social problems, think seriously and critically about alternative solutions and possible future worlds, as well as recommend strategies for achieving those solutions and worlds. One would think that this somewhat crucial albeit relatively precious sector of the world's population, more than others, is capable of avoiding too firm an anchor in the particulars of what is. 'Reality' may, for a number of reasons, constrain and overwhelm the thinking and imagination of those who have to struggle for daily existence. But surely professional thinkers and analysts have a mandate to look beyond the obvious and the immediate, and to see the possibilities open for reform and improvement.

For reasons that I suspect are familiar to most of us, social scientists are yet to adequately meet this challenge. There is initially the bias in the social sciences against work that explicitly utilizes preferences and values as a way of defining problems to be investigated, and as a standard to be used for what will be considered as adequate solutions. Research that deviates from the confines of a perspective that is viewed by its adherents as empirical and scientific is either dismissed as ideological or as being an exercise in wishful thinking. In this view, description is a proper social science concern, while prescription is not. Second, the same tradition's narrow sense of realism and empiricism operates quite decisively to inhibit futuristic thinking and orientation. If one wants maximum certainty and minimum speculation, concern with what prevails is preferable to what might or will be. If some social scientists manage to get over their reluctance to engage in futuristic thinking, their work generally confines itself to relatively simple extrapolations of current trends. The future then becomes a mere extension of the present, as though humanity has little or no ability to shape the future in preferred directions.

Two additional factors are also to blame for the lack of creative thinking about the contemporary world system and its major crises as well as about alternative systems more compatible with a humane and just world order. The crises are global in scope, yet most social scientists who pay attention to them are wedded to an analysis in which the nation-state system informs their definitions and solutions to global problems. At the same time it is becoming increasingly clear that most of the major problems confronting humankind defy national solutions and perspectives, and are generally aggravated if not directly caused by the imperatives of national sovereignty.

Finally, creative thinking about the globe, its crises, and future is hindered by an element which is inherent in the nature of social knowledge itself and the extent to which it is culture-bound and geographically circumscribed. Even the most sympathetic and globally-minded scholar can only perceive the world from a particular angle and perspective; his (or her) roots in a particular nation, race, or class help determine and shape the choice of problems and the proposed remedies to them. Certain cultural assumptions, values and concerns may sensitize a person to some problem at the same time that they cause the individual to neglect a number of different problems that other people in other places deem important. Or, the same global problem or phenomenon is frequently interpreted in different ways by observers from different cultures. Given the global dimensions of our major world order concerns, these truisms of the sociology of knowledge recommend in favour of transnational and cross-cultural perspectives being brought to bear upon the questions and problems that concern us. In short, it speaks against ethnocentric knowledge and research. While this point has long been well known, there has been much too little social science research carried out in this fashion. The work of other scholars may be available, but collaborative research across cultures and worldviews is yet to be widely practised.

Footsteps into the Future is one manuscript in the series of volumes entitled *Preferred Worlds for the 1990's* which is a result of a transnational research enterprise, the World Order Models Project. Because the World Order Models Project (WOMP) is likely to be the forerunner of many more such transnational and global enterprises, it seems appropriate to say something about its genesis, development and future.

WOMP was initially conceived in response to pedagogical needs related to the study of the problem of the elimination of war as a human social institution. The individuals involved at the outset of this programme brought to it a seriousness one associates with those individuals and groups who between the 18th and 19th centuries advocated and participated in the global movement to abolish slavery, or with those persons in this century who have been participating in the dismemberment of colonialism and imperialism.

To put the matter forthrightly, it was a conscious political act, based on a theory of social change which reasoned that most individuals on the globe, including political leadership, were encapsulated in a view of the world in which war, while perhaps unfortunate, was a necessary and permanent ingredient of human society. Thus the decision to enlist the energies of educational structures throughout the globe was partially based on the notion that the seriousness of the idea might be legitimated if the academic community throughout the world were to give it the status of a subject matter of discipline, or at least admit it was the kind of social problem which was amenable to rational analysis. Concomitantly, and certainly as important as legitimation, was the possibility of enlisting the talent and skills of the academic community in the research and education necessary for a successful global peace movement.

And so it was in 1966 we began to examine how to enroll volunteers so that our educational effort would get serious attention by scholars and educators throughout the globe. WOMP emerged as an answer.

The notion which we began to pursue was that if we were to get outstanding scholars as well as thoughtful individuals throughout the globe to become involved in the problem of war prevention, it would be necessary that they contribute actively in the inquiry. We decided to invite groups of scholars in various parts of the world to direct nationally or regionally based inquiries into the problem of war prevention. We did not proceed very far in our recruitment of individuals for the project when it soon became clear that the subject matter would have to be expanded to include the related problems of economic well-being and social justice, if we were to generate a world interest in this inquiry.

There were two reasons advanced for the inclusion of these problem areas. To begin with, there were many persons who argued that it was impossible to deal adequately with war prevention without taking into account poverty and social injustice. Empirically, poverty and social injustice are frequently so inextricably interwoven or casually related to the outbreak of international violence that they should be seen as part of the framework for defining the problem of war prevention. More importantly, however, it became increasingly clear that while peace, in the sense of the elimination of international violence, might have a very high priority with individuals in the industrialized sector of the globe, economic well-being and social justice received a much higher rating in the Third World. When we discussed these three problems, war, poverty and social injustice, as they persisted in national, regional and global contexts, and proposed examining them in the light of the next three decades, with particular reference to realizing the countervailing values of peace, economic well-being and social justice, virtually all the scholars we approached agreed to participate in the project.

We held the first meeting of the World Order Models Project in New Delhi in February 1968. At that time five research groups had been organized, representing Western Europe, Latin America, Japan, India and North America. Groups representing Africa, the Soviet Union, and some Scandinavian scholars who preferred to present a non-territorial perspective, joined in subsequent years. More recently we benefited from the involvement in the project of a Chinese as well as a Middle Eastern scholar. One meeting was held with a group of economists organized by Jagdish Bhagwati of M.I.T. This resulted in the first WOMP book, *Economics and World Order, From the 1970's to the 1990's* (MacMillan, 1972; Orient Longman, 1973) . A second book, *Africa and World Affairs* (The Third Press, 1973), edited by Ali Mazrui and Hasu Patel, resulted from a conference organized by the African research group. Altogether some nine meetings have been held in various parts of the world: India, Japan, East Africa, Western Europe, United States and Latin America.

The results of this nearly seven years of individual and collaborative work are only partially represented by this and the other WOMP volumes. We set out to create the basic instructional materials needed for a world-wide educational movement whose ultimate thrust would be global reform. No one is more aware than we are of how many more and different materials still need to be created and disseminated. We set out to do normative social research that was at one and the same time oriented to the future, interdisciplinary, and focussed on the design for social change: actions, policies, and institutions. No one realizes more than the WOMP research groups how difficult it is to do this task with competence, combined with true imagination and intellectual power.

The project has fundamentally affected the personal and professional commitments of virtually everyone who participated in it. It is fair to say that what started out for almost all the participants as a short term and secondary interest has now become a lifetime scholarly and political vocation. At a meeting of the Directors of the World Order Models Project in Bogota, Colombia, over the New Year's period in 1974, the group decided to collaborate on a series of enterprises which they hope will continue to promote research, education and a genuinely transnational social movement to realize the world order values of peace, economic well-being, social justice and ecological stability. The first of these ventures will be a transnational journal, *Alternatives*, of which Rajni Kothari will be Editor, with a distinguished Editorial Board of some two dozen scholars throughout the globe.

Secondly, a number of the individuals associated with WOMP have assumed the responsibility for issuing an annual State of the Globe Message. This Message will attempt to evaluate local, regional and global trends, rating the extent to which the world order values have been diminished or realized during the preceding year, and making recommendations as to what ought to be done in the coming years. The State of the Globe Message, issued by a group of transnational scholars independent of any formal structures of authority, should be seen as complementary to the messages which are now coming from such formal sources.

Thirdly, we have embarked upon a modest but significant research programme for measuring world order indicators based on our values, which we hope will support the State of the Globe Message and provide alternative ways for social scientists to think about and measure the quality of social life. In addition, there will be a series of transnational seminars for scholars, public figures in all professions, expanded formal educational programming, and the beginning of a mass public education movement on a global basis. All of this programming has already begun in some form and we hope will involve constructive criticism, support and participation by many people throughout the globe.

The world order images and change strategies presented in these WOMP books are strikingly diverse, reflecting the different methods, intellectual styles, and cultural/political backgrounds of their authors. Although we were able to agree on a way of stating world order problems, and establish a framework of value criteria for what we considered to be appropriate solutions, as well as devise a common methodology, it certainly would be premature to attempt to provide a consensus statement for these various manuscripts. There were, however, a set of guidelines which were stated with some precision early in the project and which, despite repeated critical examination and elaboration, have remained essentially intact. It seems appropriate to summarize these guidelines so that the volumes might be read and evaluated in their proper context.

WOMP was not principally a utopian undertaking, despite our refusal to succumb either to a complacent or a doomsday view of reality. Where our thinking is utopian, it advances what we call *relevant utopias,* that is, world order systems that make clear not only alternative worlds but the necessary transition steps to these worlds. In fact, each author was asked to attempt a diagnosis of the contemporary world order system, make prognostic statements based on that diagnosis, state his *preferred future* world order and advance coherent and viable *strategies of transition* that could bring that future into being. A straight time-frame, the 1990's, served to discipline and focus thought and proposals.

While easy to list, this set of steps impose severe demands on methodological and creative capacity. It is probably fair to say that we discovered more methodological problems than we were able to solve to our satisfaction. Some of these problems are associated with how to do each of the steps, while others arise from trying to link different steps and to integrate the normative, descriptive and theoretical modes of thought. In the end, most of the WOMP research groups chose to adopt the more traditional analytic interpretive style of research, rather than the perhaps more methodologically sophisticated behavioural science approach. The reasons for this choice varied from outright rejection of the presumed conservative biases of strictly data-based methods, to pragmatic considerations of limited time and resources. In essence we decided it was more important at this time to prepare full world order statements involving an integrated treatment of all the steps, than it was to do a more rigorous investigation of only one or two of them.

While a full report on the methodological difficulties we faced shall have to await another occasion, it might be useful if I were to outline here the major problem areas and some questions that arose in the course of our investigation. Let me begin, however, by reiterating that we were able to agree that humanity faced four major problems: war, poverty, social injustice and environmental decay. We saw these as social problems because we had values—peace, economic well-being, social justice and environmental stability—which, no matter how vaguely operationalized, we knew were not being realized in the real world. Our task then was to develop an analytic frame of reference that would provide us intellectual tools for coming to grips with these problems so as to realize world order values.

There was also general agreement that we should go beyond the nation-state system, at least in terms of the traditional categories applied to it, namely the political, military, economic and ideological dimensions of foreign policy. Instead of asking how do states manipulate their foreign policies along these four dimensions, or even, how they might move the present system to a world order value system, there was general agreement that we would have to use a much broader range of potential actors, including world institutions, transnational actors, international organizations, regional arrangements, the nation-states, subnational movements, local communities and individuals. Even here, however, each of the groups placed different emphases, diagnostically, prognostically and preferentially, on the roles of this range of actors.

Secondly, far more effort than I anticipated was put into clarifying the values implied by these problems and into making some ordered agenda on them from which operational strategies or policies could be formulated. Among the points to emerge from these efforts are:

1. The crucial importance of developing global social indicators or operational definitions of value goals.

2. The difficulty and necessity of preparing a set of decision rules for dealing with value conflicts.

3. The need for a unified approach to these problem/value areas and for more data and theory on the interrelationships among them.

4. The extent to which one's personal position on the value questions influences every other aspect of the world order research process.

5. The importance of maintaining a tension between some operational notions of 'world interest' and the deeply-felt value agenda of one's particular social group and geographic region.

Thirdly, a number of issues not associated with standard empirical research emerged because of our emphasis on constructing preferred worlds. In this connection it should be noted that the term preferred world came to have a relatively rigorous meaning. Building on the concept of relevant utopia stated above, a preferred world is an image of a reformed world stated in fairly precise behavioural detail, including a description of the transition process from the present to the new system. Since it is possible to depict a range of reformed systems and transition paths, a preferred world is the relevant utopia selected by a proponent because it is most likely to realize his or her value goals. Each of these issues that arose in this context requires separate examination, conceptual and methodological advances, and the testing of a variety of integrated research strategies before we will really be able to move systematically through world order research to preferred world statements that meet rigorous tests of workability and feasibility. To illustrate:

1. What are appropriate criteria for evaluating workability and feasibility and what are the appropriate testing procedures for each?

2. Notions of time and time horizons are critical to both feasibility and workability, yet both are far more complicated than the simple notion of years and decades. Assumptions about time seem to play a critical role in one's optimism or pessimism about the possibility of fundamental change. Also time as a key variable is surprisingly easy to forget or discount when thinking about such things as value and attitude shifts, or reorientations in bureaucratic objectives and procedures.

3. Equally perplexing is the problem of adequately defining the relevant environment and its dynamics within which one's desired changes must take place. The tendency is to define the environment as the nation-state system itself, and to ascribe relatively little destabilizing or fundamental dynamics to it. As noted earlier, this can severely restrict creative thinking about alternative futures and transition processes. But it is not easy to come up with equally detailed and useful alternatives to the nation-state image, so rooted is it in our consciousness. To really examine this question is to open oneself to the most fundamental philosophical and methodological search.

4. On a more mundane level, the presentation of a preferred world in a way that is compelling and persuasive is far more difficult than it might appear. Like good fiction or poetry, utopia writing is an art attempted by many but achieved by few. It involves crucial choices of style and form. For example, how much and what kind of behavioural detail should be used to describe the workings of the preferred world? What are the differences between revolutionary and reformist rhetoric, and more importantly what bearing does this answer have on concrete strategies and programmes? How much attention is paid to immediate public issues and how are they made to relate to the preferred future to explicate the method and perspective of the author?

Finally, there were a set of issues which arose from my guideline that each of the groups be as explicit as possible about the kinds of authority structure and formal constitutive order of the world community that would be needed and preferred, both during the transition period, as well as at the end of this century. That is to say, there was a distinct weighting of institutional-constitutional issues and approaches in the original definition of our task.

I emphasized this approach despite the obvious dangers of formalism essentially for three reasons: first, an institutional approach requires a high degree of specificity and precision and focuses attention on procedures as well as principles; second, this approach leads readily to statements in the form of models with all that it implies for comparability across models and manipulation of parts within them; third, as a form of presentation, institutional models can be easily, even powerfully, communicated. In this connection I should like to formally acknowledge my debt to the book *World Peace Through World Law* (Harvard University Press, 1956, 1962, 1966) by Grenville Clark and Louis B. Sohn. My use of this book as an instructional model and as a source of research hypotheses leads me to conclude that many social scientists, as well as lay people, underestimate the extent to which formal constitutional models can lead to clarification of issues, and perhaps even more importantly become a mobilizing instrument for social and political action. I remain convinced of the value of this way of thinking about world order, but the extent to which this view has been resisted, revised and ignored by the WOMP groups will be apparent in these volumes.

Within this context, it should also be noted that the individual authors resolve the actors–levels–authority process questions differently. Some of the issues that surfaced during our discussions in this context included:

1. The extent to which an institutional or single actor-oriented conception of the world political system is useful either for understanding how the system is operating, how it might be made to change, or how it should operate. Such conceptions seemed to some to stultify imaginative thinking about alternatives and to mask important change potentials in the current system.

2. In thinking about transition, some argued for the primacy of the domestic factor, i.e., fundamental reform in national societies, particularly within the major countries, preceding global social change. Others argued for the primacy of the global agenda and the critical role of transnational functional and political movements and institutions. This debate identified two further issues needing more attention.

3. Which problems require policy making and review at what level of social organization, from the individual to the global? How much centralization and decentralization was appropriate in various substantive arenas? What are the relevant criteria for deciding the appropriate level or mix of levels?

4. What are and what might be the linkages between these levels for purposes of analysis, policy making and practical implementation?

Before concluding, I wish to state my own view as to the significance of these manuscripts. As I see it, it is necessary to accept seriously not only the rhetoric but the reality of the term 'the global village'. The fact that the overwhelming majority of humanity understands for the first time in history that human society encompasses the entire globe, is a phenomenon equivalent to humanity's understanding that the globe is round rather than flat. This knowledge is having an enormously dramatic impact on the images and attitudes we have with regard to the authority structures of the international community, as well as those of our domestic societies. I should like to state here a conclusion, for which I will not fully argue, but which I believe needs to be articulated for an understanding of the significant global political processes that are now taking place.

It is my considered judgement that there is no longer a question of whether or not there will be world government by the year 2000. As I see it, the questions we should be addressing ourselves to are: how will it come into being—by cataclysm, drift, or rational design—and whether it will be totalitarian, benign, or participatory (the probabilities being in that order).

Since the so-called age of discovery (a Eurocentric concept which sorely needs modification in this global community), three major historical processes, or if you will, revolutions, have propelled humanity towards global community, and now towards global governance. These processes are the ideological revolution of egalitarianism, the technological and scientific revolution and the closely allied economic-interdependence revolution. It might be noted in passing that of these three, the egalitarian revolution has been least appreciated in recent times, but in fact may account for much of the disorder, dislocation and social tensions throughout the globe.

These three processes or revolutions have converged in such a fashion that five problems have emerged and been identified as global in nature. War, poverty, social injustice, ecological instability and alienation (or the identity crisis) are recognized as having a global scope. Furthermore, it is now generally understood by policy elites and observers of world community processes generally that these problems are closely interrelated and that solutions in one area affect the other four areas.

In short I believe that global community has emerged and global governance is not far behind. To my mind, this book and the other volumes in the *Preferred Worlds for the 1990's* series is a contribution to the serious dialogue about what will be the normative basis and constitutive structure of the global community. Hopefully these volumes will contribute to creating the social processes needed for a peaceful and just world order.

SAUL H. MENDLOVITZ

SPECIAL ACKNOWLEDGMENT

The Institute for World Order would like to thank the Carnegie Endowment for International Peace and the Rockefeller Foundation for the financial support which they gave to specific research within the World Order Models Project.

PREFACE

FUTUROLOGY is fast taking on the trappings of a science. The present essay does not fall in that mould. It is more in line with the classical approach to man and his future—an analysis of the predicament of man and an attempt to evolve a social order through which the good in him is realized in cooperation with other men. The predictive model that has dominated the social sciences for so long provides only a partial view of the role of knowledge in society. A more workable approach to the future, under imperfect conditions, is to seek to create one that is better than the present. The predictive method itself becomes meaningful in this context: providing data regarding feasibility of proposed goals, testing assumptions underlying policy frames that work for or against stipulated goals, and enabling actors to make the right choices under uncertain conditions by delineating the likely consequences of alternative choices. But what is basic are the values that inform both goal setting and choice of policies. There is no future except what men make of it.

This is not a scholarly treatise. All it does is to raise some questions which I have found to be critical to the future of man and provide answers to them on lines that appear to me rewarding. Others are likely to have different views, guided by different perspectives. This is as it should be. In fact that is the whole point of the World Order Models Project, of which this monograph is one among several outcomes. As I have understood it, the purpose of the project was to enable different individuals, coming from various political and cultural regions of the world, to provide diverse analytical perspectives on the evolving future of man and suggest strategies based on these perspectives with a view to realizing certain basic values on which all were agreed. As work on the project has proceeded, many of the participating individuals have found it necessary to give somewhat different interpretations to agreed values, and conceive of some as more basic than others. This has happened to *Footsteps into the Future*. While focussing on justice and non-violence as necessary components of a preferred world, the basic value that informs them both in this essay is the autonomy and dignity of man, and, as a necessary condition thereof, the autonomy and dignity of states as well. I am aware that others, including those in the project, will not agree with this particular formulation of the value dimension in human striving.

My emphasis on the value of autonomy stems from my reading of the contemporary setting of the human predicament. It is a setting in which while more and more human beings live and work under a techno-logical and organizational nexus that is becoming worldwide, the world they live in is becoming increasingly dualistic—to no small extent, precisely because they are subject to 'universal' processes. For the structures through which these processes operate have promoted division, domina-tion, injustice and violence. Two-thirds of this world is still afflicted by poverty, is denied its due share in not only world resources but also the resources that are produced in their own regions, is therefore denied the bare minima of both individual and collective security, and is subject to organized exploitation and what is known as 'structural violence'. The other one-third is subject to opposite conditions—over-development, waste of world resources leading to their depletion and destruction, and an ethic of consumption and exploitation that threatens to bring cata-strophe on the planet as a whole. Common to these two worlds—which is also a cause of the sharp divisions between and within them—is an approach to human organization that is making man a burden on the planet, work a superfluity, and machine the most potent source of life.

While the dualism pervades in nearly all societies, what has given it an enduring structure is the inequitous relationship between the two industrialized worlds that are relatively stable and comfortable and the 'Third World' that is full of misery and turbulence. It is with the problems of this latter world, the strategies it must evolve in the face of their continued state of dependence despite formal independence, and the more recent determination in its ranks to undo this state of dependence that this essay is largely concerned.

We do not share the pessimism of the prophets of doom that abound in both the over-developed and the under-developed parts of the world. The reader will find a tone of optimism in this essay which may appear unreal in the light of the grim prospects facing man in large parts of the world as is also depicted in it. Our reason for this optimism is based, first, on faith that man is capable of overcoming the ills that beset him and, second, on evidence that the hitherto exploited and dominated part of humanity has already begun to fight for its autonomy and dignity and erode the structures of exploitation and manipulation. The Europe-centred world is fast coming to an end and its effort to erect a new structure of dominance is unlikely to succeed.

We believe that the shape of the future will depend on the success with which new centres of power emerge in the Third World. We have deliberately adhered to the concept of 'Third World', despite protests from many purists, for we do think that notwithstanding all the divisions in its ranks, this is a world that is beset by common problems, and is subject to similar patterns of dominance and manipulation. If the countries in that world are to overcome the conditions of inequity and dependence in which they are severally placed, they need to sort out their conflicts and animosities *inter se* and evolve common strategies between sets of them and in some respects all of them. Unless they stand together, they are likely to fall together. And in a basic way what they do will determine the shape of the world as a whole.

Though this is not a book on India—my work so far has been mainly on India—it does provide an Indian perspective (though by no means always agreeing with Indian official policies) on man and his future, and on world issues. It is a perspective—based on the twin postulates of the autonomy of all men and states and equality between them—that, in politics, was developed eloquently by Jawaharlal Nehru and, in social engineering and man's approach to nature and technology, by Gandhi. Nehru was before his time in stressing the notion of a world order based on the equality of all states, rejecting the concept of balance of power, rejecting also the division of the world between ideological camps, predicting the convergence of great powers but at the same time perceiving the constructive role of the Soviet Union in the progress towards a multi-centred world, and of China and India in giving to the countries of the Third World a sense of dignity and autonomy. Gandhi was before his time in pointing out the hazards of modern technology, propounding an approach to nature that was based on self-restraint in man, ridiculing the elitism of the middle classes, and asking for a halt to the incipient consumerism and the growing giganticism of both the state and the modern economy that are overtaking man and undermining his autonomy and dignity. These insights are crucial to the problems that face the world today. They provide the premise on which this essay is based.

Inevitably, in writing this final version of *Footsteps,* I have benefitted from a variety of sources. My greatest debt is to other participants in the Indian team whose contributions to the thinking on this project have been wide-ranging. In fact, although the present essay has been written by me and differs in very many ways from earlier drafts, my colleagues in the Indian team have greatly contributed to this final outcome of the project. Special mention should be made in this connection of B.S. Murty who brought into the project a variety of constructive suggestions dealing with the international context of world order, Ramashray Roy who not only took on the organizational burden of the project but also contributed a number of ideas on the methodology of relating domestic and world levels of world order, the late Pitambar Pant who sensitized us all to economic realities and saved us from proceeding on unworkable assumptions. Ashis Nandy who provided significant empirical analysis of the thinking of elites and emerging elites on the future of world order, and R.K. Srivastava for his expert handling of both field work* and documentation for the project. I am also thankful to D.L. Sheth for spending long hours with me discussing various issues dealt with in this essay and reading its various drafts and commenting on them. Satish Arora helped me better appreciate some of the issues dealt with here, especially the issue of participation in modern society. Above all, I am deeply indebted to two persons: the late Professor R. Bhaskaran, perhaps the most perceptive scholar sage that Indian political science has yet produced, who was the first director of the Indian team in the World Order Models Project but unfortunately did not live to see it through, and to Professor R.C. Patel who has all along inspired me with his spirit of free inquiry and his rare insights into the role of ideas in world changes. The latter also spared the time for a prolonged conference with the participants in the Indian project and wrote a comprehensive background paper on the problems dealt with in Chapter II, and later provided a detailed critique of an earlier draft of that chapter.

The project, which commenced with the first international meeting held in New Delhi in 1968, has had the benefit of a Sponsoring and Review Committee, headed by Dr. C.D. Deshmukh who has all along provided us with willing help and guidance. Other members of the Committee, notably Pitambar Pant, M.G.K. Menon, K.N. Raj, L.M. Singhvi, A. Appadorai and Narayan Menon, attended various meetings of the Committee and gave us the benefit of their mature thoughts on the various drafts. Ashok Guha wrote a background paper for the project and Mahendra Kumar, T.K. Mahadevan, Ian Baldwin, Johan Galtung, W. Warren Wagar and Jacob Needleman provided critiques of earlier drafts. R.D. Dikshit spent a good deal of his time to provide me with a sketch for the Appendix to the last chapter. Without his expert advice as a political geographer and a student of comparative federation, I would have been unable to write the Appendix in its present form. O.P. Garkhel has struggled with various stages of various drafts. Ava Khullar

---

*As part of this work we had interviewed a cross-section of fairly high level decision-making, oppositional and emerging elites in India, with a view to understand how those in positions of responsibility think on these matters. The results of this survey are being published elsewhere. I would like to record here our deep appreciation to the respondents of this study who not only gave generously of their time but were also frank and candid in sharing their views with us on fairly controversial issues. Most of them have preferred to remain anonymous.

provided her expert handling of them and corrected many a slip. Both gave me unstinted support despite my unreasonable demands on their time and patience. I wish to record my gratitude to all.

Above all, as in all my work, I have gained to a degree that is no longer measurable from the continuous conference known as the Centre for the Study of Developing Societies where I work and where we discuss endlessly on science, politics, technology, religion—and man. A good many of the ideas and formulations in *Footsteps* were stimulated by these discussions. This does not mean that the other members of the Centre agree with me in what I have written. I know that some of them strongly disagree. But I have benefitted as much from our disagreements as from our occasional agreements. I am also thankful to them, above all to Bashiruddin Ahmed, for providing me relief from other projects at the Centre.

A word about documentation. I have kept this to the minimum in this essay, using references only when I have drawn from a data source or used someone's concept or ideal. Partly this is a matter of personal taste. For, while in one sense this essay draws upon all that I have read and discussed with others since I was a student, in another sense it bears the stamp of my own thought for which I alone am responsible. Footnotes (given at the bottom of the page) have been used mainly to elaborate a point or develop a side point, often at length. Other references have been given at the end of each chapter and indicated in the text by the use of alphabets, serially.

Finally, a word about the use of words. I have not allowed myself to depart from the facility of conventional usage according to which when I talk of the autonomy and dignity of man, I naturally assume that 'man' signifies all human beings and not only the human male. In fact, in my way of thinking the human male derives his sense of dignity from being close to femininity in both his own species and nature in general. In any case, I consider this hypersensitivity about the use of words, found in some countries, rather childish.

RAJNI KOTHARI

FOOTSTEPS INTO THE FUTURE

1

DESIGN FOR THE FUTURE

THERE is a dilemma that faces the futurist. As a reformer and a romanticist—which every futurist must be—he is guided by a vision whose fundamental credo is how to leave the past behind and remould the present towards a different world. As a skeptic and a scientist, however, he knows that a total break with the past is both an impossible and a dangerous proposition and that all he can hope to have is a *better* world. This methodological dilemma is reflected in the reality that lies before us: we live in an era of great changes, but the direction of change is by no means clear. The science of futurology, insofar as there is one, has done little more than project bright and dark scenarios of the future; by itself it provides no guidelines on whether the future will follow one course or the other.

Some have sought to handle this problem by resorting to a theory of history, an inevitable course that will presumably transform the world according to a given teleology.[1] But it is again history that has shown that in the absence of a set of determined actors united by common values, a theory of history degenerates into a myth. Unless there is a deliberate design for the future, unless there is an active principle that intervenes in the process of history, there can be little assurance of how the future

---

1. The theory of history may differ as between the liberal theory of a gradual and linear progression towards modernity, the Marxist theory of a dialectic course leading, through revolutionary change, to a classless society, or as with the transcendentalists, the fulfilment of some divine or immanent purpose through man's submission to the divine will. In reality none of these is more than a system of belief, despite some of them being couched in scientific language. It is extremely difficult to visualize the end of human, much less of cosmic, evolution. If evolution were a teleological process, there would be no way of knowing the *telos* that guided it. To claim a cognitive basis for it is most misleading. And as with power, absolute cognition leads to absolute danger.

will be shaped. The key question is: From where does the active principle come? From ongoing structures and established processes of change (acquisition of modern technology, raising the rate of economic growth, maturing to a place in the world balance of power) or from basic acts of will emanating from a consciousness of the real conflicts and issues that divide men and nations? It appears to us that without deliberately undertaking the latter kind of change, the process of history will continue to be determined by ad hoc manipulators of events (bureaucrats in power, military establishments, international technocrats, professional managers). If we are to free ourselves from this drift, the need is to outline a realistic design on which to fashion the will to change. History obliges only those who have a sound perception of the options open to them and have a will to exercise their options.

In large parts of the world, politicians and administrators (still mercifully free from the aspiration of attaining big power status) are groping for a proper perspective on the issues that face them, either as rulers or as dissenting groups. By and large, however, the present intellectual effort and style provide little assistance to these people. It is a style that is process-bound, prognosticating from the known and the familiar, 'objective' and thus presumably scientific. It hesitates to question, let alone seek to reconstruct, the structure of reality.

Diagnosis of Emerging Trends

The nature of this reality manifests itself in all dimensions of the emerging scenario. New developments in science and technology (beyond the crude manifestations of the machine age) hold the promise of ending exploitation of man by man based on an obsolete technology and an organizational theory that continue to hold sway. There is also taking place a demystification of the laws of economic management, so that ordinary men and women are in a better position to make choices governing their lives. Also in the political sphere there are in evidence secular tendencies towards greater democratization of society. At the international level there is a slow but irreversible shift from an oligopoly of political and military power to one in which there are a greater number of effective centres of power. Intellectually, too, there is a growing realization of the excesses and dangers released by the technoeconomic model of industrialization and urbanization, an increasing skepticism about the claims of the theory of progress, and an expanding search for alternatives to both capitalist economy and the socialist state towards something at once more humane and more just and peaceful. Above all, the greatly increased role of politics in human affairs, aided by the revolution in communication, has enabled man to think in terms of an ever widening span of empathy and loyalty—from the nomadic conception of isolated group existence to a conception of the human community in terms of hundreds of millions, and gradually of the whole of humanity. The emergence in Europe of the nation state phenomenon and its spread throughout the world constitute important milestones in this growth of consciousness. And the nation state system is itself undergoing important modifications under the impact of new necessities that are impelling man to think in terms of the entire species to which he belongs.

But while these long-term trends toward freedom and diversity and a new basis for human solidarity are at work, the short term is full of ominous signs that may put insuperable impediments before the realization of what the long run holds in store. GNPs are rising everywhere but their benefits are being confined to small metropolitan elites who derive a good part of their legitimacy and political support from external linkages rather than by identification with their own people. The spatial distribution of land and other resources (except population) continues to work against the poorer regions of the world. The gospel of modernization has released forces that produce ethnic cleavages, internal violence (civil wars, political excesses, and the brutalities of military juntas) and armed conflicts between neighbours encouraged by the big powers. The economic gap between rich and poor nations continues to widen while the achievement of minimum conditions for all human beings is becoming increasingly difficult to achieve in large parts of the world despite phenomenal advances in science and technology. And patterns of dominance are escalating as a result of "aid" and technical assistance that have resulted in a distortion of economic policies and political structures and in heavy burdens of debt repayment on future generations. Poorer countries are being told to engage in family planning to restrain their populations, to integrate their ethnic minorities and 'motivate' their illiterate farmers—if neccessary, through coercive methods—and to leave the real problems of power and its organization to be tackled by the big powers through appropriate 'balances' and spheres of influence.[2]

2. The genesis of this incongruence between the theoretical postulate of equality of 'sovereign' states and the reality of a world stratified between a handful of imperial powers and a periphery of dependencies goes back to the age of European expansion. But the situation did not change much after the physical withdrawal of these powers from large parts of the colonial world and the establishment of a United Nations committed to the principles of equality and self-determination of all states. As Jawaharlal Nehru saw so clearly at the dawn of India's independence (which followed closely on the heels of the adoption of the United Nations Charter), precisely when the bells of freedom were ringing over large

Contd. on next page

The scenario for the near future that emerges, then, is one of a growing dualism in the world reflected in a widening hemispheric North-South chasm. As it cannot be resolved militarily—thanks to the development of a weapons system that has become at once far too deadly to be usable and far too concentrated in the hands of a few to be subject to rational control—and as the technoeconomic structure of the world militates against an economic solution, the easy course adopted by most of the ex-colonial countries is to engage in militant anticolonial postures and an empty ideology of confrontation while the lot of their people, who are fast multiplying, continues to worsen.

PATTERN OF DOMINANCE

The system that prevails in the world today is structured not simply along a division of the world between dominant and dependent states but also along deep divisions within the latter. The widely accepted teleology provided by the modernization model has produced a basic schism between a tiny modernist elite and the people at large, between the urban centres and the rural periphery, and between the educated and the uneducated, cumulatively producing a privileged class that reiterates the gospel as preached by their political and academic mentors, that concentrates power in its hands, and that turns into willing agents of the metropolitan powers of the world by suppressing the demands and aspirations of the rest of their countrymen. In a number of under-developed countries, national power and economic success are increasingly measured by a race for amassing large aggregate GNPs irrespective of how they are distributed (indeed, the bias is against distribution as it would allegedly lower the 'rate of growth', though this has never been adequately demonstrated), by an increasing preference for strong central authority that 'mobilizes' the periphery for its own parasitic ends, and by a growing reliance on the coercive potential of the state and the army for security against not only external threats but also internal discontent and upheavals [A]. Meanwhile, the grounds for this discontent are on the increase with a fast-growing world population, an increasing proportion of which is unemployed, young in age, concentrated in a few countries, huddled in urban areas, politicized but lacking in genuine self-regard, and

parts of the ex-colonial world, the adoption of a model of stratification of the nations of the world by the U.N. had created a system that threatened that very freedom. For a discussion of this theme and how it unfolded for a nation striving hard to retain its autonomy and peaceful policies under world conditions threatening them, see Chapter X of my *Politics in India*, New Delhi, Orient Longman, and Boston, Little, Brown & Co., 1970, pp. 343-418.

consequently possessed by a pervasive sense of futility and powerlessness and general breakdown of self-control.

Thus the way world power patterns and social and psychological trends are developing, there seems to be little ground for optimism for contemporary human beings, large numbers of whom are likely to experience a growing sense of isolation and cynicism. In the absence of a determined intervention in ongoing processes, based on widely shared values that are capable of reversing the prevailing pattern of dominance and exploitation, the world may well feel threatened by the spectre of a state of nature depicted so powerfully by Hobbes and may decide to buy its peace and security—and the advantages of technology—by agreeing to live under a superstate provided by an agreement between the big powers somewhat on the lines of the post-1815 Holy Alliance in Europe, only more subtle and cunning. The resulting system will indeed be a 'world order', managed by the metropolitan centres through an array of system analysts and information processors who will put an end to both domestic and international disturbances as soon as they arise. It will be a perfect state, more perfect than the one sketched by George Orwell. Far from the state withering away, all that will remain will be the state.

But in this very condition of a growing sense of despair there perhaps lies a hope. The widespread discontent with existing reality among large numbers of sensitive persons round the world can lead to a sense of futility, but it can also produce a desire for action thus proving once again man's oft proven ability to overcome the crises that face him. The very factors that appear to be liabilities—a 'surplus' population, an increase in the proportion of youth in the population and the state of unrest in which they are, a surfeit of unemployed technicians and educated manpower, a paucity of capital goods and industrial fuels—can be turned into resources for creating a more happy and harmonious world, provided of course that such an effort is informed by an appropriate set of values and an institutional and technological model based on those values. We are at a time in history when, given a proper understanding and an appropriate theory of action, we may well succeed in reorienting the world social and political structure toward preferred directions.

There are moments in history when long needed changes which were only dimly felt for decades are vividly felt and offer a chance of being carried out. The present is such a moment. It provides a peculiar combination of *necessity* born out of a sense of crisis (that the human species may become extinct) and *hope* born out of accumulating evidence that if only men would be prepared to act, it is possible to move towards a better human order. The threats posed by the possibility of total annihilation through war, through the collapse of the environment, through energy exhaustion or through mass starvation, or a combination of all of these, provide the sense of urgency. At the same time new scientific findings point to the fact that not even a fraction of human potential is being utilized, that the human planet is full of still untapped resources and there are new possibilities in technology which will conserve rather than destroy the environment, and that it is possible to move towards a social model that will produce a world based on equality rather than inequity. This is a particularly propitious combination that can provide a spur to bold thinking and action. (Without a sense of urgency humans are not likely to act, nor do they act if there was no hope for a way out.) It is a moment in history that should be clinched. It may not come back again. The history of man is full of lost opportunities [B].

PROBLEM OF AUTONOMY

As we look at the totality of the problem, it seems to us that the main tasks are not technological but are political. The basic issue in restructuring world reality is to establish the autonomy of nations in the Third World and on that basis to promote a sense of collective self-regard among them so that we can realize the values of individual freedom and dignity, justice in the distribution of worldly goods, and opportunity for participation in decision-making structures at various levels. Men must live in autonomous political communities that provide minimum conditions of life and equity for all so that they may pursue their own material and spiritual ends. The ultimate idea that has guided us in this work pertains less to some perfect model of social order and more to the quality and character of the individual being and his search for the higher values of creation.[3] In order to achieve this, it is necessary to promote conditions of autonomy at all levels.

As we look at the larger political and cultural processes that have been at work during the last few centuries, we find a basic conflict between alternative civilizational worldviews, between a positivist, manipulative, expansionist and man-centred worldview whose essential aim is the creation of an ideal and perfect social order, and a view of life and its purpose that is familial in orientation and is supportive of naturalist and feminine qualities [C], seeks to subdue the will to power, considers all life sacrosanct, and has as its ideal the achievement of individual autonomy and self-realization rather than the perfection of a social

---

3. We reject the supernatural view of creation, however, as we do not find adequate intellectual reasons for supporting it. At the same time we reject the dominant Occidental perspective of man based on an imperfect understanding of the relationship between knowledge and ethics. For a full discussion of this and related philosophical themes, see Chapter II.

order. The former worldview derives its strength from the Hellenic-Judeo-Christian tradition (from which Islam also derived its credo), whereas the inspiration for the latter comes from the ancient civilizations of the East. The real failure of the latter worldview over the centuries was that those who held it were not able to fulfil the necessary materialistic urges and needs of man. They failed to erect a viable political order that could withstand external pressure that came in the wake of the Industrial Revolution and its colonial expansion. The dilemma that these societies face—and to them can now be added the large number of countries from Africa and Latin America that suffer from a serious identity problem arising in part from their religious affiliations but also from a growing realization that the game is lost if they continue to ape the West—is that it is not until they assert their political autonomy (their *power*), erect viable states, and handle the problems posed by modern science and technology in terms of their own needs that it may become possible for them to give new life to the best in their own traditions [D].

Reflecting this clash of civilizations and regions is the duality of the present-day political reality. This reality is composed of two sets of nation-states—the early arrivals to independent nationhood as well as economic development who are past the stage of achieving political autonomy and material prosperity, and the late arrivals to these processes, thanks to the colonial interlude, where both autonomy and development are still aspired to. Such a hiatus in the structure of world reality makes all task of a radical system change in the international order—or the talk of a massive transfer of technology and resources for bridging the gap between rich and poor nations—appear at once farfetched and opportunistic. Its very loudness suppresses the fact that it may become a means of getting around the depth of the schism that divides the world, for any generalized formula of institutional overhaul or technological transformation will only result in continued dominance by the technologically advanced culture of the Northern Hemisphere. Perhaps, this time—if they succeed in their revolutionary designs—the dominating elite will be radicals, not conservatives, although there seems to be little hope for this. Essentially, they are both myth-makers utilizing modern mass media and communication and conference facilities for building elaborate defences around basic structures of political and intellectual domination. Some of them are, of course, highly sincere and committed people—even if frightfully naive.[4]

---

4. The 'establishment' of the world against which the radicals are beating their breasts is busy laying out a powerful design for their continued dominance of the world, taking care in the meanwhile to co-opt in their system the very powers who were once supposed to be the bastions of radical change.

There is a need to adopt a more diversified approach to the whole problem of national autonomy and international control, to centralization and decentralization, to schemes of participation and representation, to distributive and redistributive policies, and to the definition of what is parochial and local and what is universal and more than local. To adopt a blanket formula of limiting the sovereignty of nation-states— irrespective of the level of already achieved state-ness and nation-ness and without discriminating between powers that are able to destroy the independence and integrity of other states and those who have not yet achieved the means to defend their independence and security—will not only be an exercise in naivete but also positively undermine the very interests and ideals that the one-worlders have in mind. The same kind of argument applies to the most recent flood of prescriptions for limiting growth after the much publicized Club of Rome study [E]. Applied to the poorer countries this may, if uncritically accepted, well become a formula for continued impoverishment and domination. On the other hand, if such a debate can lead to desirable correctives to the equally uncritical acceptance of the dominant model of technoeconomic growth, it will become possible for us to avoid the kind of malaise into which Western society has fallen and will make us all sensitive to a different kind of perspective. There are some rather hard choices that are involved. On the one hand, considerations of survival may legitimize persistence of inequality, both between and within states (as it may be argued that equality in material standards may prove detrimental to ecology). On the other hand, pressures from the deprived strata—again between and within states—for emulating the life styles of the rich will mount, unless the rich themselves give up their wasteful ways. The consequence can be a bitter struggle for the goodies promised by the model of high indus- trialization. There is need for a new kind of consensus based on a new model of life to be accepted by the world as a whole.

Design for the Future

From this general diagnosis of contemporary reality follows our preferred model of a world order. Our model is informed by the values we seek to realize [F]. In order that the individual should enjoy maximum autonomy and freedom, in order that political communities maximize social justice for their people, and in order that the dangers of violence be minimized, we have to admit at least three different levels of goal- fulfilment—the individual level, the national level, and the world level—in our scheme of preferred arrangements. To realize autonomy for the individual human being and to forge satisfactory states of community among men, it is necessary to provide greater rather than less autonomy to a majority of individual states who at present are not autonomous. (Without a free collectivity a free man is not likely to emerge.) At the same time we must find solutions to problems of production and distribution, choice of technology, prevention of both international and internal violence, and containment of the deleterious consequences of economic growth and consumption patterns all of which are becoming ever worldwide in scope and ought to be treated as such.

Indeed, our whole rationale for thinking in world order terms stems from a realization that it is no longer possible to bring about successful change of an enduring kind in one area or country, except in very marginal ways, without taking account of the world context. Even revolutions suffer from this limitation. Similarly, no amount of either pleading or moralizing to restrain standards of consumption or curb 'chauvinist' tendencies is likely to go far in the poorer regions unless at the same time a similar onslaught is directed at the citadels of affluence and the centres of political and military dominance. We are convinced of the need for a global approach to the economic and political problems facing human beings. Our only difference with the one-worlders is that for us the social reality of the nation-state is integral to any movement towards a better world.

Curious though it may sound, the one-worlders are rather conservative thinkers. For what they are proposing is a simple extension of the characteristics of the nation state on to a world state, accentuating all the deficiencies of the nation state by making it unmanageable and grotesque. The abstract ideal of one world will ever remain a non-starter. If men are to develop wider allegiances—as we argued earlier, they have already come a long way—there will be need to build on available networks of deep loyalty: of family, of community, of nation. This should be done not by mere extension of an existing institutional model but rather by forging new kinds of institutions that cover larger and larger numbers of human beings without undermining the great diversity which gives them strength and a capacity for love and loyalty. What should emerge from this is a new *network* that will continuously transform present solidarities and discords at various levels into a system that at once admits the validity of each and transcends the limitations of all. We shall deal with this problem more concretely later in this chapter and in greater detail in Chapter V. Each major step in the evolution of human society has called for new institutional innovations—it was never in the style of mere extension of earlier forms—that fit new situations. The crisis that the human race faces today calls for yet another innovation in institution-building without undermining existing structures of loyalty. A world state is not an answer to this crisis.

Thus the perspective that has guided the Indian team in the project, of which this essay is an outcome, is one in which we are moved by

attitudes that are somewhat different from those that move either the
liberal internationalists intent on somehow eliminating conflict from
human affairs or the revolutionaries on the left keen on building a world
free from all vested interests. We are motivated by efforts to build autonomy, freedom, well-being, and justice *at a number of levels* so that
ordinary men and women can realise these values. The fundamental value
that moves us is that of the autonomy and dignity of ordinary men and
women, its necessary corollaries being the value of diversity of cultural
traditions and political forms on the one hand and of equality in access to
basic necessities on the other. Neither the spectre of an overriding world
government in the image of some transcendental ideology nor some
smashing operation in the hope that it can do away with all encumbrances
holds any attraction for us. Perhaps such an attitude comes from the
background of an ancient civilization seeking to realize preferred values
through active intervention in the process of time without rejecting what
is good and of enduring value in its traditions. Our very realization of
the stupendity of the task that faces contemporary man makes us averse
to the hollow sounds of comfortable angry men from the Northern
Hemisphere hopping from one continent to another in a bid to transform
the whole world—the latest edition of the white man's burden. Hence
our somewhat different perspective.

VALUE PROFILE

Our preferred world is a world in which the individual enjoys
autonomy for his self-realization and creativity—what is generically known
as freedom. This is our principal value. So we can move towards such a
world, several other values have to be simultaneously pursued. First, the
primary condition of freedom is sheer survival, a protection against
violence—local, national, and international violence, as well as violence
tending towards either annihilation of the properties of life or towards a
deadening uniformity of all forms of behaviour and social structure.
Both the needs of survival and diversity may thus be subsumed under the
value of *nonviolence*. Second, all men ought to be able to liberate themselves from economic deprivation and misery, irrespective of their ethnic
or national origin or their social status. For this to become possible, it
will be necessary to achieve as much equality among human beings as is
necessary for the realization of common goals. Operationally, this may
be translated into the value of *justice* through which both the formulation
and the implementation of common goals are to be evaluated. Third, the
individual should be able (to the extent he wants) to *participate* in the
making of decisions that affect his life; he must be a member of a functioning democracy in which he not only exercises choices between given

alternatives of policies and leadership at various levels but also is able to exercise initiative in making new decisions and persuading others about the desirability of certain community actions. This means that the democracy in which he lives is neither just an institutionalized scheme of competition between limited alternatives that are predecided by small elites (as is the case in most liberal democracies) nor some version of democratic centralism (as is found in most socialist regimes), but is one in which there is sufficient scope for personal initiative at different levels and in different sectors of life.

Alongside the values of autonomy, nonviolence, justice, and participation,[5] there is a need to ensure a larger ethic of behaviour that we may call the ethic of self-control. Our preferred world should not be a consumption society, aggressive in the cultivation of ever growing wants, destroying nature and ravaging land, plants, and the nonhuman species, and dehumanizing social relationships. In such a world there should not only be a *minimum* standard of material living for all but also a *maximum* standard beyond which resources must be transferred, first to those that have not yet achieved the minimum, and after everyone has achieved it or a tolerable multiple of it, to the production and consumption of nonmaterial goods. The notion of a constantly rising material condition that men and nations are aspiring to achieve everywhere is not a utopia but in reality a disutopia. A better standard of life in our preferred world will be measured in terms of not only material standards but also cultural and ethical standards. This involves limiting wants (restraining artificial stimulation of needs) and making it possible for the individual to aspire to not simply freedom from inequity and exploitation but also to a higher freedom in which he seeks liberation from dependence on material acquisitions and attachments. Eventually, the exercise of autonomy must be subject to self-control, a sense of modesty, and a continuing

---

5. We have used a number of concepts above in outlining our value profile, largely with a view to laying out our rationale for our choice of values but sometimes also with a view to elaborating on the values. The values themselves are four—autonomy, justice, nonviolence, and participation—each of which is an operational value for a design of the future and for political action. (Our concept of value is something that is concrete and capable of being translated into reality.) The more abstract concepts provide the theoretical rationale for these values. Thus both freedom and self-realization are translated into the value of autonomy, survival and diversity into the active principle of nonviolence, the theoretical postulate of equality into the operational value of justice, and the more inclusive institutional concept of democracy into the behavioural norm of participation. Some concepts have been used for expanding the meaning of a given value—thus dignity and self-reliance amplify the value of autonomy—while others (economic development and welfare) have been used as necessary means to the realization of a value (justice).

quest and wonder about the ultimate causes of reality. In order to realize such a state, however, it is necessary first to create the conditions of autonomy outlined above.

Changes from the Present

It can be seen that the principal stumbling block to achieving these conditions of life is not the absence of some centralized and benign world authority but, rather, the presence of structures of dominance and inequality and the absence of real autonomy in large parts of the world. Our preferred world would do away with this inequality and this dominance or, what is perhaps more realistic, bring them within tolerable limits. This has two implications for action: restructuring world politics to remove conditions that perpetuate inequality and dependence, and devising institutions—at various levels—that will consolidate a world based on the principles of autonomy and equality.

TERRITORIAL STRUCTURE

In regard to restructuring world politics, it is necessary to come to grips with the reality of international politics. As long as the less powerful and poorer nations of the world remain disunited and fall prey to the manoeuvres of big-power politics,[6] there seems to be little chance of achieving real autonomy for them or attaining even the necessary conditions for internal social and economic development. There is need to evolve a sense of a common stake among them, to resolve mutual conflicts that are in reality marginal and have only been enlarged out of proportion because of the tendency of many a country to look for support to one of the big powers, and together to seek to bring an end to outside dominance and exploitation. In this some help may be forthcoming from dissenting intellectuals and certain truly civilized men within the dominant nations, but the real initiatives for building strength and a sense of unity will have to come from within the dependent states themselves.

6. This is, of course, an oversimplification. The system of dominance has become sophisticated in recent years. It does not merely operate through the big powers. There are a number of intermediate powers and scores of nonterritorial (intranational and extranational) actors through which the system operates. Mexico is by no means a big power but is part of the dominance system. So is, clearly, Brazil. So was Israel until the Arabs decided to assert themselves in their own region. South Africa and Rhodesia continue to provide strong bases of imperial domination. The nonterritorial actors include the powerful economic enterprises that operate multinationally, 'foreign return' elites, and large numbers (though by no means all) of United Nations and other international civil servants all of whom seem to be part of a single complex.

Most of these states are too small and too poor to do anything very effective for realizing their autonomy and putting an end to their dependence and exploitation. At the same time the more powerful nations are getting consolidated into regional superpowers. Indeed, it is noteworthy that after 1945, precisely when metropolitan powers were seeking to undo old boundaries and historic animosities in their own regions, they were imposing artificial boundaries and creating new bases for conflict in other continents with a view to keeping them divided and weak. There is clear need to undo this mischief by promoting a federalizing process in the latter regions, starting modestly through economic cooperation and the removal of cultural barriers, and leading in due course to more integrated political entities, greater equality among them, and between them and the more powerful and prosperous states. In other words, there is need to make the number and diversity of nation-states more rational and manageable than is the case today if the structure of world politics is to be conducive to the values stated earlier. In our preferred world to be realized by the decade of the 1990s, we would like a smaller number of nations or federations ("communities") of nations, each large in size and strong enough to be self-reliant, so that progress towards the twin conditions of autonomy and equality that we have postulated becomes possible. This will also make for nearly equal representation at the world level so that the various institutions at that level can operate in a truly participant manner, in contrast to the present situation in which the plethora of weak and atomized political units can be manipulated to serve the interests of a narrow oligarchy of international power.

Our preference would be for between twenty and twenty-five political units of the world community, though of course there is no magic in any particular number and what is suggested here is only meant as a heuristic device. In Chapter V and the appendix to the book, we have tried to suggest lines of a possible federalizing process, but even that exercise is largely heuristic and is meant to serve no more than as a basis for debate.

INSTITUTIONAL STRUCTURE

Apart from such a structural change in the world political configuration, there is need to institutionalize certain processes at the regional and world levels. As we see it, there should be a complex of institutions geared to the promotion of autonomy and equality among both individual national units and individual citizens of these units. These institutions are to be viewed not as parts of some monolithic world authority but, rather, as catering to diverse functional needs that transcend existing boundaries and call for larger, more unified, efforts.

1. There should be a set of functional authorities of a multi-state kind dealing with technical and welfare needs of the world population that build upon the structures that have already emerged—e.g., in health, communications, aviation—but extending much further with a view to eliminating gross inequalities in access to technology, in means of production, and in the relationship between land and living beings. These institutions should, subject to the agreement of the states concerned, plan and undertake economic enterprises in the less developed regions and be backed by sufficient resources to balance and counter monopolistic corporations.

2. There should be regional and world political structures in which all the nations of the world are represented that will provide the technical and welfare bodies—which should be the core of the worldwide institutional drive [G]—with sanctions and resources. Thus, in our preferred world model, while the institutions of a participant democracy will function mainly within national communities, they will also be significantly supplemented at higher levels.

3. There should be regional as well as world-level specialized agencies for dealing with functions whose scope extends beyond existing states, such as resource planning, development of new—as well as some old and wholesome—energy sources, ecology, and population and migration policies. These agencies should promote research on alternatives to the present technoeconomic model, communicate the results of this research widely, and bring authoritative pressures on national governments to carry out agreed-upon measures.

4. There should be a world security system that will at once restrain regional military pacts sponsored by the big powers and act as a catalyst for a significant transfer of resources from the war industry located in the technologically advanced regions to both defence and development of the vulnerable regions so as to minimize conditions of violence in these regions. There should be at the disposal of the world body an armed force on a continuous basis, small in size but expandable when the need arises, such as to curb genocidal acts of violence as occurred in Vietnam, Bangla Desh, and Mozambique, by calling upon countries who have demonstrated their commitment to the values of peace and justice to contribute their forces, as was done in the Congo crisis in 1960.

5. There should be a set of institutions designed to protect human rights and standards of justice wherever these are violated.[7] This

---

7. There is at present a U.N. Commission of Human Rights but, lacking a world based on genuine autonomy and accountability based on such autonomy, it is largely ineffective. So is the present Council of Jurists, which is not an authoritative juridical body in any case.

should include a high-powered world court of justice to which are organically linked an authoritative council of world jurists and an active commission for human rights, both equipped with appropriate secretariats and regional field agencies.

Apart from these basic structures, there will, of course, be need to strengthen and develop various institutions at the regional and multi-regional (world) levels to perform functions whose logical locus is beyond the national unit—both preventive functions (such as against environmental destruction) and promotional functions (such as diffusion of information and sharing of scientific and technological research). The purpose of such institutions should be to neutralize economic and political structures that prevent the growth of genuine autonomy and self-reliance in political and economic spheres among the different states of the world. As argued above, there is need for the invention of new kinds of institutions on a continuous basis in response to a fast changing—and endangered—world without undermining deeply laid loyalties and solidarities. Only thus can still wider loyalties, extending to the species as a whole, emerge and a just and nonviolent world be brought into being.

Thus, as we conceive of the world in the 1990s, we visualize a system in which the autonomy of the national political community is both retained and (in the case of the large number of dependent nations) considerably augmented. However, this will be in part supplemented and in part modified by (1) a large reduction in the number of sovereign units comprising the world community, enabling each of them to have a minimum size of population, territory, and natural resources, as well as enough diversity of culture and of material and scientific skills, and (2) an authoritative complex of regional and multi-regional institutions that will prevent exploitation and dominance. The world political system will thus, in its operating ethos as well as in its institutional structure, function at both global and national levels, with appropriate intermediate levels built into the system. In other words, the system will be an operating world federation without centralizing power in the hands of one apex unit. Also, while we place high value on the autonomy of each of the constituent political units, we hope that (thanks largely to the intellectual environment created by the spread of new values) there will be widespread consensus among these units in at least one respect—namely, the agreement that individual survival, worth, and autonomy are the final end of social organization—and, hence, in the desirability of having participant structures at various levels of the world social reality. Justice and nonviolence, the other two values of such a world, will follow as behavioural components of this fundamental consensus on the value and meaning of autonomy.

THE DOMESTIC LEVEL

For the kind of world we prefer, it is clear that appropriate processes and structures for the realization of our values will have to be evolved within domestic political systems as much as, and perhaps sooner than, at the global level. While we should strive to remove glaring injustices of the world political and economic order we would be deluding ourselves if we were to ignore the same issues of autonomy, equity, and justice within existing national communities. Few will deny that man's attempt to devise rational modes of government and justice has far to go even at micro levels, let alone in evolving more inclusive structures of freedom and justice in the world.

In the model we are proposing, national political communities will have to provide for the following essential conditions:

1. Institutions for optimum participation of people at different levels, ensuring both representative structures of responsible government and more direct structures of deliberation and consensus at the level of the work place, the local community, and cultural institutions.

2. Institutionalization of the principle of equality among men as a condition of justice though not as a doctrinal principle, this being an area where politics and economics intersect.

3. A balance between enlightened, centralized national institutions that can take a total perspective and are responsible to the people as a whole and a decentralized structure of decision-making, planning and implementation, so as to maximize individual freedom, social justice and cultural diversity and thus to give rise to a vibrant federal polity [H].

4. A fundamental obligation that the nation-state and units within it should preserve human rights, violation of which should lead to legitimate intervention, certainly by the national central authority where it is enlightened enough to recognize its obligations, but failing that and in cases of mass violation of human rights (to be decided upon by legitimate world information and communication agencies), by regional and world agencies as outlined above.

ECONOMIC MODEL

This brief statement of preferred conditions at the national and subnational levels opens up a number of aspects that we intend to treat in the last three chapters. But there are two aspects that may be spelt out a little more here because they have a bearing on the general model for the future and are relevant to both national and world levels. The first aspect is that the economic system entailed in our preferred world must be changed from the present growth based model aimed at an aggregate production target to a need-based model defined by the principles of individual autonomy, social justice, and nonviolence. This calls for a revision of many basic perspectives that have guided the model of industrialization and that seem to have been accepted by intellectual and political elites in most parts of the world—for instance, perspectives on rural-urban proportions, on the role of agriculture, on the type of industrialization, on the strategy of employment, on the presumed economies of scale, and on the consequent choice of technologies. Much more attention needs to be given to rural and semiurban as against large metropolitan units, for attaining minimum satisfaction levels as against constantly expanding consumption standards, for minimizing dependence on scarce world resources, and on the other hand for evolving a policy of transfer of skills and resources from developed to underdeveloped regions, classes, and ethnic groups *within* nations. We shall go into these issues in more detail in Chapter III.

SIZE AND AUTONOMY

The second aspect that has a bearing on the general model for the future relates to the problem of size of political units, an issue that is again relevant to both domestic and world considerations and which we, following the classical thinkers on politics, consider crucial to the realization of our values. As we perceive it, national political units ought to be federal in character combining the advantages of both large and small sizes. Our own preferred model is for somewhat large-sized national communities composed of (1) somewhat small-sized subnational units arranged along two or three levels vertically, each enjoying a measure of self-government, and (2) a large number of autonomous groups arranged horizontally that are by definition self-governing. Within the national polity it is necessary to maximize participation, social justice, and economic development as means of providing a fair deal to all and a nonviolent mode of managing and absorbing conflicts and tensions. All this is best achieved if the constituent states or provinces of a nation-state are small, compact, single-language units, characterized by ease of travel and communication, and are dynamic enough to minimize elite-mass distances. On the other hand the advantages of large scale will be ensured by the total size of the national federal community being large.

In our preferred world we consider the structural issue of optimum size somewhat important. We would like to have 20 to 25 states instead of the present more than 150 of highly unequal size and potential for economic and political power. We prefer our model of size and number for a variety of reasons. First, as distinct from maximizing goals of participation and justice *within* nations, we would also like to maximize the goals of power and its optimum distribution *between* nations. Of course, it is neither feasible nor desirable to have the various federalized units of equal size or uniform in any other respect (one is not building a system from the world level downward but from the present national level upward), but we would like them to be at least *comparable* in one or more of several ways—territorial size, population, natural resources, productive potential—so as to ensure a measure of equality and respect for each other's integrity while still retaining considerable diversity in culture, politics, and social development.

Second, viewed from the perspective of two or three decades from now—not a very distant future—the aim should be to minimize the dominance of a few powers, as is the case now, for this would militate against our operational values of justice and nonviolence. Twenty to twenty-five states is a large enough number not to degenerate into a balance-of-power situation and a small enough number not to permit domination of a colonial type. It should be remembered (from what has been proposed above) that whereas in our model we mean to develop world institutions performing substantial welfare, judicial, and security functions, we do not wish to underrate the reality of *power* in the world setting even of the year 2000.

Third, what we are proposing is not entirely new. Various models of federating into larger units have already been proposed, within Latin America, the Middle East, East and West Africa, and Southeast Asia, and in each case for the purpose of augmenting regional power equations (both political and economic). Of course, there are still many hurdles to face—of psychological identity, the vested interests of existing elites, and the present system of alliances and balances engendered by the big powers. However, considered with other parts of the model proposed here, the proposal is not too fantastic to put into effect.

Like all other designs of a preferred world, the proposals made here are likely to be amended and modified as different elements of the model are brought in touch with reality. However, we are convinced that some restructuring of the present political map of the world is necessary to realize our values though, of course, the restructuring will make sense only as part of a series of interrelated measures designed to promote the basic goal of autonomy.

Limits of Order

The outline of a preferred world that we have just considered (and that we shall try to elaborate on in subsequent chapters) is of a system that involves a progressive combination of autonomy and unity without, however, leading to centralization. The structural principle of our model is to produce enough unity that will ensure enough autonomy and *vice versa*. Autonomy is not to be confused with individualism. While autonomy involves the principle of diversity, it also involves the need to modify the ill effects of diversity in the form of domination of the many by the few by admitting the complementary principle of integration. For it is necessary to ensure that autonomy does not degenerate into the privilege of a few.

The model we have presented to realize such unity in diversity attempts on the one hand to prevent interactions whose outcomes are harmful—dominance, exploitation, violence—and on the other hand to respond to needs and demands of individuals and political communities the world over through structural changes and innovations at various levels of world reality. But it is still a limited institutional system, leaving much to spontaneous and voluntary efforts at various levels, and allowing the human individual enough scope to pursue his own design for himself. The vision that has guided us in this essay is not one of a perfect social and political order where everyone is made happy according to a set format. It is rather one of a state of creative anarchy in which there are a large number of units operating at many levels, each enjoying a large measure of autonomy and all of them interacting for the realization of ever new ends as these are discovered. We have no great attraction for fixed and grandiose schemes of unification, whether for peace or for plenty. The world has already learnt at great cost that all such designs become insufferable leviathans.

Notes

A For a critical analysis of the prevailing theory of modernization and its implications for political autonomy in the Third World, see my "State Building in the Third World: Alternative Strategies", *Economic and Political Weekly*, Annual Number, 7(5-7), February 1972.

B See Margaret Mead's 1973 Nehru Memorial Lecture on *Prospects of World Harmony: An Anthropological View* (New Delhi, Nehru Memorial Fund, 1973) for a lucid analysis of some of these points as seen by an anthropologist. The lecture helped me clarify my own position on these issues.

C　Many in the West are slowly becoming conscious of these distinctions. Most important among these are Lewis Mumford and Erik H. Erikson. Still the most important of Mumford's statements in this respect is in his *The City in History: Its Origins, Its Transformations, Its Prospects*, London, Secker & Warburg, 1961, especially his treatment of the neolithic age, dominated by woman and the organic principle, its fusion with the paleolithic culture, and its ultimate subjugation, in pp. 11-54. Erikson has dealt extensively with this theme in his various writings. See especially his "Reflections on Womanhood", *Daedalus*, Spring 1964, and "The Golden Rule in the Light of the New Insight", in *Insight and Responsibility: Lectures on the Ethical Implications of Psychoanalytic Insight*, London, Faber and Faber, 1966, and his most recent work on Gandhi, *Gandhi's Truth: On the Origins of Militant Non-Violence*, New York, W.W. Norton, 1969.

D　There is much in these traditions that is just not worth preserving. We shall deal at some length with this issue in Chapter II.

E　Donella H. Meadows *et al., The Limits to Growth: A Report for The Club of Rome's Project on the Predicament of Mankind*, New York, Universe Books, 1972.

F　See the next section, under the heading "Value Profile", for a statement of these values.

G　The details are given in Chapter V.

H　For a more concrete description of such a balanced system and answers to inevitable skepticism about it and to the widely prevalent point that a major development effort is not possible in a decentralized polity, see the detailed analysis in Chapter III.

2

INTELLECTUAL
PERSPECTIVE

OUTLINING a model for a preferred world would be an empty exercise unless it were informed by a deeper probe into the crisis of the present world. To move from a world as it would be, if present and expected trends continue, to a world as one would like it to be, given one's value preferences, involves an intellectual understanding of available options on the one hand and a political understanding of the issues involved in translating intellectual choices into concrete reality on the other. This is not an easy combination to achieve. It calls for a relevant theory of change that combines practical sensitivity with normative imagination.

The Dominant Worldview

For undertaking such a probe, it would be instructive to examine the dominant perspective that has guided social and political developments in the recent past and to evaluate the intellectual and philosophical movements that have shaped it.

If we take a very broad sweep of history in order to put contemporary developments in some perspective, it appears that the basic divergence in worldviews and political cultures that ultimately led to a long period of conflict and domination that has come to be known as the age of imperialism was between those civilizations that were inherently secure, self-contained, inward-looking, and nonexpansive and those that were insecure, aggressive, outward-looking, and expansive. The civilizations of the East, of which China and India provided the core, lacked in basic expansionist drives, valued harmony and balance as virtues in themselves, were possessed by a religiosity that lacked a proselytizing ethos, and generally placed a relatively low value on intellect and rationality (the accent was on tradition and wisdom) and failed to measure up to the demands of power (the accent was on duty and decorum).[1] The Occidental civilization, on the other hand, put power on a high pedestal, considered knowledge to be an instrument of pragmatic pursuits (at least since the dawn of the modern age when the Socratic thesis that knowledge is virtue gave place to the Baconian one that knowledge is power), and was, in time, able to overpower the religious urge toward realizing the City of God by the secular assertion of man and his mastery over nature and his repudiation of any principle above man. (Even the organization of religion in the West, as that of the Catholic Church, quickly took its cues from the principles of imperial Rome rather than from the message underlying the gospel of Christ himself. The latter was, in essence though not in its doctrinal details,[2] Oriental.)

Such a classification of civilizations is, no doubt, oversimplified and somewhat arbitrary. For all major civilizations have within themselves the two elements in our theoretical framework, self-control and the drive for power. Similarly, no civilization can thrive without a measure of expansionist drive. (It is in the nature of life itself to expand.) The differences that are found arise from diverse historical confrontations. It

1. This is not to say that these concepts necessarily led to desirable results—at any rate not from the point of view of our values. Thus, in Hindu thought "duty" became an impersonal concept, used by the Brahminic elite to suppress deviance. In course of time it became the basis of the caste system. Also in the Confucian structure of thought duty became a conceptual basis for social stratification, though there was much more openness there because of the complementary principle of merit. (The Chinese civilizational thrust has always been more secular than the Indian one.) Similarly, wisdom—in the East as well as in the West—has often degenerated into a static concept and has been used to impute authority to a socially sanctified proposition and hence to apply a closure to further questioning. Decorum is a basically Confucian proposition that has often been misused to suppress diversity. Mao's lifelong concern to undermine the Confucian legacy has been based on his reading that it systematically suppressed protest and rebellion.
2. In terms of doctrine, of course, Christianity lends support to the homocentric thrust of the modern West. The biblical gift of nature to Adam has to no small extent both legitimized and facilitated the technological leadership of the West from early medieval times. In the Oriental cultures religion urges man to live in harmony with nature, which is often conceived in transcendental terms. In the Judeo-Christian tradition man is appointed master of all creation, which exists only for his use. On this see Lynn White, Jr., *Medieval Technology and Social Change*, New York, Oxford University Press, 1962, in which the author brings out in great detail how such a religious legacy provided sanctity to Western man's exploitative view of nature, and hence of his enormous technological lead over others. In the Oriental cultures, which in fact were ahead of the Occident in the technological field until the middle ages, this drive was absent. Hence they ceased to develop their tools further. In the words of a Chinese scholar as reported by Paul Valery, "we invented gunpowder—but for shooting off fireworks in the evening".

appears to us that faced by different historical and natural conditions, Occidental and Oriental civilizations developed different orientations to power. In the West the orientation to power took the form of control over nature, territorial expansion, and later as both these were achieved (and civil society was consolidated), distribution of secular power between different estates and classes. In the Orient either consciousness of power did not fully emerge except for short periods (as in India) or it did emerge but was still considered dangerous and was therefore concentrated in a small ruling class (as in Confucian, though not Taoist, China). In both India and China the legitimate expansion was not of the state (though no doubt this also occurred for short periods) but of the mind.

When the initiative in science and technology shifted to the European continent, they enabled Western man both to liberate himself from outward authority and then, through a worldview that first put man at the centre of all species and then European man at the centre of all men, to bring other societies under the European domain as part of Europe's civilizing mission. The Occidental worldview had the great merit of infinite intellectual curiosity that sought to discover regularities ('laws of nature') underlying a seeming flux. But, unfortunately, this accent on the intellect gradually shifted from being valued for its own sake (the true essence of *science* as a search after truth) to something that man used in his conquest of the environment and in fulfilling his own acquisitive and dominating instincts (the essence of *technology*, or rather, of a science based technology which is a product of the peculiarly Western approach to knowledge).

While this aggressive approach to life gave to the Occident its enormous power, the other great civilizations were unable to stand up to the challenge posed by it. Their somewhat more comfortable existence, thanks both to the bounties of nature and to their relatively passive approach to it (which was at times worshipped and at other times conjured up as inactive and hence irrelevant), led to fundamental deficiencies in their approach to power. This accounts for a variety of responses: breakdown in the face of Western expansion (as in the case of India and Southeast Asia), self-delusion by just refusing to face up to the new facts (as in the case of China) or a clever and cynical handling of the situation by both making a virtue of inferiority and taking steps to overcome it by mere emulation without waiting to consider the consequences of this approach (as in the case of Japan). On the whole, the great civilizations of the East succumbed to the onslaught of the West.

There are some thinkers, most important among whom is F.S.C. Northrop[A], who have traced the reasons for the expansion of the West as against the shrinkage of the East in differences in the quality of thought in the two. Western thought, since the Greeks, is predominantly rationalistic,

Eastern thought predominantly intuitive. The West stresses the cognitive component of knowledge, the East the aesthetic component. The ability of the West for sustained analysis and 'abstraction' has facilitated its gains in the field of science and technology, which in turn made for its expansionism and imperialist spread. There seems to be something in this argument though we would ourselves attach greater importance to the direct linkage between knowledge and power in the West at a time when the East persisted in both viewing knowledge as a superior activity and thinking of power as potentially dangerous and something to be contained. For, after all, abstraction has been a quality of the Eastern mind too. It is there that mathematics and a study of the stars got a start. Even today the Indian mind, for instance, is more at ease with abstract thought and much less with empirical inquiry. Perhaps the two abstractions are of a different order, the Western type more related to building systems of inquiry into the real world than the Eastern where the discovery of zero got transformed into a philosophical concept (that of *sunya*, of nothingness) and the study of the stars turned into the metaphysical system of astrology instead of a sustained scientific inquiry that modern astronomy represents leading to the conquest of the space.[3]

The scientific and industrial revolutions gave new directions to European universalism, which had already acquired a secular slant because of the battles waged within the Christian Church, and laid the foundation of a new civilizing mission in which the state, the Church, and the fighting and trading classes of Europe found common ground (despite conflicts between them in some regions). There followed the long period of colonial expansion and the age of European imperialism with which we are all familiar and remnants of which still continue, especially in Africa. As a historical epoch, it represents a turning point that has transformed the nature of the world.

3. Instead of a contrast between abstraction and intuition as such, it will be more useful to distinguish between two types of abstraction: the capacity to symbolize and the capacity to generalize. The former represents the mathematical mode of thought while the latter relies on empirical observation. This distinction may set apart the Oriental from the Occidental ways of thought, one stressing the mathematical mode and the other the empirical mode though both are found within each. These two modes have always competed in the process of knowledge, including in modern science. With the advent of nuclear physics and the emergence of the science of psychology, both of which rely on observations that are more inferential than direct, attention has been focussed on the complementarity of the two modes. Yet, the proper nature of this complementarity is not fully understood at the level of philosophical thought. This lies at the bottom of the still persisting tension between rationalism and empiricism. As man's consciousness comes to grip with the problem of knowledge in dealing with the human condition, it will have to evolve an appropriate philosophy that links the two modes of abstraction.

SEARCH FOR A SOCIAL ORDER

It is with this transformation, its basic leitmotifs, and the forces it has released that we ought to be concerned. As one ponders over the malaise that has overtaken humanity in recent times—the malaise of organized and accelerating violence, of the decline in human empathy and compassion and the growth of exploitation and cruelty, of the co-existence of corrupting affluence and dehumanizing misery on the same planet—one is forced to take a hard look at the peculiar worldview and philosophy of life known as 'modernity' that first evolved in Western society and has since spread throughout the world.

In general, the history of Western society is that of a struggle for discovering a viable social and political order to minimize the capriciousness of nature and the solitariness and inherent brutality and evil in man himself. This has been the concern of almost all influential thinkers in the West, despite the Socratic concern with virtue and Pascal's counsel against unlimited rationalism. What has mattered most in Western thinking is how to evolve a perfect society, a good society, a beneficient and affluent society. Under this powerful quest, the concept of freedom also got gradually transformed from freedom to some higher end to freedom from want and scarcity and from unpredictability.[4] So did the concept of reason, supposed to be the distinguishing feature of man as against other species. Instead of conceiving reason as a quality embedded in the evolutionary process through which man can integrate the diverse components of his own being for a deeper understanding of life and its meaning, Western man turned reason into an instrument in man's mastery over nature, in creating institutions that would make man himself subject to laws, and in general producing conditions of control and predictability at all levels.

Finally, there is the concept of empirical truth—the ennobling search of Western man that has led to the impressive achievements of science and technology. An attitude of wide-ranging curiosity and search

4. It is true that the concept of freedom as seeking a higher end ('freedom to') is there in the Western tradition, too. Martin Luther used the concept in this fashion and so did Hegel and, among the liberal philosophers, John Stuart Mill. It is after the rise of utilitarianism and positivism that the negative view ('freedom from') for reducing uncertainty in social arrangements took hold. But it is the latter view that has since held fort despite existentialist and other forms of dissent. This point applies more generally also. In the West, as in all other cultures, there have been many strands—spiritualist, romanticist, materialistic, and nominalist, as well as latterday hedonistic and positivistic thought that gained in power since the eighteenth century and has come to dominate the Western worldview of man and society. It is no doubt a simplification to assess a culture by reference to only the more dominant strands. We confess to this charge. But it is by dealing only with them that a realistic critique is possible. There is not much to be gained by spending time on fossils.

after empirical universals has given to the Occidental man his distinctive capacity to manipulate the external environment. It has taken the form of reducing the mysteries of nature into observable laws, and similarly resolving the 'predicament of man' (posed so brilliantly by Thomas Hobbes) by reference to a law-governed social order whose commands are binding on man and whose role is to liberate man from his natural condition of isolation, want, and strife.

To seek in this manner the great and noble expressions of the human mind—reason, truth, freedom—and to reduce the whole of reality into a manageable set of paradigms was, according to the Occidental worldview, what distinguished man from other beings. But as there was evil in man himself that resulted in strife and in wars, it was necessary not to view these great expressions of the human mind as ends in themselves but to bend them to the creation of a good society—free from strife, violence, arbitrariness, and unpredictability. Hence the need not only to discover laws of nature and to subject nature to human control but also, as with Hobbes, to discover laws of *human* nature and to subject its vagaries to covenants governing all men, or alternatively, as with Hegel and Marx, to uncover the laws governing history—the laws of motion of society—and to realize the progressive principle in history that is at once good and inevitable.[5] The good, in all such thinking, is essentially reduced to the common good. The concern all along is to create not just a viable but an ideal social and political order. The Oriental civilizations, on the contrary, went for a minimal view of social and political order. Perfection was to be sought for the individual (and that too for the inner man), not for society. Impressed by the perennial flow of time and the fact that a particular era or social form was inevitably transient, the Oriental thinkers saw folly in man's search for a better and still better life in society. Such an approach, on the other hand, lent too much stress on continuity, produced a cynical tolerance of inequity and

5. It would have been better if, instead of making Hegel 'stand on his head', Marx had parted company with him. For Marx, in his search for a scientific basis to man's search for freedom, had the supreme opportunity of integrating the cognitive and the ethical components in man—a problem until today unresolved in Western rationalism—and thus of moving towards a new consciousness. His concept of historical materialism did not permit him to extend his search far enough. Indeed, the ethical problem seems to have continuously evaded him. Marx's concept of *law* compelled him to make it emerge below the threshold of *consciousness*—which he as a philosopher was interested in but as a 'scientist' was forced to despise as a bourgeois prejudice. Here, of course, Marx is in line with the Western concepts of rationality and science that are designed to attend to the problem of empirical truth alone and not allowed to enter the realm of ethics. Hence the failure to evolve an integrated view of the human being—except for the 'early Marx' whom many are currently busy restoring but who is in fact the Marx before Marxism. It is the latter that provides a full system of thought, not the early moralist.

injustice in social relations, and on the whole underrated the role of power and of human consciousness in moulding man's future.

MAN AND NATURE

The enormous energy that has been released by an application of the Occidental view of man's place in the universe has brought a powerful sense of mastery of *man over nature*. The knowledge of the laws of nature has become an important condition of man's freedom. The model of scientific cognition and manipulation of the environment has been with equal force applied to the problem of human nature and its potentiality, to the building of social and political institutions, and to the conquest of time itself.

In spite of all sense of mastery over nature and in spite of all confidence in building an efficient social order, however (and perhaps in a sense because of this), modern man's capacity to relate himself to the universe is limited in two major respects. The first respect involves *man himself* and his ability to exercise control over his desires and passions, not necessarily by reference to some super-human sanctions but as a quality of his own being, as Confucius would have put it. Although modern biology and psychology have made some spectacular advances in exposing the process of human evolution[6], it appears as if the very instruments of domination and control that modern man has perfected vis-a-vis his environment have taken on a Frankensteinian quality and made him the

6. Sigmund Freud's general diagnosis of the human condition (as distinct from the particular method he developed in dealing with mental sickness) still holds as a classic statement, or rather a twentieth-century restatement of Thomas Hobbes's diagnosis of the predicament of man. There is a basic aggressive component in human nature that cannot be wished away, and it is the task of civilization to tame it. The tragedy is that this basic aggressiveness enters into the institutions that civilized man has produced. Indeed, to no small extent, the insulations that the most modern of these civilizations has produced appear to enlarge and accentuate the expression of violence. It is against this that Freud was trying to fight. His *Future of an Illusion* and *Civilization and Its Discontents,* London, Hogarth Press, 1928 and 1930, respectively, although addressed to the typical Western audience and utilizing characteristically Western concepts such as 'guilt' and 'sense of sin', still remain classics of human prose—full of concern for the human species and its future. As regards research in biology, our knowledge is still inconclusive. It appears that violence is a deeply ingrained characteristic in human evolution and there are severe limits to our ability to control it. We do not yet know enough about the motor mechanisms through which ideas exercise control on the total action of man. Those who have persisted to inquire into this problem almost think that short of a deliberate change in the genetic structure of man, aggression and violence will continue to afflict mankind. Meanwhile, the inconclusiveness of knowledge in this direction has led many to seek refuge in mysticism. Hence the cult of yoga, the guru, Zen Buddhism.

prisoner of his own accomplishments. Science and industry themselves—the presumed agents of man's liberation—have been transformed from being means to man's self-realization to being ends in themselves.

The other major respect in which modern man's capacity is limited involves the very relationship between *man and nature* that has been the main concern of science. Modern man is in continous tension with the rest of nature. The relationship is not based on an integral view of nature but, rather, is based on one of manipulation of 'external' objects that become instruments of man's power and righteousness. This is a serious shortcoming in the phenomenological perspective that underlines both modern science and modern philosophy. Underlying it is a divorce between science and morality. The axiology of the latter still falls outside the scope of science. Reason, the principal instrument of the scientific method, is limited to the problem of truth in the cognitive sense and has not yet been extended to cover the fields of ethics and aesthetics. Given this limitation, the problem of an integrated human consciousness remains unresolved. To us this appears to be a basic weakness of the scientific worldview, at any rate as it has developed so far.

Implicit in this perspective is the assumption that moral phenomena cannot be integrated with natural ones; hence the bifurcation of man between body and mind. Interestingly, however, it was through this dualism between mind and matter, worked out cleverly in René Descartes's attempt to accommodate the claims made on behalf of the supernatural order, that the *primacy* of mechanistic over natural phenomena was in fact established and the way paved for affirming the superiority of scientific over intuitive truths and for asserting man's independence of all external constraints.[7]

The belief in each man being an end in himself, that ever since Immanuel Kant has characterized Western humanism, led in time to the idea of free will and to a gradual separation of the world of values from

---

7. Descartes, sometimes described as the father of modern philosophy, was mainly interested in establishing a mechanistic system based wholly on reason and in getting rid of final causes altogether. However, too conscious of the fate of Galileo, he stopped short of asserting complete supremacy for the mechanistic principle and hence set up a sharp dualism between mind and body (thus saving the face of the exponents of God's will). Later system builders diverged on two paths: some like Baruch Spinoza towards a man-in-nature position by denying to mind any superiority of substance and others by suppressing the mind-matter dualism in favour of universal mechanism. The latter tendency was complete with Hobbes and David Hume, though these belonged more to the English empiricist tradition which also denied any transcendent position to the mind, than to Cartesian rationalism. See the excellent treatment of dualism by Irving Babbitt in Appendix A to his *Democracy and Leadership*, Boston, Houghton Mifflin, 1924.

the world of nature. Underlying this schism is the splitting of the human psyche into two isolated components of cognition and connation, and in turn the separation of law from the entities of which it is a law. The concept of free will thrived on such a separation and in secular life gave rise to the meaningless problem, first posed by Plato, of uniting the philosopher and the king. (In the East, too, such a split took place, as between the Brahmins and the Kshatriyas in India or the Mandarins and the laity in China, although it was based not on a philosophical separation but, rather, based on a concept of nature as something mysterious that only the learned could fathom.) The split continues to our own day in both East and West and has, in the name of knowledge, become a handle for privilege and exploitation.[8]

Such a separation between man and nature, body and mind, intellect and feeling has produced a mental climate of arrogance; man is supposed to live in a condition of splendid isolation without any sense of an organic relationship to the rest of existence. The most striking evidence of this thinking is to be found in the way the findings of Charles Darwin were used for social and philosophical ends. Instead of heeding Darwin's central thesis on the animal origins of man and his demonstration of basic unity and continuity in the evolutionary process, his interpreters (not just the social Darwinists like Auguste Comte and Herbert Spencer and their later followers but also a host of others) were more impressed by the concepts of natural selection and survival of the fittest that have appeared to them to establish man as a superior being.[9]

This disembodied and amoral conception of man was bound to have far-reaching political consequences. It provided the philosophical basis for a transformation of the rational self into an impersonal self and

8. In the West, Marx sought to put an end to this split while in the East both Gandhi and Mao Tse-Tung have vehemently argued against such a division between knowledge and action, between intellect and labour. However, Marx, who posed basic problems facing contemporary man through his concepts of alienation, reification, and commodity fetishism, and his attempt to trace the crisis of modern times in the fragmentation of man from the totality of human reality, still believed that these conditions can be checked when capitalism gives place to socialism and the state withers away. For this he relied on further developments in technology that will liberate man from the 'realm of necessity'; he even idealized leisure and in the end considered physical work as something that is debasing. Gandhi and, later, Mao parted company with him on this point.

9. It is interesting to note that when Jagadish Chandra Bose, a leading Indian scientist who shot to world fame in the early part of this century by his biophysical and physiological research, highlighted the other aspect of Charles Darwin's work, namely, his discovery of basic unity and continuity in the living world, he surprised many of his Western contemporaries. On this see Ashis Nandy, "Defiance and Conformity in Science: The Identity of Jagdish Chandra Bose", *Science Studies*, 2 (1), 1972, 31-85.

of individual moral authority—which needed no higher sanction—into a collective will that also needed no higher sanction.[10] The ground was thus prepared for exploiting the expansive streak in science and technology and legitimizing the urge for dominance in politics. The idea of freedom as a condition of moral life was the great strength of the rationalist tradition, but to have made man's freedom an end in itself pushed him into an amoral position and made him the instrument of a new transcendentalism, that of secular power—and in course of time, of economic power—that was not answerable to any higher law [B].

THE THEORY OF PROGRESS

The most remarkable offshoot of this conception of man and reason is the theory of progress, one of the most important mainstays of the Occidental worldview [C]. A definitive formulation of the theory, namely that science and rationality have made possible continuous advance for man and put an end to the shackles of tradition and religion that bound him, came from the work of the Encyclopaedists in the eighteenth century, although the conception of such a goal was greatly influenced by the rediscovery of ancient Greek classics, the dawn of modern science, and the Reformation. Much that has transpired since the Enlightenment in the Western world—and from there, through the economic and political energy generated by the liberal state and its Utilitarian doctrine, to the rest of the world—has been informed by the basic postulates of the theory of progress. This theory is at the root of the impact of science on society, and has provided fundamental spur to the economic achievements of modern man, the technological transformation of the earth—and now the conquest of space—and the great advances in empirical knowledge about the world. It is also at the root of a fundamentally linear concept of time and space in modern man, has driven him on to an incessant striving for material acquisitions, and accounts for the increasing accent on dynamism, constant innovation and change for the sake of change. It is responsible for the consolidation of secular authority and for its spatial expansion, for the drive for power, for the emphasis on efficiency, and for the at once absolutist and instrument view of knowledge.

The theory of progress has gradually become the basis of a new popular faith—more powerful than any religious faith. In its self-confident

10. "Higher" does not have to be religious or supernatural. It could be a higher law that man himself accepts as emanating from his understanding of the ties that bind him to other men, to other species, and to nature as a whole. The particular metaphysic through which an individual relates his own existence to the universe is something for him to work out, given his cultural background and his own intellectual understanding.

sweep, man has lost his equilibrium and his composure. Though the theory is based on a conception that placed man at the centre of the universe, it has, thanks to the institutional framework that is deemed necessary for continuous economic and technological expansion, produced a world in which man is being constantly driven by forces beyond himself. At the same time, he has lost his sense of mystery and wonder about the universe and the ultimate meaning of life (except, of course, for a few gifted men). The ordinary individual in such a world has become *free*—from the shackles of tradition and the excesses of nature. But he has ceased to be *autonomous*—self-possessed, able to opt of the organizational nexus when he wishes, and seeking his self-realization according to his own wits and values.

Such a perspective on the world, based at least in part on popular faith in the theory of progress[11], has had powerful political and social consequences. In the West it has led to the creation of a mass society that is continuously 'mobilized' for productive efficiency and the corporate state, is 'educated' for carrying out the necessary functions of the productive apparatus, is homogenized through the mass media, and through all this, is enabled to enjoy a growing package of shopping, the precise quantum of which is to be decided by a given individual's propensity for social and psychic mobility—for movement is the essence of modernity. Outside the West the perspective has led to massive economic and political expansion, to domination of the natives in order to liberate them from their traditions, and in general to homogenization of the world through the doctrine of modernization. All men are equal, hence, they must all be uniform—literate for carrying out given functions, urbanized for the sake of efficiency, and socialized into a growing scale of need-gratification as stimulated by the commercial and advertisement media fashioned in the major centres of the industrial world.

11. 'At least in part' because the theory of progress and the popular faith in it cannot account for all that is undesirable in the West and its impact on the rest of the world. The expansive streak in the West owes not a little to romanticist and messianic doctrines of will, of manifest destiny, of the mission of the Christians in 'uncivilized' lands. However, there is no necessary contradiction between these traditions from an earlier age (brought to life by German romanticism) and the expansionism to which the Age of Enlightenment (with its own evangelism and messianic zeal) gave rise. Perhaps in the absence of romanticist traditions, Western progressivism might have proved less menacing. Perhaps in their absence a new metaphysic based on science and rationality may have been born. But one is not sure how this would have happened in the absence of a tradition of humility in man. Science alone does not ensure it. For, after all is said for the scientific spirit, the question does remain: Why have these archaic traditions survived? Can they survive without a fertile soil that continues to nurture them?

THEORY OF MODERNIZATION

The gospel of modernization—that package of urbanization, achievement motivation, mass-media exposure, specialized education, spatial mobility, and a rising consumption of finished goods—that is overtaking and intoxicating the Westernized middle class in these societies has been the principal vehicle of contemporary processes of economic expansion, cultural domination and political manipulation. Its universalizing credo is deeply affecting the autonomy of individual human beings, of diverse cultures, and of most states as well. It has also shaken the self-respect of peoples, made them feel ashamed of their own traditions, and given rise to a high degree of ambivalence in their relationship to their own societies. Contemporary concepts of universalism and world culture are based on this precarious and potentially totalitarian perspective [D]. There may be a lot of condescending concern and evangelical piety for the lot of the poor and the underdeveloped in it, but there seems to be little regard for the dignity and freedom of human beings and the diverse social systems and states that give them their identity.

In institutional terms, the doctrine of modernization, the latest incarnation of the theory of progress, has given rise to a growing faith in centralized institutions. Subtly, both the liberal doctrine of a free society and the communist doctrine of a classless society have endorsed the role of a centralized bureaucracy for achieving social ends. During the very decades when participation has become the dominant value with people everywhere, in actual practice it has not meant much [E]. The capacity of citizens to actively intervene in the social process that the value of participation enjoins has become severely limited because of the high degree of centralization of most institutions resulting from the growth of a technocratic state. In this there is not much difference between formally democratic countries (at least most of them) and countries that avowedly believed in 'democratic centralism'. Increasingly, it is also found that the liberal emphasis on freedom of expression at constituting the essence of liberty is somewhat misplaced. The impotence of liberal intellectuals and the liberal press in the United States on issues like Vietnam and Bangla Desh has shaken this faith.[12]

12. Freedom of the press and of open expression are, no doubt, important; their absence in some of the socialist countries and in many of the developing countries constitutes a major weakness. All the same, the earlier faith in the compelling influence of 'public opinion' has been belied in the face of a state apparatus that has become immune to criticism and the simultaneous development of new methods of communication that manipulate the public mind through the inculcation of personality cults and chauvinist feelings. It requires an extreme measure of irresponsibility and public fraud (*a la* Watergate) for the traditional forums of freedom of expression to become even moderately effective.

Similarly, the idea that the existence of highly organized interest groups will further the cause of freedom has not been realized in practice. No doubt, interest groups have emerged—some of them very organized and able to get their demands fulfilled—but they have proved more potent in fighting for the cause of the already established than for the disestablished. The most important of these associations in which socialists the world over had placed a great deal of faith, namely, the trade unions representing the interests of the proletariat, have turned out to be one of the most conservative elements in the modern state.[13] And with it has gone the expectation that the working classes of the world will unite and overthrow capitalistic forms of dominance.

It is necessary that we understand the class ethos emerging in modern society almost everywhere. In the major countries of the world both capitalism and communism have been increasingly modified by a common middle-class elite to converge into the model of a bureaucratic state in which political, industrial and military power is concentrated [F]. It is significant that the economic ethic underlying capitalism has undergone a major shift. Capitalism no longer depends on the habits of thrift and saving that were highlighted by Max Weber. It now relies on a diametrically opposite economic ethic, the ethic of constant want and waste that are so necessary to keep the industrial machine and its managerial elite going. It is also significant that communism is increasingly basing its appeal on its capacity to demonstrate technological power and industrial efficiency, not on its original rationale of freeing men from the reified constraints of wage labour, class and the state [G]. Curiously, it is this urge to catch up with the more advanced technology of the West rather than any resolution of ideological conflict that has led to the so-called spirit of *détente* among the major communist powers.

On the whole, barring the experiment in evolving a participatory form of economy and a federal polity based on real diversity that is under

13. This may be a hard judgment delivered in a somewhat blanket fashion. One should not underrate the role of the labour movement in changing the nature of the state in Great Britain though its role has often been more 'conservative' (in the philosophical sense of the term) than 'revolutionary' (as Marxist theory had postulated). The same can be said of the labour and socialist movements in the Scandinavian countries and in Israel where, as in the U.K., the trade union movement is a dominant force. However, since achieving their basic economic and political demands, these movements have become parts of the establishment and have often added to the processes of bureaucratization and centralization of decision-making. There are, no doubt, important exceptions and also some indications of new currents in the world labour movement consequent upon the growing power of the multinational corporations. We shall return to this theme in Chapter V when we deal with agents of change.

way (though not without strains or ambivalences) in Yugoslavia [H]
—and of course, leaving out the large rural land masses of Asia and
Africa where poverty reigns and the bureaucrat finds it uncomfortable
—there seems to have taken place a general growth in centralization and
an increase in the manipulative component of the modern state and its
industrial mainstay, both of which are dominated by a class of bureaucrats and professional managers. This class has firm command in the
developing countries too, partly because it is in control in the metropolitan centres. In fact this is the only truly world class—not the workers
of the world shaking off their chains from below but the bureaucrats of
the world operating from command positions at the top. In this situation the role of politics as an exercise of options by ordinary human
beings has disappeared.

Thus the basic values of a scientific humanist culture—freedom,
equality, a classless society—are increasingly subjected to concentration
of power in a few hands. This is inherent in the hedonistic worldview
that, ever since it was propounded, has taken charge of modern man
and his productive apparatus. The result is that the great advances of
modern science and technology have only succeeded in reiterating the
elementary problem of human survival—now on a world scale and with
the aid of more massive instruments of destruction than the human race
has ever known. A war with nuclear weapons or a collapse of the environment may annihilate a large part of the human race and in the
meanwhile their threat has started wearing it out psychologically.

Towards an Alternative Perspective

Before we seek an alternative worldview, it is necessary to pause
and reflect upon the human condition. In a fundamental sense this
condition has not changed very much since Hobbes formulated the issue
in his own search for an end to the human predicament through the
instrumentality of civil society. But in a practical sense it has become
much worse thanks to the inability of the present civil society (which
has taken on a global character) to turn the revolution in knowledge and
communication unleashed by science towards a just, peaceful, and
integrated world order. Basic to the new context of the human predicament is the problem of large-scale violence. The solution is basically
political and cultural—to evolve human forms and educational processes
through which violence is minimized if not eliminated. Biology itself
provides little guide to action—except perhaps in the negative sense of
exposing the depth at which the violent streak in man exists—unless
one resorts to the optimistic belief that the evolutionary process will in
time issue to man a more rational disposition or that man will be able to

restructure his genes so that the aggressive instinct in him is either eliminated or tamed.

It is only in the West that the problem of overcoming strife and violence has been conceived in a secular manner—that is, as something that man himself can achieve in this world and in civil society. The great Oriental systems of philosophy, barring a few deviant thinkers [I], have sought to deal with the predicament of man—of which all of them have been deeply aware—by either invoking supernatural sanctions or undermining the individual urge to power by resorting to a finely worked-out system of social stratification so that each person knows the scope and limits of his personal endeavour.[14] (The two approaches normally have gone together.) While the limitations of the West in respect of controlling the sources of war and violence are all too obvious, the Oriental systems hardly provide an alternative for today's world.

We must all come to terms with the West, the crucible of modern scientific achievements without which an overcrowded planet cannot survive. The issue in coming to terms with the West is whether the growing violence in the human species (and in its relationship with other species and forms of life) is because of the persistence of the nonrational, transcendental tradition from an earlier age despite the rise of science and rationality, or whether it is the culture of science itself, with its exaggerated sense of mastery and conquest and its undermining of the basic religiosity of man, that is responsible for the present crisis. The argument is still going on. However, it seems to us that the two positions are not as contradictory as they appear, that the religious tradition in the West is in tune with its scientific tradition, that the two are woven together in a symbiotic relationship, and that both have propagated a homocentric worldview. With the phenomenal strides made by empirical science, such a worldview was bound to produce a climate of arrogance and exploitation, the ethic of survival of the fittest, and a basically dualistic view of both nature (*Homo sapiens* versus others) and human nature (the cognitive versus the ethical).

It is *only* in this respect that there is perhaps something to be gained by capturing the spirit of some of the more integral perspectives developed by Oriental civilization—their stress on inner harmony and

14. The West also has had a strong tradition of thinking in which the principal interest is to curb the evil in man—from Plato through Christ and in modern times from Friedrich Nietzche and Henri Bergson to Albert Camus and C. S. Lewis. While exponents of this tradition have always been there and it is of late again gaining ground thanks to the excesses of modern technology, the dominant trend in the West continues to draw its inspiration from the secular-rationalistic tradition. For a hard-hitting critique of this tradition that does not fall prey to the temptation of 'embracing the East', see Jacques Ellul, *The Technological Society*, London, Jonathan Cape, 1965.

self-control. We have already made it clear (see the detailed notes to this chapter) that we do not approve of using these concepts in a way that imputes a higher status to nature than to man; this will only perpetuate the alienation we wish to avoid. Nor do we subscribe to any supernatural metaphysics. Basically, both harmony and self-control are concepts that belong to man himself, in respect of the diverse and conflicting elements within him. It is only on the basis of an inner harmony —and the consequent control on undue expansion or gratification of the self—that harmony vis-a-vis the external world becomes possible.[15]

What we have said above does not conflict with the basic postulate of the scientific worldview. Indeed, inherent in that worldview is both the notion of humility and the notion of integration. It is only in the absence of a philosophical disposition of restraining autonomy through an exercise of self-control that the forces released by science can become subject to unrestrained hedonism as has happened so far in the West—and its numerous outposts elsewhere. We place high value on man's autonomy and his sense of power. But it is necessary to ensure that *all* men are assured of their autonomy and power. This makes necessary both equitable distribution (the dimension of justice) and cultural and institutionalized restraints on the use of power (the dimension of violence). For, lacking this distribution and restraint, power that is so necessary for man's freedom and self-regard (its denial in Oriental cultures led to their undoing) can become an end in itself and undermine not only individual freedom but also survival of the species. The crisis we face today is one born out of the issue of species survival. The possibility of total threat on which this crisis is based is new. It was never there before. It calls for a totally different intellectual climate.

It is necessary to dwell further on this. For, the human predicament has acquired new dimensions with the rise and spread of modern technology—which must be distinguished from modern science. The power it has generated has an impact on objects that have no voice in the decision-making processes of modern society, least of all in the representative systems of government. Thus, as the growing economic, energy and environmental crises have shown, decisions taken at one point in time have the

15. Similarly, by an 'integral perspective' we do not wish to advocate an anthropomorphic approach in which man loses his own identity and merges himself with nature. Rather, we have in mind an approach in which there is neither merger nor alienation. To the extent that nature enters into man and binds one man with others, it enters into the very scheme of values that he evolves. The point is to consider man as a conscious component of nature, as 'self-mediating nature' as Marx put it, a concept that Georg Lukacs and Istvan Meszaros (see Meszaros, *The Marxist Theory of Alienation*, London, Merlin Press, 1970) have developed at some length in their work. The problem is to search for the place of intellect in the system of nature. We shall return to this point later in the chapter.

power to affect future generations in very vital and largely irreversible ways. Far from sacrificing gratification in the present for a better future—the common assumption of planning—modern society is constantly sacrificing the prospects of the future for gratification in the present. How is one to assure that the interests of the unborn generations of the future are somehow represented in the present? What applies to the time dimension applies also to the dimension of space: decisions taken in the metropolitan centres of power and their ever rising consumption of finite resources affect millions of people in far-off places. How is one to assure that the interests of the latter are duly represented? And, cutting across both time and space, is the whole question of what man by his wasteful and destructive ways is doing to the rest of the species, to vegetation, to inanimate sources of life. Who is to represent these? Serious problems have arisen for which the prevailing theory of participation has no answers. It is here that the role of the intellectual and the futurist lies—empathizing with these unborn, distant and inarticulate beings, taking a total view of creation, and intervening in legislative and administrative processes at various levels without, however, degenerating into another Brahminic clergy that arrogates to itself all knowledge and wisdom. It is only in this fundamental respect (rather than in the sweeping claims of social science theory) that the true basis of universalism—encompassing all beings—is to be found [J].

Such universalism must combine the scientific spirit as developed in the West based mainly on the assertion of man's primacy over other beings with the eclectic philosophical worldview of the Oriental civilizations based on a recognition of the fundamental unity of all existence, thus drawing from both these past traditions with a view to meet a totally different future. In doing só one should not aim at a mere synthesis of unchanging elements but rather a new integration that is relevant to a new situation. The assumption in all this is, of course, that the human intellect is capable of absorbing and integrating the best that experience has to offer, that cultural divergences do not have the inevitability of natural laws, and that history is no more than a guide to the future in the shaping of which the human actor intervenes decisively. Such a future will have to be built on foundations and a paradigm of action different from any that the various pasts have offered. The role of the latter is no more than heuristic.

The paradigm of action must, while availing itself of the best that modern science has to offer, move beyond the progressive creed and the doctrine of modernization to which it has fallen prey. Basically, the need is to move from a concern to create a perfect society in which all men enjoy goods and liberties provided by the social order, to a conception in which the individual can exercise a wide range of choices in pursuing his self-realization, according to ideals of life that he himself deems proper and in cooperation with other individuals for whom he is moved by feelings of kinship and a shared political destiny. The point of departure of such a worldview should not be the provision of a maximizing social and political *order* in which individuals enjoy uniform comforts and a negative right to express dissent but, rather, should be a condition in which individuals and human collectivities are bound together by a *consensus* on values and a set of institutions and usages that incorporates this consensus.

The purpose of the institutions themselves is to provide minimum conditions of life for all so that men of diverse background and capacities can pursue their own interests and their obligations to others. To the extent that the attainment of these conditions *for all* necessitates restraints on the more fortunate or privileged members of society, the restraints should be exercised and the necessary regulative and redistributive measures backed by social and political sanctions. But all such measures are to be conceived as part of a more general process of building a truly participant community based on a consensus on values.

Justice, not equality, is our operational value, and even justice is to be perceived in a progressively nonmechanistic fashion, as promoting a certain quality of life. Left to itself, the concept of equality can become a dogma, lead to demagogy and tyranny from above, and reduce individual men and women into uniformities called masses in whose name power is concentrated in the hands of a few. A proper concept of justice should, instead, foster respect and preserve diversities in human propensities and preferred social arrangements.[16] Acceptance of diversity will also lead to an awareness that whatever one does—individually or socially—is bound to be imperfect and that he who enjoys autonomy must also exercise self-control and act with humility toward others. Autonomy should not degenerate into unlimited expansion and gratification of the self.

The hedonist concept of individualism (based on the pleasure principle) confused autonomy with free will, and equality with the greatest good of the greatest number,[17] which in turn undermined the

16. We do not wish to be misunderstood. Equality is important as a concept informing the relationship among men as men—that is, in their respective status and mutual regard for each other. But it is justice that provides the political condition for realizing this ideal. Actually, justice provides the form (the process) through which equality (the ideal) can be realized in practice. If equality were to be made the *form*, chaos would follow as spelt out in the text.
17. The utilitarian doctrine, which later provided a justification of authoritarianism in the name of the majority, is in fact no more than a *reductio ad absurdum* of the Kantian doctrine of each man being treated as an end in himself and not a means

liberal spirit that had associated the rise of modern science. The concept led to a potentially insatiable urge to power, heightened the acquisitive instinct in man, and laid the foundations for a spirit of expansionism and dominance. These values still shape the world.[18] If we are to move towards a better world, it will have to be not in terms of creating still stronger authority structures that would optimize values for all. It should rather be in terms of undoing the conditions of dominance and restraining powerful men and states from assuming the role of being society's or the world's gendarme, so that people throughout the world can realize their diverse potentialities and live in peace with each other.

For a fellow-feeling among all men, it is necessary to build on organic networks of love and affiliation—from family to nation. We know quite a bit about man and what spurs loyalty in him. We know about the influence of the way a child is reared on his capacity for love. We know about the impact of cultural and political institutions on man's capacity for deep loyalty. We know about the bundle of emotions that accompany man's capacity to exercise reason as a social being. We know about the value of diversity in building durable human communities. We know about the springs of aggression and the processes through which they can be sublimated. We know how deep loyalties emerge and how they extend from immediate to increasingly wide-ranging networks. The sum of all this knowledge leads to the conclusion that in order that humans can think in terms of the species as a whole, they should first be able to develop loyalties to the family, the community in which they live, and the nation which provides means of self-extension. Concepts of love of mankind and world peace are no substitutes for these. There is no abstracted love for an abstracted mankind. In fact it is dangerous to think so (to love mankind and not men). Indeed, it has often been found that, lacking an environment

to another man's end. For Kant, of course, the right to be so treated was based on the premise that all human beings were expressions of a divine reality and were subject to its imperatives. No such sanctions obtained in the case of the later utilitarians and their positivist and totalitarian offshoots.

18. To be sure, the concept of autonomy that is our primary point of departure in this book has been an important element in Western philosophy. More often than not, however (at any rate, since the nineteenth century), it has been closely associated with the pleasure principle and unrestrained expression of it. For us autonomy is the operational form (value) of the basic postulate of freedom. In that form the function of autonomy is to assert *power* in its most conscious form and to make such consciousness an element in the causal process of history. Self-control, which is our corrective to the value of autonomy, consists in accepting the limit to one's own power in this causal process and admitting the similar power of others. The whole problem of autonomy turns on a wide distribution of enough power without which the autonomy of some turns into dominance over others. This is what has happened in the modern world.

of love and loyalty around them, the votaries of peace tend to be rather violent persons. The effort that is called for by the new crisis that faces man will have to be built on the insights mentioned above. Peace is not something that can be built in the air.

There are two aspects involved in this effort. The first of these is to achieve political autonomy for all states in place of the present condition of debility and dependence for a large majority of them and, on the basis of such autonomy, to ensure the autonomy of all individuals and a relationship of mutuality between them so that the individual and the collectivity are informed by the same set of values and derive strength and dignity from each other. The second aspect relates to promoting the widest possible dissemination of these values so that a solid cultural foundation is laid and so that the actions of men and states are made accountable to these values. The two aspects are related: one is to be conceived as a perspective for political action, the other as an intellectual effort. Without the latter the former will lead to elaborate institutional structures of political and economic order that in the absence of corresponding values informing them, may well be distorted and undermined in practice. On the other hand, the latter activity without the former will become an abstract exercise in sermonizing in which the real political actors will not be interested and which may indeed create a false sense of complacency among the propagators of the new values as if some kind of a revolution were round the corner or, contrariwise, may lead to widespread frustration and a sense of futility and powerlessness among them.[19] In what follows we attempt to combine the two aspects.

INTERVENTION IN HISTORY

The basic issue concerns the ability of man to exercise choices, to actively intervene in the process of history. Our conception of politics is based on such a possibility. Politics, according to us, ought to be neither *ad hoc* manipulation of events as they come nor adherence to

19. The basic point is that no culture (except, perhaps, the most static ones) can be evolved on the basis of abstract values. It can only evolve through an active interaction between actions and the experience of those actions. Value preferences, for us, are not some *a priori* postulates that stand neatly above the ordinary processes of life. Nor do they stand for some absolute and precise standards. For us they are no more than normative guides to action that are constantly being evolved and indeed constantly negotiated in the context of actual life processes. Values, as other forms of empirical reality, are first objects of cognition and then—based firmly on such cognition—of consciousness. In practice they are subject to change and mutation as any other form of life. This perspective must be kept in mind throughout the book.

a predetermined purpose as laid down in some closed system of thought (whether mystical or scientific). It should rather be an exercise of choice in the light of the concrete situation that faces man and the future that lies before him.

To be sure, one cannot wish away all 'laws' or even determinism for that matter. There will always be an element of determinism in the universe, in the arrangements of this planet, in the workings of a polity, indeed in the behaviour of any individual or group. These laws are not limited to the domain of science and the world of nature; they operate in an even deeper manner in the domain of culture and tradition, in the mores governing the collective consciousness of a people, and what is most relevant to us in this essay, in the degree to which man can control his own or his fellow men's instinct towards violence. It is necessary to recognize such regularities and constraints and to understand the scope and limits of the possibilities facing the observer or the actor. The acts of human intervention in the historical process mentioned earlier must be informed by this understanding and the fundamental issues and choices posed by it. However, the whole point about the relationship between knowledge and action, as we now understand it in the twentieth century, is that we should move from the notion of *discovering* either a pre-existing order or a given direction of change (linear, dialectical, mutational) and then simply conforming to these compulsions, to one of *designing* a preferred future within a given range of choices as informed by a set of values.

The search for causalities in the social process, in other words, is to be found through values that have been evolved as a result of the interaction between consciousness and reality.[20] Further, as values provide the causes, the real agent of change is no impersonal or inanimate force or some system of thought but is man himself. Both causation and moral sensibility are to be traced to man, his values, and the power at his command to translate his values into reality. The social process does not operate inexorably and independently of man's consciousness. In evolving his actions, man will no doubt be guided by the regularities and probabilities that govern the universe as well as by the constraints of the particular time and space configuration in which he finds himself, for it is wisdom to do so and folly to just rush into an act without adequate understanding of the forces that are at work. But neither these constraints

---

20. In reality, of course, values may not be and often are not the sole or even the prime causes of the historical process.   But they happen to be the only basis for conscious action. The rest is independent of us. The structure of causation that has a bearing on human action is highly complicated, and we are just beginning to understand it.

nor one's reality perception about them determines one's course of action in any closed manner.

The scheme of values that has guided this essay was stated in the first chapter. Our basic concern is with the development of autonomy —in men as well as in states. To achieve this we must put an end to the fetters that bind contemporary man. These chains are of two types— political and economic structures of dominance and exploitation on the one hand and the limitless stimulation of wants and desires by the irra- tional uses to which technology is put on the other. It is clear to us that the two are related and, further, that it will not be possible to curb either by simply capturing state power, even if this were to be done in the name of the people as a whole (whatever that may mean in practice). We must evolve a cultural environment—through politics and through education —that will inculcate in human beings both the need to end exploitation and the need to limit wants, the need for self-control. Self-control, according to our view of a sane life, is a corollary of man's freedom. Lacking control by the self, there is bound to be control and manipula- tion from the outside.

MAN, NATURE AND TECHNOLOGY

A combination of the principle of autonomy and an ethic of self- control necessitates a proper approach to the relationship between man and the totality of existence. This relationship has to be conceived as one of active union,[21] not one of conquest and exploitation. (Man's

21. By this we do not mean that there is a 'whole' and there are 'parts' and man is such a part. We do not think that the universe is such a rational whole, with a purpose and end of its own; at least we do not know, on the basis of present know- ledge, that it is. Those who have posited such an end (as in Greek rationalism, Indian mysticism, Taoism, and Christian theology) have ended up in both a justi- fication for inequality and an attitude of arrogance that we, in this book, have rejected. In such a metaphysic the most powerful 'part' arbitrarily identifies itself with the 'whole' and arrogates to itself the duty of maintaining the whole, as hap- pened with the Brahmins in Hinduism and the Churchmen in Christianity. (The position is a little more subtle in the case of the Chinese, but in effect the Mandarins assumed the same role.) In our view each being is a whole, reality is plural, and the unity we talk of is a unity born out of a consciousness of diversity on the one hand and perception of common goals and a readiness to work for them on the other. There is no prior assurance of such unity—it is not pre-existing—or indeed even of security, development, or progress. Hence the problem of the 'human condition', a continuous challenge to reason and intellect. Where man may differ from other species is in his intellectual capacity to symbolize in the abstract, a capacity that can be turned into a moral imperative encompassing the whole of humanity, in- deed the whole of existence. Hence the possibility of unity without destroying diversity, or rather by building from diversity.

exploitation of man is only a part of a larger ethic of exploitation.) The modernist view of evolution and the place of man in the hierarchy of living species arrogated to *Homo sapiens* a higher place—as the only embodiment of reason that could fathom the mysteries of nature, master them, subjugate other species, and kill them for the ends of civilization.[22] It was a small step from this arrogant view of the structure of the universe and the place of civilized man in it to the view that some men were more civilized than others and the division of the human species between advanced and backward peoples, between masters and slaves, between the chosen and the subject races. Thus the concepts of *übermensch* and *üntermensch* are inherent in the modernist worldview, at any rate as it has been developed so far in the West.

The roots of this arrogance in modern man are to be found in the movement from a conception that views society and technology as instruments for a deliverance from nature and its sinister quality which may have been a legitimate view to begin with—as Hobbes masterfully perceived it, though he did not anticipate the uses to which his analysis was to be put later[23]—to a conception in which society and technology have ceased to be instruments and are looked upon as the essence of civilization. Thanks largely to the environmental crisis, it is now being realized that such a perspective will bring nemesis on man himself and undermine his survival.

Our point of view is that we must replace the prevailing perspective that assigns to man a position of superiority in relation to other species—thus paving the ground for imputing similar superiority to only some men and races [K]—by one that respects life and its needs and potentialities in whatever form it is found.

22. We do not yet know enough about the rationality of all beings, and whether it is innate in the evolutionary process. But the claim that only the human race has been endowed with the rational faculty is already beginning to be challenged by biological research. What does appear to have emerged from man's sustained search after truth (whether mystical or scientific) is that there is need for some unifying principle. But it is difficult to define it in any precise manner. From the point of view of this book, reason is not devoid of moral sense, and its ultimate criterion is respect for life in its infinite diversity. Such a view may not be scientific in the strict sense of the term (though, after all, it is based on the principle of life itself), but it is the only basis for an enduring civilization. The present instrumental and exploitative use of reason has no place in such a perspective.
23. If anything, Hobbes sought to evolve a mechanism that would enable man to inhibit and control his passions. His more hedonist followers lacked his deep understanding of the baser instincts that man had biologically inherited and had proceeded to give to these instincts a rather long rope. Contemporary man is still hanging by this rope, but it is not clear for how long. There was also no doubt in Hobbes's mind that society was an instrument (in fact, according to him, a contrivance). The end was man, the creator of the commonwealth.

This brings us to the problem of scarcity that has underlain man's quest for mastery over nature and over other species, as well as underlain man's exploitation of man. The great advances in technology, it is said, have the potentiality of putting an end to all this by taking man from the realm of necessity to the realm of freedom. Now it does appear that modern technology is poised to end the condition of scarcity that has characterized all earlier epochs, provided, of course, that man can make the right kind of technological choices for the fulfilment of human goals, which today means a prudent and parsimonious use of resources, a judicious combination of techniques and skills for a wide distribution of opportunities and income and, with this in view, liberation from undue dependence on remote sources of sustenance. The promise of abundance by itself does not guarantee any of these.

The accent on abundance as a value in itself has led to an utter neglect of the political dimensions of technology arising out of the growing divorce between production and consumption, and hence between work and man. Indeed, the vision of liberation from the realm of necessity is guided by a conception of work as essentially an encumbrance. The vision is one of producing for the people but not by the people. It is the vision of a highly organized mass society and of a centralized welfare state. It is also the vision of a total alienation of man from the rest of existence and the rise of a wholly synthetic man. It is in many ways a frightful vision [L].

From the perspective of our values of autonomy, justice, and participation, we would prefer a quite different approach to the problem of scarcity and the nature of work and technology. For us science and technology are, as everything else, natural phenomena. To posit these activities as apart from and over and above nature constitutes the root of the loss of control by man of his own destiny. The tragic consequences of modern science are to be found not in science but in a philosophy of life that has turned science into a religion and made it the source of a new obscurantism. In the process, man, the presumed master of all things, has lost his moorings. There is need to adopt a more integral view of man, nature, work, and technology.

As we see it, the basic objective of technology is to make man self-reliant rather than having him barter away his autonomy in exchange for an increasing consumption of goods and services. We would prefer a far less centralized system of production and technology even if this means less abundance of consumption items. We would prefer a system in which, as Gandhi put it, production is not only mass production but also production by the masses. This perspective has become far more relevant today: while scarcity may be on the decline, this is made possible by making more and more men idle and superfluous to the social process [M]. In our way of thinking, we would posit a close relationship between man and work, and stress the necessity for man to work if he is to preserve his sanity and integrity. A total end to the realm of necessity will, far from ushering in a realm of freedom, put an end to whatever freedom man already enjoys. Let there be less aggregate affluence and greater equality in life opportunities, a measure of self-control in this, and some restraint on man's acquisitive instinct. An end to scarcity is within man's reach, and there is no mystery about it—provided, of course, the present structures of inequity and exploitation are put an end to, and provided an end to scarcity is not conceived in terms of vulgar and wasteful affluence. Technology will be a great aid in bringing such a world about provided that man knows how to control it—and control his own self.

CONCEPTION OF POWER

Involved in the profile of values and perspectives outlined above is a conception of power that at once emphasizes man's capacity to intervene in the social process and obliges him to build ethical and institutional safeguards so that such intervention does not result in unrestrained expansionism and self-indulgence. While we believe in the autonomy of politics, our conception of politics is one of translating values into reality, thus making the normative dimension of the human enterprise the basis of the emprical dimension. Unrestrained empiricism leads to a blind emphasis on power for its own sake and results in a manipulative view of man's relationship to nature, to society, and ultimately to other men. This is what happened to the theory of progress. Among other things, that theory led to the vulgar conception of a division of all men between progressives and reactionaries, a conception that is still going strong and has become the basis of a great deal of both intellectual and political tyranny in our world. In our conception of progress (we do not deny validity to the *concept* of progress or of modernization; it is the prevailing *theory* that we reject) we assign a central role to the human consciousness in defining the ends of politics and hence, of power.

This means two things. Power should be purposive and not an end in itself; and it should be rationally distributed. As mentioned earlier, we consider power a necessary condition for autonomy. But for it to play that role it is imperative that its concentration be put to an end. Neither justice nor nonviolence (our major operative values) can be realized without an adequate distribution of power—between men and between states.

In advancing the perspective described above, we are less interested in translating abstract notions like equality or fraternity into some institutional superstructure and more interested in realizing man's autonomy and a responsible exercise thereof, where life is found to be meaningful and man is in harmony with himself,[24] where justice prevails and the sense of injustice is minimized if not removed, and where the individual is able to sit back and ask—provided he is disposed to ask such a question—if he is in fact living the life he wants to. The specific values and institutional arrangements of our preferred world would have meaning only in the larger context of providing conditions for the self-realization[25] of individuals in cooperation with other individuals, in the process imparting strength and dignity to human collectivities known as states.

We offer this integral view of man, society, and nature as a possible alternative to the prevailing perspectives. In developing it we have drawn from both Occidental and Oriental worldviews both of which have had powerful impacts on the minds of man. (If we have given more space to the Occidental one, it is because it has drastically changed the world we live in and has confronted it with fundamental issues.) We have found both of them wanting. But we have also sought to combine, to the extent such a combination is possible, worthwhile elements from both. At the present stage of human knowledge it is difficult to arrive at a preference for either of the two modes of civilization. What is somewhat less difficult, bold though it may sound, is to move beyond both of them. It appears to us necessary to do so. For while the basic human predicament continues to be as it always has been, the conditions in which it has to be dealt with have been drastically altered.

24. It is meaningless to talk of harmony between man and nature as such. That can only be a reflection of harmony *within* each natural unit—above all within man, who is the cause of much disharmony and tension both for himself and for others.

25. As with the concepts of self-control and harmony, our concept of self-realization does not refer to a supernatural purpose in which man finds his realization. We are aware that there are many—both in the East and in the West—who use the concept in that manner, and we respect their point of view. But their metaphysic is different from ours. For us the only basis and evidence of the existence of self is in one's consciousness. Self-realization is rooted in this consciousness. It is realization of man's purpose in life in a conscious manner. We are, of course, aware that these days even the term 'consciousness' is used in somewhat mysterious (often mystical) ways. We do not blame those who do so. When the whole world around one seems to be falling apart, perhaps the only way to survive psychologically is to identify with something unknown and mysterious.

Notes

A F.S.C. Northrop, *The Meeting of the East and West*, New York, The Macmillan Company, 1946.

B On this whole theme, and especially on how Kant's conception of freedom paradoxically provided the germs of national chauvinism, see the illuminating Humayun Kabir Memorial Lecture of Isaiah Berlin, "One Philosophical Source of the Idea of National Freedom", New Delhi, Indian Council of Cultural Relations, March 8, 1972.

C The most authoritative statement to date on the theory of progress is, of course, J. B. Bury, *The Idea of Progress*, New York, The Macmillan Company, 1932. But see also the critical study of the idea as it worked itself out in recent times by W. Warren Wager, *Good Tidings: The Belief in Progress from Darwin to Marcuse*, Bloomington, Indiana and London, Indiana University Press, 1972.

D I have dealt with this problem in greater detail in my paper "World Peace and Human Dignity" in Christoph Wulf (ed.) *Handbook on Peace Education*, Frankfurt, International Peace Research Association, 1974.

E For an analysis of the limitations of the participation model as found in practice, see Satish K. Arora. "Participation and Nation-Building", in Rajni Kothari (ed.) *State and Nation Building: A Third World Perspective*, forthcoming. For a comprehensive treatment of the implications of the Western model of modernization, see Satish K. Arora, "Pre-empted Future? : Notes on Theories of Political Development", *Behavioural Sciences and Community Development*, 2, September 1968, 85-120.

F For analysis and documentation of how "state-management" has taken command of a society based on free enterprise and a democratic constitution, see Seymour Melman, *Pentagon Capitalism: The Political Economy of War*, New York, McGraw-Hill, 1970.

G That the theory of progress and its modernist developments is shared by socialist thinkers has been ably shown by Wagar, *op. cit.*, pp. 325-333.

H A few other experiments in workers' management deserve notice, especially the one in Peru. For a rigorous treatment of the model of decentralized industrial economy that avoids the pitfalls of both capitalism and state socialism, see Jaroslav Vanek, *The General Theory of Labour-Managed Market Economies*, Ithaca, N.Y., Cornell

University Press, 1970, and *The Participatory Economy: An Evolutionary Hypothesis and a Strategy for Development*, Ithaca, N.Y., Cornell University Press, 1971. On Peru, see Michael Anderson, "New Forms of Worker Participation in the Peruvian Economy", New York, The Ford Foundation, September 1972, *mimeographed.*

I The most well known of these is the extreme materialistic school of the Charvakas, approximately, 600 B.C., which anticipated Western hedonism by several centuries. But both the Sankhya cosmology of knowledge and the Nyaya methodology of science also reflect a strong tendency toward empirical sensitivity and the freedom of the intellect. Both Jainism and Buddhism (as well as the philosophy of the Ajivakas), though mainly interested in salvation from the bonds of the finite world, were highly rationalistic and rejected supernaturalism. There are many good works on these schools of thought. For a good critical survey, see D.P. Singhal, *India and World Civilization*, 2 vols., London, Sidgwick & Jackson, and Calcutta, Rupa, 1972. For a Marxist analysis of Indian materialism and atheism, see Debiprasad Chattopadhyaya's two studies, *Lokayata: A Study in Ancient Indian Materialism,* New Delhi, People's Publishing House, 1959, and *Indian Atheism: A Marxist Analysis,* Calcutta, Manisha Granthalaya, 1969. The intense realism of pre-Buddhist Confucian thought is, of course, well known.

J For a penetrating analysis of this whole issue from the point of view of ethics, see Hans Jonas, "Technology and Responsibility: Reflections on the New Tasks of Ethics", *Journal of Social Research*, 40 (1), Spring 1973.

K More recently, biological research has been summoned to justify claims to ethnic superiority. See, for instance, C. D. Darlington, *The Evolution of Man and Society*, London, Allen and Unwin, 1969. For an excellent critique showing how a great deal of biological research (not just Lysenkosim) is used for political and ideological ends, see Robert M. Young, "Evolutionary Biology and Ideology: Then and Now", *Science Studies*, 1(2), 1971. Watson Fuller (ed.), *The Social Impact of Modern Biology,* London, Routledge and Kegan Paul, 1971, provides a number of good studies on this theme.

L We shall return to these issues, including a discussion of Marx's conception of the end of progress as a movement from the realm of necessity to the realm of freedom, in greater detail in Chapter IV.

M For an extensive treatment of this problem, see Chapter IV.

3

ON JUSTICE

THE MOST outstanding obstacle to the realization of a just and nonviolent world is to be found less in the capriciousness of nature that modern man seems to have "mastered" than in the social and economic order that he has contrived in pursuit of progress and civilization. It is an order that has condemned large sections of mankind to live in poverty and degradation subjecting them to shame and humiliation, and reducing the societies and states of which they are inhabitants to a condition of dependence and servility.

This is the most glaring indictment of the prevailing world order. For in it, despite all the advances of modern society and the industrial and technological revolutions of which it is so proud, a large part of mankind lives in destitution and misery. The world we live in is above all a world characterized by massive injustice. Moreover, it is injustice that is becoming increasingly conspicuous and hence painful because of the growing duality of world economic and political conditions. Before we propose our own prescriptions for removing both the objective sources of such injustice and the subjective *sense of injustice* that is found all around us, it would be worthwhile to make a diagnosis of the historical process that has brought about this condition.

Diagnosis

THE COLONIAL IMPACT

The dynamic historical process that has led to the sharp duality of the contemporary world can be traced to the ascendancy and expansion of the industrial civilization in the eighteenth and nineteenth centuries, thanks to its systematic mastery over the material culture of man and its development of highly centralized political structures that were appropriate to the new era—at a time when the other great civilizations of the world had fallen prey to social stagnation, spiritual complacency, and political in-fighting. The ascendancy of the industrial nations and their expansion abroad were the results of a complex of revolutionary changes that took place in Europe not only in the fields of religion, science, and the art of government but also in agriculture, commerce, and industry (which is why the European impact on other regions turned out to be more comprehensive than was the case with earlier colonizations). But our main concern in this chapter is with the political economy of this encounter that has produced growing affluence of one part of mankind and immiserization of the other.

The reasons for this are not mysterious. Whereas the industrial revolution in the region where it originated in due course produced an economy based on skilled labour and growing productivity per labourer, which in turn led to a steady rise in real wages and thus a slow distribution of wealth and welfare (typically through the joint stock corporation, the trade union and the welfare state), the same technoeconomic forces produced quite different results in the colonized regions. In the latter, whose economic penetration and political control were motivated by the interests and needs of the colonizing countries in the form of raw materials and markets, the supply of primary goods and raw materials for export became the dominant economic activity, the traditional rich handicraft industries suffered eclipse as a result of deliberate colonial policy, while the modern sector that came into being in the course of time was very small and narrow in its base, catering mainly to the consumption needs of a fraction of the people and unable to provide employment to a fast-growing population. The result was that an increasing proportion of this population was thrown on the backward sector of an economy based on subsistence farming and other primitive occupations, thus giving rise to the phenomenon of growing under-employment and poverty in these regions—as a result of being drawn into a common world economy.[1]

1. In the words of Dadabhai Naoroji, an early leader of the Indian nationalist movement and a very original thinker who propounded the theory of economic drain during the colonial period, there were "two Indias" created by an internal drain on the one hand and an external drain on the other, the internal drain being an instrument of the external drain. "In reality there are two Indias—one the prosperous, the other poverty-stricken. The prosperous India is the India of the British and other foreigners. They exploit India as officials, non-officials, capitalists in a variety of ways, and carry away enormous wealth to their country. To them India is, of course, rich and prosperous. The more they can carry away, the richer and more prosperous India is to them....The second India is, the India of the Indians—the poverty-stricken India. This India, 'bled' and exploited in every way of their wealth, of their services, of their land, labour and all resources by the foreigners —this India of the Indians becomes the poorest country in the world after one hundred and fifty years of British rule." See the authoritative study of Naoroji's

Under these conditions a process of growth based on domestic purchasing power was out of the question. The effort to boost export earnings as a basis of development also turned out to be a mirage because of increasingly adverse terms of trade for the poorer countries and growing barriers to trade imposed by the rich countries. The only available impetus for breaking the blockage to development was a massive transformation of the agricultural sector which was not forthcoming because of the nature of the elite to which the colonial system gave rise. The situation was strongly reinforced by the nature of the educational system, which was designed to turn out a small middle class to occupy junior positions in the administration and designed to leave the bulk of the people illiterate, who were thus denied the skills necessary for moving into the modern sector.

AFTER INDEPENDENCE

These conditions continued even after the end of the colonial period and after the advent of the era of conscious planning by the newly independent nations. There were many reasons for this. The technology that was borrowed and imported from the "developed" countries was inappropriate to the needs of the poorer countries, being capital-intensive and promising a fast rate of growth in the aggregate but unable to alleviate the most crucial dimensions of poverty, namely, extremely low incomes for a large part of the population, a growing scale of unemployment and an even more increasing scale of underemployment. Moreover, this technology called for levels of skill and know-how that were simply not available indigenously and had to be imported, also in the name of technical assistance. Even where the skills were available to some extent, as for example in India, the dynamics of "aid" and international trade made those equipped with these skills closely dependent on the metropolitan areas which have held firm control over research and development. This further widened the gap between the professional-bureaucratic elite and the people. The economic priorities pursued by the former turned out to be impediments to a substantial transformation of the agricultural and other backward sectors. Furthermore, the consumption pattern and demand for goods and services tended to be set by the prevailing norms of the highly developed countries that were blindly accepted by the rich and the not-so-rich of the poor countries.

Under such conditions of stagnation, all sections try to adjust to the inevitable. The industrial entrepreneurs are satisfied to work for low

drain theory by B. N. Ganguli, *Dadabhai Naoroji and the Drain Theory*, Dadabhai Naoroji Memorial Lectures 1964, Bombay, Asia Publishing House, 1965.

wages and to accept limited markets, enjoying non-competitive and monopolistic positions. The professional middle classes adopt a consumption
ethic and a style of life that are inimical to growth and that set them apart
as a privileged class that feels culturally superior to the general population.
Those living on agriculture get divided between an absentee landowning
class living in urban areas and the mass of poor peasants, neither of whom
are inclined to introduce reforms and innovations in this crucial sector.
And the labouring classes in the cities who have jobs develop a vested
interest in maintaining and improving their bargaining power, which
in turn restricts the growth of employment and impels the employers
to adopt labour-saving technology. Meanwhile, the ranks of the unemployed and the poor keep swelling, despite the overall growth of the
economy, as the small and mechanized industrial sector absorbs a diminishing proportion of every increment in the labour force and the rest
are thrown onto the backward sector of the economy whose already
depressed state is made worse by the influx. All this is not only out of
tune with the real needs of the majority of the people; it also drastically
cuts into the saving potential of these countries, shifts resources and
production priorities toward satisfying the luxury needs of a parasitic
class, and altogether distorts economic development, despite the much-
talked-of industrialization and modernization of the economy.

THE TECHNOECONOMIC MODEL

During the 1950s there came into being a persuasive doctrine of
economic development that was supposed to lay the foundations of the
above-mentioned industrialization and modernization and take the poorer
countries of the world from underdevelopment to a rapid take-off
into sustained growth and, in the process, bridge the gap between
the rich and the poor nations. According to the new design the
government was to occupy the commanding heights of the economy;
control the allocation of resources and production priorities in other
sectors; step up the mobilization of resources, internally through heavy
taxation and externally through "aid" and foreign investments; raise the
accumulation of capital and investment in the modern sector; radically
alter capital-output ratios through controls and rationalization of the
economic structure; and through all this, give rise to a rapid growth of the
GNP and *eventually* of the standard of living of the people as a whole.
This approach to the removal of poverty in the countries of the
Third World has turned out to be a chimera, leading in fact to further
accentuation of disparities and injustice. Perhaps the principal reason for
the failure has been that the doctrine of development relied exclusively
on economic factors and neglected critical dimensions of the power

structure of the society, the bureaucratic structure of the state, the distribution of educational opportunities, and the nature and orientations of dominant elites, all of which were reduced to the status of *ceteris paribus* or at best treated as residual factors. The doctrine relied heavily on the governmental bureaucracy as its principal agent of change at a time when, administratively, most of these bureaucracies lacked the requisite entrepreneurial talent. These bureaucrats also came from a class that was culturally closer to the small group of local industrialists and landed gentry, as well as to foreign investors and technical experts, than to the bulk of the poor people for whom the plans were supposed to help.

Centralized planning and decision-making, imported models of growth and consumption patterns, and corresponding technology and managerial culture that resulted from handing over the development process to such a class also distorted economic priorities. Instead of a substantial transformation of the really backward sectors of the economy and the generation of increased productivity, employment, and purchasing power in those sectors, what took place was super-imposition of a small modern sector that absorbed the bulk of savings and capital but whose capacity to absorb ever growing additions to the adult population turned out to be quite small.

The overall result of such a doctrine of development is for everyone to see. In country after country one witnesses the spectacle of positive and in some cases accelerating rates of growth of aggregate national incomes coupled with both absolute increase in poverty and unemployment for the people and widening disparities in incomes and wealth—all of this as a direct consequence of economic development. The much noted gap between the rich and the poor nations has its more disturbing reflection at the domestic level in a widening gap between a small privileged class that gets all or most of the benefits of development and a large and growing mass of the poor and the destitute the linkage between the two kinds of gaps being provided by the much publicized transfers of technology, homogenization of elite cultures the world over, and the new doctrine of international cooperation based on "aid" and collaboration. The great organizational *tour de force* of our time, the multinational corporation, has cemented this linkage into a dynamic relationship. The overall result of this great thrust for the ostensible purpose of stimulating development in the poor countries has been an economic structure of the world that has become more sharply dualistic than it ever was, with nearly half the population of the world below or close to the poverty line [A].

The dualist character has been brought forth by many studies, including those carried out by the United Nations. Thus, according to the *1970 Report on the World Social Situation* published by the Department of Economic and Social Affairs of the United Nations [B],

Structural dualism—while a far from unknown phenomenon in advanced countries—has thus emerged more plainly than ever as a crucial dimension of the social situation in developing regions, where it is manifested in severe and generally growing disparities between higher and lower income groups, between the *elite* and the masses, between urban and rural areas, between regions within countries, between the modern and traditional sectors and above all, between the minority who enjoy full remunerative employment and the vast majority who lack adequate (or any) means of earning a living.   By depriving large population groups of equitable shares in the material fruits of progress, in opportunity for advancement and in political influence, such dualism has in some countries posed a rising threat to stability and social integration, while also constituting a major disincentive to popular participation in development plan implementation.   These are the realities which underlie the observation, made by a recent United Nations meeting, that the concept of dualism is more appropriate than that of aggregate growth models as a framework for understanding the social problems and social aspects of development [C].

The indicators of this dualism are evident within all major underdeveloped regions of the world (not just between them and the prosperous regions).   Thus, in Asia, which accounts for more than half the world's population and the largest concentration of poverty in the world (the per-capita annual income being around $100 for most of the countries), income disparities are very large [D], the living condition of the low-income groups is worsening [E], there are large regional disparities that are getting worse with progress in economic development [F], and the social pyramids are assuming an increasingly modern character in which higher-middle-class bureaucrats, entrepreneurs and professionals are getting closely linked into a common *elite* who have "profited most from the tendency toward an increasing concentration of income and other development benefits" [G] while the masses are still reeling in not just economic poverty but also in ever deteriorating physical conditions[H].

In Latin America, which manifests extremes of correlation between high rates of growth in GNP and concentration of wealth and income in a small upper-class living in a few favoured regions and cities [I], the estimated unemployment rate (based on a much larger and growing rate of underemployment) is over 28 per cent of the active population [J], the underutilization rates taking on staggering proportions in agriculture even in countries like Mexico with "consistently favourable rates of growth both in national income and in agricultural production" [K]. In Africa, where even the rudiments of self-reliant nationhood are yet absent in most

countries, a truly indigenous elite has not yet emerged while the bureaucracy has become a privileged class, devouring a "disproportionate part of
the budget in many African states" (the salary of a high level civil servant
in Uganda is 112 times the *per-capita* national income) [L]. Efforts at
improving the lot of labourers has resulted in unemployment [M], provin-
cial and regional inequalities are on the increase with development
frequently concentrated around major cities[N], and all of this is resulting
in growing unemployment among the rural poor[O]. In the Arab region,
otherwise a reservoir of massive wealth in the form of oil, the educated elite
has become most powerful, resulting in rates of urbanization that are much
ahead of rates of industrialization [P], consequent neglect of rural development, low wage rates thanks to the continuous influx of unskilled persons
from the rural areas into the large cities, and high rates of unemployment
and underemployment among the rural poor [Q]. In all these regions
the impact of modernization has resulted in growing disparities, a pervasive dualism in cultural and economic levels, and expropriation of the
benefits of modernization by a small upper-middle class.

ELITE AND MASS

Thus the same technoeconomic factors that led to a progressive
improvement (even if unequally) of living standards of almost all sections
of the people in one set of countries has led to a confinement of such
improvements to a small section of the people in another. Such an
imbalance in the outcome of the same historical processes has in turn
produced mounting social cleavages and tensions within the poorer
countries arising out of an almost total cultural dissociation between the
elite and the people, the growing economic dependence of these countries
on metropolitan centres, and as a direct consequence of this dependence
but also helped by converging trends in military and security arrangements,
a dependent political status for all but a very few of them. Meanwhile,
the ravages of localized wars, the ever growing stockpiles of nuclear armaments and their continuous testing, and the aggressive exploitation of
natural resources by the purveyors of the new technology have begun to
erode the health and well-being of coming generations in the poorer regions. (To top it all, pressures are now being brought on the latter to
slow down their development for the sake of ecological preservation.)

The model of modernization based on technoeconomic transformation that has bewitched the leaders of the poor countries in their search
for making up with the richer countries has thus turned sour for the former.
Among other things, the modernization model gave rise to the illusion that
centralized planning and a regime of economic controls can be the principal catalysts of far-reaching social change. What in fact happened

was the growth of an insensitive and heady bureaucracy far removed from the people, an increasing concentration of crucial decisions into a few hands, and more often than not, a demagogic leadership and an authoritarian political regime. A number of these regimes have received artificial respiration from abroad, most notoriously from the United States, which took on the role since the Truman Doctrine, of being the world's *gendarme*. Military dictatorship, frequent *coup d'etats*, and a constantly fattening and parasitic elite have been the main features of many of these states—in Latin America and Southeast Asia in particular.

RADICALISM

The situation has not been much better in countries where avowedly leftist regimes have come into being. The radical pretenses of these regimes have released expectations that can be scarcely realized, given the nature of the model that has been adopted and the nature of the elite through whom it is sought to be implemented. Most of these regimes are pseudo-socialistic in their ideological makeup. They lay more stress on brave slogans designed to earn international goodwill than on domestic performance, create artificial crises to cover up basic inadequacies, and generally produce a climate of instability arising out of failure to perform, which only leads to demands for still-more-adventurist policies. The usual labeling of political regimes in these countries as 'conservative' or 'radical' provides no meaningful clue to actual performance. For, with the exception of Julius Nyerere in Tanzania and Mao Tse-Tung in China, the leaders of all these regimes seem to share the same technoeconomic assumptions and the same general perspective on social change—and the same neglect of the political-institutional dimensions—that we have found responsible for continuing poverty and injustice in the world. This striking similarity in basic doctrine owes itself to the fact that the elites of all these regimes come from one homogenous class throughout the world, namely, the highly educated and urbanized middle class. In the words of a perceptive observer from Latin America [R],

> In most Third World countries, the population grows, and so does the middle class. Income, consumption, and the well-being of the middle class are all growing while the gap between this class and the mass of people widens. Even where per capita consumption is rising, the majority of men have less food now than in 1945, less actual care in sickness, less meaningful work, less protection. This is partly a consequence of polarized consumption and partly caused by the breakdown of traditional family and culture. More people suffered from hunger, pain and exposure in 1967

than they did at the end of World War II, not only numerically, but also as a percentage of the world population.

Alternative Perspective

Fortunately, the technoeconomic model discussed above has not, despite its general appeal and a powerful demonstration effect, acquired an exclusive hold on man's quest for a better life. Equally potent have been the values associated with such a quest, awareness of which has spread to large sections of the world population thanks to their affirmation by both the proponents and the critics of the reigning philosophy of progress. These values—of freedom, equality, participation, and justice— have acquired the autonomy of powerful ideas, provided yardsticks by which the claims and pretenses of elites and counterelites are measured, and are gradually giving rise to alternative perspectives on preferred conditions of life.

The diffusion of these values has produced an awareness of both absolute and relative deprivation, produced a growing *sense* of injustice, and led to a consciousness of conflicts of interest between groups and nations. These perceptions have brought the value of social justice to the forefront of human aspirations; the concomitant and equally pervasive value of participation has begun to loosen up power structures and disturb the political status quo in various countries. With this the norms that had so long sustained inequitable social arrangements and legal orders have gradually suffered erosion and lost their legitimacy and authority. Men and nations, especially in the Third World, but perhaps also in the other two worlds, are looking for a new basis for consensus that can translate the absolute values of freedom and justice into operational goals, a spelling-out of the strategies needed for realizing these goals, and a new institutional model for implementing these strategies in the real world.

A DIFFERENT REALITY

Much of this groping, however, is still at the level of expressing a generalized discontent with the existing state of affairs. In order to arrive at a comprehensive understanding of the contemporary world social situation, it is necessary to grasp that the conditions that obtain in large parts of the world today are very different from those that obtained in nineteenth-century Europe, in Meiji Japan, or in post-revolutionary Russia. The elemental social problem that is crying for solution today is not one arising from exploitation of labour by overexerting it but, rather, is one of simple nonparticipation in the productive process by millions of human beings who have no useful role to play in society. Similarly, the main source of cleavage in the world today is not one arising from a conflict between classes on an international scale as was the case in nineteenth-century Europe but, rather, is one between those living in metropolitan areas and having access to the world's resources and those that live in the vast countryside—which includes entire nations—where the only important resource (land) cannot absorb growing numbers of people in any productive manner. Furthermore, the world context in which these cleavages and barriers operate today is not one of vast distances and primitive colonization but is one of ever shrinking size and collapsing levels in which the whole world is becoming divided between a few centres and a vast periphery [S].

NEED FOR FRESH THINKING

These are conditions in which a model of social and political development that is based on large-scale technology and organization, homogenization of the world productive process, international division of labour based on comparative costs, and a communication technology based on spreading the latest in everything is likely to accentuate rather than alleviate patterns of economic backwardness, social injustice and political domination. The way to counter these tendencies lies in rejecting certain prevailing assumptions and replacing them by some fresh thinking. Thus it is necessary to self-consciously admit the value of diversity in human aspirations and technological choices instead of suppressing it at the altar of universalism, to arrest the centralizing trends in modern technology that create growing disparities and cultural barriers within single societies, to shed the idea that cities are coterminus with civilization or large size with progress, or think of economic welfare in terms of achieving minimum conditions for all and not just in terms of aggregate growth targets, and, finally, to appreciate that the issues of social and economic justice that now face the world cannot be handled by experts alone and call for an involvement of the people in shaping their own lives.

These considerations suggest the following preferred framework of policy perspectives and structural reform, at least for the next quarter century of world development. At the end of that period there may be need for further fresh thinking on the problems that then face the world, although the nature and magnitude of those problems will in good measure depend on what is done between now and then.

1. *Focus on Man* : The prime concern of economic policy for a just social order ought to be to generate employment that is able to absorb at least the new additions to the adult population, and where there is a

substantial backlog of unemployment and underemployment, to absorb that as well. The major source of injustice today is to be found not so much in a condition of general scarcity as in the fact of diminishing marginal utility of man as such, in the fact that hundreds of millions of people throughout the world find themselves idle and useless, often in their very prime of youth. The problem has been stated in no uncertain terms by the present President of the World Bank,

> The cities are filling up and urban unemployment steadily grows. Very probably there is an equal measure of worklessness in the countryside. The poorest quarter of the population in developing lands risks being left almost entirely behind in the vast transformation of the modern technological society. The "marginal men", the wretched strugglers for survival on the fringes of farm and city, may already number more than half a billion. By 1980 they will surpass a billion, by 1990 two billion. Can we imagine any human order surviving with so gross a mass of misery piling up at its base?

2. *Agricultural Transformation:* The major impetus for such employment [T] will have to come from a transformation of the agricultural sector, converting it from an area of stagnation to a catalyst of growth. This can be achieved, first and primarily, by introducing and rapidly implementing the new technology associated with the green revolution. The green revolution does seem to us to have provided a major breakthrough for nations wanting to achieve self-sufficiency as well as for raising the status of agriculture in national priorities. However, there is need to adopt these practices with conscious care and try to adapt them to fulfil social goals. They must substantially raise employment and the incomes of the poor, not just aggregate output. Beyond availing of the new inputs there is need to attend to other practices: crop differentiation that can increase the amount of labour needed per acre of land and raise the income of labourers, development of water resources that are suited to the needs of small farmers and tenants, encouragement of farm practices that are labour-intensive, discouragement of mechanization that is labour-replacing and the provision of relevant credit and infrastructural inputs for the small cultivators. This, in turn, calls for the other package of measures known as land reforms, so that the benefits of the green revolution are widely dispersed instead of being pre-empted by the well-to-do farmers as has occurred in so many countries, so that the rural social and economic structure becomes more egalitarian, and so that the available land is able to provide employment and a minimum income to millions of more families than is presently the case in most poor countries [U].

3. *Rural Industrialization:* In large parts of the world it is safe to predict that the sum total of reforms involved in the new agricultural technology and redistributive legislation will not be enough to sustain a growing population on land. Studies from several countries on manpower absorption by different sectors of an economy show conclusively that, except in places with very low density and large surpluses of land, there comes a stage when agriculture begins to absorb a diminishing proportion of the rising population. This critical stage will be reached in most of the poor countries between 1975 and 1980 [V]. It does not follow from this, however, that those not engaged in agriculture should take to the cities for jobs in modern industries, for the fact is that the latter are not as great employers of men as they are of machines; and, in any case, the investment needed to generate the needed employment through modern industry is of a scale that few among the poorer countries can afford—except by large-scale import of foreign capital, which is neither feasible nor desirable.

If we consider various other trends in resource use, congestion, breakdown of city life, and growth of crime and violence, it is necessary to restrain large-scale migration to the cities. There is need, therefore, to provide nonfarm employment in the rural and semirural areas. This can be done, first, through massive public works programmes for constructing durable community assets (building roads, canals, wells, and various other infrastructural facilities for rural development) for which there is great scope in millions of villages and tribal settlements round the world. Employment in these public works can take on a role quite different from short-term relief operations; they can become a basis for long term investment and reduction of costs in such spheres as water use, land consolidation, and marketing of farm output, in turn generating more productivity, employment, and incomes. A large part of these activities can be supported from increased food output, thus also restraining inflationary tendencies. Improvements in agriculture can also be used as a stimulus to a whole line of processing and refining industries in the rural areas.

Second, such a combination of increased farm output and increased employment on land and public works should provide the basis, through its stimulation of demand for consumer necessities, for the growth of small towns close to the rural areas where medium- and small-scale industries can be located. The usual haphazard growth of towns and cities that takes place in the absence of conscious policy renders them into essentially parasitic spots where middlemen bring the flashy output of industries from large cities (and imports from foreign lands which, of course, continue to tantalize men and women in many ex-colonial countries) and tempt villagers into buying them at exorbitant prices. This should give place to a conscious policy of decentralized industrial development and location so that urban growth becomes complementary to rural development and contributes further to the growth of employment and incomes of the poorer strata. The chief casualty of the colonial period was a whole range of rural and semirural industries and a number of non-agricultural occupations that were means of livelihood to large sections of the people —and which in fact made for a society that was far less unequal and unjust than is the case now [W]. It may not be possible to revive the whole spectrum of these occupations, but it is possible and necessary to provide a new basis for fulfilling the same economic functions, namely, making available work other than farming. The encouragement of self-employed artisans, the cultivation of the finer arts and crafts according to different national traditions, and the growth of new and small-scale industries for the manufacture of goods needed by the local people can provide the basis for this regeneration.

4. *Social Continuum:* The crux of such a combination of policies designed to raise employment and alleviate mass poverty is to put agricultural and rural development at the core of public policy. But there is a counterpart of this approach in the area of urban development and industrial policy as well. Apart from heavy industries that require large capital inputs and centralized organization, industrial development should be employment-oriented as much as possible, should produce goods that are needed by large strata of the population rather than by a small middle class, and should be widely dispersed in the country so that the employment that it generates benefits all areas rather than is concentrated in a few cities or regions as is the case in large parts of the world today. Regional disparities constitute a crucial dimension of social injustice— and its visibility—in most of the ex-colonial countries. Most of the favoured regions are those with large urban centres.

Socially, this means that the present duality of city and country-side must give place to a continuum in which the green revolution (and its necessary concomitants in livestock and horticultural development) regenerates the villages, small-scale and medium industries are located in the towns, and large-scale industries that necessitate heavy inputs of capital and high technical efficiency are located in the cities. As such a fusion between industry and agriculture takes place, further intermediate links in this continuum—rural social structures in towns, urban amenities in villages—will develop, thus combining the best-traditions of both rural and urban life and producing a composite and integrated culture.

Our preferred world is not one made of millions of self-contained villages (as was Gandhi's dream) but, rather, is one of thousands of small nucleating towns toward which the rural landscape gravitates, thus doing away with both the present duality of metropolitan and rural cultures, limiting the large size and concentrated location to just the industries that cannot do without them, while at the same time enlarging the size and horizon of rural communities, and providing them with the necessary infrastructure of welfare and communication facilities. Such a spatial structure—supported by a decentralized structure of community decision-making as argued below—would provide the necessary framework for the technoeconomic alternative to the present dualist model of city versus countryside.

5. *Policy on Education:* It is not simply by altering the economic basis of rural-urban relationships that a more just social order will be created. We also need to alter the cultural underpinnings of the present patterns of dominance and disparity. An important aspect of the sharp duality of life styles and living standards found in most poor countries is the nature of the educational system whose aim continues to be to produce colonial-type gentlemen, disoriented from the larger society and constituting a class apart. ·

In most ex-colonial countries, formal education was initially meant to produce an *elite,* mainly to fill the ranks of the bureaucracy, the law-and-order establishment, and in some countries the technical positions in public administration and private enterprise. This orientation still persists in a large number of these countries in spite of the achievement of independence and, in some of them, in spite of the political elite's commitment to democratic and socialistic ideals. Education, far more than property or income, is the basis of privilege in these societies.

Meanwhile, a majority of the population continues to be illiterate and unskilled while the ranks of the highly educated in the urban areas keep swelling. Studies in this area suggest that whereas expansion of literacy and primary education produces very rich and rapid dividends, after a point higher education turns out to be a huge waste [X]. Acquisition of a minimum educational level greatly raises a person's skills and his capacity to enter the employment market; it also raises his sense of potency and his ability to relate himself to the outside world, his sense of political efficacy, and his general self-confidence and sense of dignity [Y]. In contrast, an undiscriminating expansion of higher education beyond the absorptive capacity of the economy produces an alienated class that is unable to relate meaningfully to the rest of society,[2] rapidly inhabits various levels of the bureaucracy making it increasingly inefficient and

---

2. We do not share the diagnosis that the main fault in higher education in the developing countries is that universities are far too oriented to liberal arts and general science training and do not give adequate attention to technical education. In our view, the universities (perhaps everywhere) have gone too far in accommodating this view and have in the process lost their character. It is the function of a university to train the minds of its members and provide basic analytical skills for facing concrete problems in life. Rather, the fault lies in the fact that universities are turning out engineers and technicians, economists, and social scientists who are

insensitive to the needs of the people, and, with growing unemployment in its ranks [Z], loses self-respect and becomes aggressive.

This polarization between a large mass of illiterate and totally unskilled and *hence* unemployed people on the one hand and a class of people who are overeducated and *hence also* unemployed on the other is a natural culmination of the hiatus between the elite and the people— and between parasitic cities and a depressed countryside—discussed earlier. We must alter this condition by a major allocation of resources to mass literacy, primary education, and adult education programmes, by giving special attention to the economically weak and socially handicapped strata whose major avenue of mobility seems to be education,[3] and by a re-orientation of the job market so that employment to a large spectrum of nontechnical jobs is available to those without college degrees, thus deflating the importance of higher education and the disparities that result from insistence on degrees.

Higher education itself needs to be reoriented, by restricting university education to what its logical role is, namely, to provide basic grounding in main sources of theoretical knowledge, and to develop a vast network of functional education located in the vicinity of institutions and enterprises where knowledge is to be used. Except for a few advanced courses for specialists, these should impart intermediate skills through short-duration programmes, for use in the rural and semiurban areas where the real work is. Only thus can the present spectacle of the highly educated queueing up for jobs in the cities while the villages are starved of technical manpower be brought to an end. Several commentators appear to dismiss higher education (and institutionalized education generally) as largely unnecessary [AA]. We do not share this view. In almost all developing countries there is need for a very large number of doctors, engineers, geologists, architects, designers, managers, even economists and sociologists. What is at fault is not their availability but their placement, their location. Most of them are unwilling to go where the real jobs are, the institutions where they learn are unwilling to train them for

basically illiterate and who are taught from obsolete texts dumped by multinational publishers into the colonial markets. Graduates come out of these mass factories wholly unprepared for dealing with the problems they are likely to encounter in their work.

3. One of the unfortunate consequences of the recent attack on schools and education in some developing countries is that upper-class elites who have already cornered educational resources and occupy bureaucratic and professional positions (and have sent their own children abroad for studies) have been busy pruning down educational programmes—just at a time when such programmes were beginning to spread to backward regions and lower classes. Though the motivation of its authors is clearly different, the "deschooling" thesis poses the same danger as the "limits to growth" thesis.

use in local conditions, and the leaders of these countries are unwilling to tell them candidly about their duties and their responsibilities.   There is need to look upon education as a political process, upon the attainment of a degree or diploma as a social good that must be capable of being socially used, and upon the relationship between educational output and available work as part of a conscious plan of development.   Higher education, instead of becoming an instrument of class privilege and exploitation and a source of disparities, must be made an integrator of human resources and human needs.

There is also need to undertake a major review of the whole institutional approach that has accompanied the modern view of education—classroom-based, bookish, graded, and located in large campuses in large cities.   This approach needs to be replaced by a closer relationship between education and work—including intellectual work where education is sought for scientific and literary pursuits—and by bridging the gap that divides the location of one from the location of the other.   City-based education must be largely for city folk.   For others, schools and other institutions must go where the people are, not the other way around. Unless these various aspects of the educational scene are approached with some perspective on the changing social reality, it is difficult to see how the deep cultural barriers that divide different classes and accentuate economic disparities can be overcome. Education can be made to bridge these gaps or to accentuate them.   The need is to move from the latter orientation to the former.[4]

There is need to give special attention to the education of women. In most parts of the developing world women are less educated than men, in countries with low literacy levels women are far less literate than men, and within the depressed social strata and ethnic minorities in these countries the gap is even more pronounced.   Meanwhile, daughters of the rich are flocking to the universities and some of them are leading women's lib movements (aping their counterparts in affluent countries), which in the developing countries mean the liberation of the privileged. These gaps in education among women and between them and men are an important source of the persisting duality of cultures, economic levels, and consumption standards, the latter more often than not being a direct

---

4. There are practices outside the educational sphere that contribute to the inequitous role of education.   One is the wage and salary structure that obtains in a society—the enormous gap between the top and the bottom of salary scales, the wide disparity between payments in private and public sectors (the former being very high), and similar gaps between urban and rural jobs, even of the same type (the rural being underpaid).   These differences provide a powerful rationale for prescribing higher (and foreign) degrees for the better-paying jobs, something that the poor and the weak can never afford.

function of the perennial shopping to which the educated women are so addicted. These differences also account for the wide divergences in the way children of the rich and the poor are brought up, thus perpetuating sharp disparities for decades to come. A greater attention to raising the educational levels of women and mothers from poor, underprivileged, and conservative[5] strata of society can spin off a major process of social reconstruction.

6. *Ethic of Consumption:* Even more fundamental than the gaps in the literary culture are the gaps in the material culture that divide the urbanized upper and middle classes from the people. Perhaps the most important and glaring contrast in the poor countries of today is caused by the extraordinary consumption levels and material possessions of the richer and high-status groups, following almost *in toto* the standards set by the high-consumption societies. The lust for things and for more and more things has become so myopic that it has given rise to all kinds of unethical practices, chief among these being a large incidence of corruption among public officials and a thriving black money economy that is sustained by the availability of a large array of consumer goods.

Apart from the vulgarity of such ostentatious living in societies characterized by massive poverty and malnutrition and apart from the creeping corruption to which it gives rise, such standards of consumption also undermine the whole fabric of economic policy. If a massive pro- gramme of employment and social welfare is to be generated, a high rate of savings and capital accumulation will be necessary. This implies a high rate of savings among those with large incomes as well as implies a res- traint on salary and wage increases among the employed classes, including the working class, so that resources can be transferred to employing the unemployed (in a poor country to be employed is itself a privilege) and raising income levels of the poorly employed and the underemployed.[6] There is also need to encourage voluntary savings among the working class, the farmers, and the lower-middle classes who have already reached an

5. Apart from the poor and the underprivileged, in some societies there are specific ethnic groups in which women are assigned a subsidiary status, and this condition is perpetuated by wide gaps between men and women in their access to cultural institutions, economic opportunities, and political movements. Educational de- privation contributes substantially to this condition. Thus, in India both the general standing of the Muslim masses (as distinct, of course, from the small urbanized and educated elite) and the status of women among the Muslims have suffered from the low educational standards of the women.

6. Underemployment is even more of a curse than unemployment. After all, the choice to remain unemployed is not available to the really poor who must take whatever comes, however little, intermittent or degrading. For a fuller discussion, see my "Political Economy of Employment", *Social Change* (New Delhi), 3 (3), September 1973.

income level that provides for basic consumption needs [BB]. At the same time the consumption of the really poor sections must be raised substantially both for increasing productive efficiency and for equity.

All of this calls for an *ethic of consumption* that discourages ostentatious living, cuts down the production and consumption of non-essential items, and shifts production priorities toward fulfilling the needs of the poor. It is, of course, necessary to encourage saving among the peasantry, the lower-middle classes and even the labouring classes as mentioned above. But this will be an impossible task unless the pace-setters of society themselves adopt a consumption ethic that encourages austerity and reduces the gap in material culture between the different classes. Gandhi put his finger on the most crucial dimension of moving toward a just social order when he called for *a limitation of wants* and warned his countrymen against falling prey to an industrial machine that not only reduces a majority of men into labouring slaves but also dictates what and how men should eat, wear, dress, sing, and dance. Today his insights are even more relevant than when he lived. If there is to be peace and harmony in the world and an end to exploitation among men and nations, the present norm of a high-consumption ethic must give place to one that on the one hand meets the minimum needs of all men and on the other hand limits the needless expansion of wants that have no relationship with the basic requirements of body and mind.

7. Nature of Production: Built into such an ethic of consumption is also an ethic of production that is critical to the achievement of justice in society. The current notions of social justice derive from a concept of economic equality that is essentially distributive. It is not surprising, therefore, that both theoretical understanding and empirical evidence have underlined the need for first expanding the cake and then distributing it.[7] Part of the problem is that both production and distribution are thought of in terms in which the mass of the people are reduced to a position of subjects and onlookers. An economic ethic that seeks to meet the consumption needs of all while limiting the flow of inessential commodities involves a simultaneous increase in the incomes of the poor and the output of goods that they will need to buy with those incomes. This means that instead of conceiving production and consumption as two separate activities, one aims at an economic system that (to repeat Gandhi's dictum) not only produces for the mass of the people but one in which the mass of the people are also the producers.

---

7. Even in the socialist countries committed to the creation of a classless society, there has been a tendency to allow economic disparities to grow for a considerable time. Only later, as for example after 1948 in the USSR, have they moved towards greater equality.

As all visions, perhaps this, too, is an ideal type. All that one can hope to initiate is a movement toward such a state. In practical terms this calls for a location policy that, while permitting large-scale organization where it is unavoidable, will encourage the growth of small-scale, labour intensive, decentralized pattern of industrial development. Similarly, the market economist's retrogressive concept of *effective demand* (that only the needs that are backed by the existing distribution of purchasing power are worth producing for) will have to give place to a concept of *need effectiveness* so that the real needs of the people as a whole determines what goes into the package of production. A combination of such a production system and the consumption ethic outlined above will lead to a climate in which progress toward dispersal and decentralization of economic power becomes possible. As this happens, the orientation to social justice will become less technocratic and become more political and thus capable of initiatives from below.

8. *Social Minima:* A major casualty of the present structure of consumption and production is the fact that large numbers of people living in poor—as well as in some rich—countries suffer from acute malnutrition and resulting physical and mental deficiencies. Their numbers are likely to increase in the next few decades. While national and international bureacurats are busy propagating birth-control measures to ward off an "explosion" sometime in the next century, the problem of enabling those who are already born and will be born in the next twenty-five years—only after which population planning is likely to have an impact—to live a normal life and put in sustained work for their livelihood is receiving inadequate attention.[8] The picture of the poor that emerges from various studies is highly depressing: it is a picture of large families exhibiting physical and psychic abnormality, incapacity for sustained work even for a few hours, a pronounced inferiority complex, a tendency to deal with patterns of exploitation and coercion by directing them inward and against their own dependents, and a vicious cycle of parents inducting children into these characteristics of deprivation and degradation, turning them into the same kind of adults when they grow up, and thus almost *ad infinitum.* We must give top priority to a programme of providing basic health care and an adequate supply of protein and other nutrients to the poor and especially to their children. Internationalist and humanitarian sentiments found among the rich of the world may be channelled into this one simple task. It is only after a minimum standard of health

---

8. This is not to underrate the importance of reducing population growth. For in a already highly populated country the burden of dependency on the income-earners becomes much too heavy and the *sense* of dependency among the young brings in feelings of rejection and humiliation.

is assured—and the benefits of education are widely spread—that people's perception of survival of infants and family size will change and the problem of population growth will be tackled on a rational basis. Alongside minimum levels of income there is need for certain essential social minima (varying, of course, according to diverse cultural and climatic conditions[9]) that should be provided for all men everywhere.

Political Economy of Justice

We have deliberately gone to some length in outlining the precise policy perspectives and corresponding ethic of behaviour needed for the realization of justice in a world marked by extremes of disparity and inequity, both between and within nations. It is only on the basis of such detailed considerations (discussion on which is already in progress in many quarters) that a more general perspective on goals and strategies for the future can be concretely stated. We shall do the latter now.

DEVELOPMENT FOR JUSTICE

We reject the notion that nations of the Third World ought to follow policies that will bring them to the same level as the industrially advanced nations. Such an aspiration is both unrealizable and undesirable. It is unrealizable because, as pointed out by a devout planner from the Third World, the only way to get anywhere near the national incomes of the rich countries is:

> to accelerate as much as possible the growth of GNP in developing countries and decelerate the rate of growth of population so that the growth rate of GNP per capita in developing countries is much higher than the growth rate of GNP per capita in developed countries. The task is not at all easy. If this rate is assumed even 3 per cent during the course of next 30 years for developed countries as a whole, it will take a rate of growth of 12 per cent for developing countries to catch up with the average GNP per capita of the

9. This point should not be overstretched. It has sometimes been used as an alibi for continuing the present disparities in standards of nutrition between the rich and the poor countries. At the same time adherence to standards developed in the richer countries can produce such high and unachievable requirements that no effort whatsoever will be forthcoming. (As has often happened before, extremes of relativism and universalism produce the same results for the lot of man.) A study of varying needs of diverse peoples is likely to both ensure action—because it is within reach—and lead to new discoveries, such as by rediscovering indigenous vegetable and other resources for quickly raising standards of nutrition and health.

developed countries by the end of this century.... If the rates of growth of GNP per capita are 5 per cent and 6 per cent for developed and developing countries, there will be a gradual reduction in the relative disparity but the absolute gap will be more than doubled at the end of 30 years [CC].

Apart from the impracticality of such an approach under conditions of rising populations and the growing scarcity of resources crucial to rapid industrialization, it is also not a desirable goal. Bridging the gap with the rich nations in a short span of time entails exclusive concentration on growth rates and nelgect of progress toward social justice. And yet it is only the latter that constitutes development. At any rate, that is how we look at the problem. It is necessary to make a distinction between growth and development. Although there is no necessary conflict between the two, they need not go together. By itself, to aim at a high rate of growth of GNP is unexceptionable; indeed, a noticeable increase in the employment and incomes of the poor is not possible without a significant increase in GNP. But it is equally true that one can have a fairly high rate of growth of GNP without increasing employment and incomes of the lower strata of the people. In other words, whereas social justice *entails* a high rate of growth of GNP, such growth does not *ensure* justice.

This is clear from the history of the economic development of a large number of countries in the underdeveloped areas, especially in Latin America and Southeast Asia. Even a country like India, which has tried from the beginning to reconcile the objectives of growth and justice as well as the objective of economic self-reliance, had for a long time depended on a model of industrialization and of planning that concentrated more on raising the rate of growth than on spreading employment and raising the incomes of the lowest deciles of the population. It is only recently, with a more clear commitment to removal of poverty and expansion of employment opportunities, that it is groping toward new a model of development. China has had greater success in evolving a model of development that ensures minimum income and employment for large masses of the people, though in terms of rate of growth of GNP it continues to be one of the less rapidly developing countries of the world. There is reason to believe that a number of other poor countries are beginning to realize the serious limitations of the growth model that aimed more at bridging the gap with richer countries than at closing the wide gaps that existed in their own societies. But the full implications of rejecting a model that relies exclusively on the rate of growth and moving toward one that conceives of it as merely a statistical summation of a series of concrete goals are yet in the process of being worked out in all these countries.

MINIMA AND MAXIMA

Our analysis in this chapter provides the elements of an alternative model. The objective of development, according to us, should be to achieve minimum conditions of material welfare for all the people, the *minima* to be defined according to local conditions and norms, some societies fixing them higher than others but all of them providing at the least a package of minimum items of human necessity such as food, clothing, shelter, nutritional needs of children and mothers, and socially approved minima of health, education, drinking water, and public transportation for all. The extent to which these minima should be translated into personal or family incomes or be combined with social welfare and social security programmes of the government will depend on local conditions and the nature of the political system. But it should not be difficult for any system to work out a minimum-income policy as a basic component of development planning.

A policy of minima entails a policy of *maxima*. Indeed without the latter the former is, in practice, impossible to realize in reasonable time. Also, beyond a certain point, incomes ought not to be allowed to grow nor human wants allowed to be artificially stimulated by the aggressive salesmanship of modern industry or the demonstration effects from the rich capitalist countries. There are two reasons for this limitation, one of which is relative and the other absolute. No one has a right to amass more and more income and riches when large sections of the population live below subsistence standards. Also, it is morally undesirable to go beyond a certain level of fulfilment of human needs. For an unlimited gratification of wants leads to individual decay and social disharmony, an unnecessary destruction of natural resources, a fouling of the human environment, and hence a bartering away of the health and happiness of future generations for the present pleasure and lust of a few. Hence, our emphasis on "limitation of wants" as a necessary principle of our preferred world.

There should be a reasonable *scale* connecting the minima and maxima, that is to say, an admissible ratio between the two, thus limiting disparities and enabling society to implement the principles of natural justice. Entailed in the norm of such a scale is the further norm of *transfer* of surplus incomes and wealth above the maximum to those who have not yet reached the minimum.

Together, the notions of minima and maxima, a reasonable scale between the two, and transfers from the rich to the poor provide us with an economic philosophy not just for a particular country but for the world as a whole. For it also suggests that countries that have already achieved prescribed levels of material well-being have no right to bottle up resources in the name of national sovereignty and self-aggrandizement. On the other hand, we have no intention of suggesting that international transfers of resources and wealth should take the form of "aid" from the rich to the poor countries as we understand the term at present, for it is clear that aid policies have seriously compromised the autonomy and self-respect of recipient countries and of individuals living in them. Such autonomy is an integral part of our conception of justice. Instead, a reversal of the policies of self-aggrandizement of the richer nations should be realised by social and ethical movements led by sensitive intellectuals and public figures within those countries, movements that will bring about changes in trade patterns and ecological policies, put a halt to the ravaging of distant lands and extracting their fast depleting resources for the indulgence of already over-developed nations, stop wars of aggression waged by these nations that maim and destroy the populations of poor countries, including their future generations, and enforce restraints on high-consumption behaviour with a view to stopping the destruction of natural resources and the human environment of this planet, if necessary by imposing strict fiscal and punitive sanctions. We are not interested in bridging the gap between rich and poor countries as an end in itself but, rather, are interested in seeing that the acquisitive spirit that has taken hold of the richer countries does not become a vehicle of injustice and destruction on a world scale as is the case at present. (The oil crisis forced by the Arab nations on the highly developed regions of the world in 1973 has, in the light of our analysis, provided a major opportunity to the latter to put their own house in order and, by so doing, enable the other regions of the world to come into their own.)

ISSUE OF PARTICIPATION

Implicit in our preferred model for social and economic justice are also a number of other issues. The norms of minima and maxima are not mere economic formulations; they are part of a certain conception of a good and desirable life. Not only should an individual be entitled to a minimum level of living; he should also be able to participate actively (though he ought not to be forced to do so) in the way things are produced and decisions are made. It is not just a minimum wage that one thinks of here in some kind of a contractual relationship, alienated from the work process and the total scheme of ownership, production, and distribution of the means of livelihood. Rather, one thinks of an apparatus that man himself controls, finds meaningful, and derives a sense of personal power and significance from. Furthermore, to the extent that economic activity is managed and mediated by political and administrative agencies, the whole problem of effective participation in decision-making, at the desirable *level* and in optimum *units*, becomes real. Without such participation the economic aims may indeed be difficult to achieve.

There is also the question of not permitting the economic process, and what is now tellingly called the "industrial-bureaucratic complex" of modern society, to take on an automation of its own and destroy every other value in its inexorable march. In other words, as the values of a participatory democracy and of nonviolence in man's relations to man and to the environment are joined with the values of autonomy and justice, it may well be that we should ask ourselves equally basic questions about the kind of institutional superstructure that we want to build. Three major dimensions of this issue are (1) the rural-urban structure of the economy, (2) the territorial structure of the state, and (3) the participatory structure of the polity. As we pose these questions, it will become clear that the available model of modernization is not conducive to our goals; that the norm of a necessary shift from a predominantly rural to a predominantly urban structure based on large-scale industrialization may not be the best thing that human intelligence has devised; and that urban metropolitan life, far from being a "civilizing" instrument, may turn into a structure of manipulation, exploitation, and destruction of the very properties of man's natural environment that are essential to human survival.

Similarly, we may also question the norms of centralized government, large-sized states, and big bureaucracies as necessary instruments of national integration and political accountability; and as we question these, we may begin to answer with greater clarity the problems raised about local autonomy, about decentralization of functions, powers, resources, and talents, and about optimum size for genuine participation of the people. Perhaps there is something to be gained in the very short run from large-scale enterprises, modern communication media, and centralization of planned initiative, although the real issue here is less of scale than of control. But it is also necessary not to close all options for the generations to come concerning the quality of life they would like to have. As the prospects of the future are vitally affected by what is done in the present—it is no longer possible to think in terms of just a few months or even a few years ahead—it is a matter of considerable responsibility that these various consequences of present actions are borne in mind.

It is necessary to consider here a widespread belief that rapid development cannot be carried out in a participatory framework, that only a determined and authoritarian elite can bring it about, that this indeed is the lesson of contemporary history. Our answer to such a position is that it mistakes appearance for reality, that the issue is not one of choice between liberal democracy dominated by machine politics and state socialism in which a small bureaucratic elite seeks to perpetuate itself, that both these systems are authoritarian as far as the large numbers of the people are concerned (there is far greater similarity between the two than appears at first sight), and that the real issue relates to the classic predicament of political life, namely, the relationship between those in power and those out of power, between the government and the people. Seen in this light it is not surprising that the demand for authoritarianism has normally come from members of the privileged classes (the intellectuals, the bureaucrats, and the technocrats), often reinforced by the analyses and prescriptions of foreigners and, not infrequently, of foreign powers.

It is, of course, difficult to devise a decentralized society in a world environment in which national security and aggregate economic power become the prime demands on national resources. This indeed is the principal dilemma, not just of individual societies but of the entire human species. It is the new scenario of the classic Hobbesian problem, still unresolved. And yet one must pose an alternative to the present system and work towards it. We have tried to do it in the present essay. (The argument will continue in the chapters that follow.) Our model of a participatory system is not conceived in terms of simple political reforms. Rather, it is expressed in a number of sectors—concerning economic organization and its governance, the nature of education, location of work and enterprise, choice of technology, size of units (economic, political, demographic, communications), and the nature of work. Participation is not some process of involving everyone and reducing all to a common denominator. Rather, it consists in evolving institutional structures from which diverse individuals get a sense of dignity and self-respect, as beings that are able to determine their own destinies. (Poverty and inequality are themselves reflections not just of prevailing relations of production but rather of structures and values that deny dignity to the human being.)

Nor is our thinking on participation conceived in terms of establishing idyllic and isolated small communities. Our conception (outlined above) of a social and spatial continuum goes against such a utopia. We are also convinced that given the numbers of human beings we have to deal with, such a utopia is no longer feasible. Our concern, rather, is to imbibe into structures at various levels and of various sizes the *value* of participation as integral to our model of a just society and our conception of autonomy and dignity of all human beings. It is only through such an integrated view of the various components of our model that an alternative political perspective can emerge and policy issues can be discussed in a meaningful manner.

It would be folly, however, to look upon such a perspective as in any way smooth sailing on some neat path. Nothing is more difficult to realize than changes in the social framework of politics—except for the worse.   Every step on such a path needs to be fought for, by organizing for it and building sustained pressures from below in the form of social and intellectual movements. And it is, of course, clear that these will need to be conceived and carried out in not one but many spheres, at not one but many levels, and in not one but a large number of societies.

These, then, are the issues that arise when specific problems of economic strategy, political structure, educational policy and the reconstruction of the human space are considered from the integrated perspective provided by a set of values and the criteria that follow from it.   Involved in such an approach is what may be called a design for living in which reason, compassion, and a regard for the equal worth of all men are joined in the cultivation of a truly civilized life.   And as we do this, the distinctions between economic and political issues disappear and we begin to see the real linkages that underlies any effort to produce a better world.   Our conception of justice entails such a comprehensive perspective on the future.

Notes

A We do not subscribe to the extreme view that all aid programmes and collaborative agreements between local and foreign investors are solely motivated by a consciously worked-out design for exploitation. There are some who have genuinely believed in the utility of such programmes for the development of underdeveloped countries (e.g., Lester Pearson, *Partners in Development: Report of the Commission on International Development*, London, Praeger, 1969). We do think, however, that even the latter—ranging from national and international technocrats and the economists who are making a living out of "aid" to idealists keen on banishing poverty from the world—have been insensitive to world political and economic realities and have, often unconsciously and naively, aided the trends discussed by us here. For a comprehensive debate on the issue sponsored by the World Order Models Project, see Jagdish N. Bhagwati, (ed.), *Economics and World Order: From the 1970's to the 1990's*, London, Collier-Macmillan 1972, and New Delhi, Orient Longman, 1973.

B U.N. Publication E.71.IV.13, New York, 1971.

C The meeting referred to is reported in United Nations, *Social Policy and Planning in National Development: Report of the Meeting of Experts on Social Policy and Planning held at Stockholm from 1st to 10th September, 1969* (U.N. Publication E/CN.5/445).

D *1970 Report on the World Social Situation, op. cit.* See Table 2 on p. 7 and analysis based on it on p. 8. Income disparities are wider in urban than in rural areas. Thus, according to the well-known *Report of the Committee on Income and Levels of Living (Part I)* published by the Indian Planning Commission in 1966, the top decile of the urban tax-paying households accounted for 42.4 per cent of pretax income while the entire lower 50 per cent of the households accounted for 17.5 per cent. The rural counterparts of the top decile and the lowest five deciles was 33.6 per cent and 20.7 per cent. The U.N. Report also cites (p. 9) similar findings from the Philippines and South Korea.

E According to a plan evaluation study undertaken by the Indian Planning Commission (*Regional Variations in Social Development and Levels of Living—A Study of the Impact of Plan Programmes*, New Delhi, Government of India, Planning Commission, 1967), the average monthly *per capita* consumption expenditure was almost the same in 1963 as in 1951, while the official consumer price index moved up from 125 to 132 over the same period. As a result, a third of all rural families are living below a household income of Rs. 100 (about $18) per month, which is officially defined as the "poverty line". There are large regional variations, of course. Thus, in the six states with a poor record of performance, the proportion living below this family income ranges between 50 per cent and 73 per cent.

F In Thailand 70 per cent of rural families in the populous agricultural northeast region had annual cash incomes of less than 3,000 baht as against an average family income of nearly 39,000 baht in the national capital. In the Philippines, average family income in metropolitan Manila was 4,790 pesos in 1961 while in Eastern Visayas the corresponding figure was 1,166 pesos. In India the percentage of population living below the poverty line varied from 9 per cent in Assam to nearly 45 per cent in Kerala. U.N. 1970 Report, p. 10.

G U.N. 1970 Report, p. 11.

H Thus in India less than 2 per cent of the villages are served with protected water supply, whereas out of about 2,700 towns and cities, 1,153 have access to such water.

I "Decision-making is centralized in the upper reaches of the public administration in the national capitals, with a consequent lethargy or paralysis of initiative in the organs of local government and sectoral administration in the rest of the country. In this respect, the large commercial and financial institutions follow patterns similar to those of the public sector. The upper-income strata, constituting the main markets for the new consumer-goods industries, live in the great cities, and the industries themselves fall into patterns of concentration governed by their markets and sources of financing. Higher education, modern medical facilities, mass communication media and the manifestation of culture have been concentrated in the same way and along with them the more lucrative and prestigious sources of employment. The great cities receive the lion's share of public expenditures on social programmes such as housing. Lastly, on a scale that threatens to negate the advantages of concentration for the cities themselves, comes a flood of migrants seeking crumbs from the concentration of wealth, sources of employment, and sources of social assistance." U.N. 1970 Report, p. 35.

J   *Ibid.*, p. 39.

K   The estimated rate of underutilization is 71 per cent. U.N. 1970 Report, p. 40. The calculation applies to 1960 but "the situation does not seem to have improved" according to a study conducted by Manuel Aguitera Goméz, quoted at length in the Report cited.

L   U.N. 1970 Report, p. 66. The corresponding ratio in Ghana, however, is 24.

M   The Tanzanian government has undertaken the most conscious measures to reduce income disparities but not with great success so far. Thus the officially commissioned "Turner Report" (cited in the U.N. 1970 Report, p. 67) came up with the fact that the rise in wages and general labour costs since independence had been associated with a decline in the number of wage earners.

N   Examples are the area around Dakar in Senegal, Abidjan in the Ivory Coast, and Addis Ababa in Ethiopia. In Kenya the regional disparities are most acute: whereas the per capita monetary product is £252 in Nairobi E.P.D. with a population of only 315,000, it is £6 and £5 in the populous Nyanza and Southern Kenya, respectively. The U.N. 1970 Report that cites these facts concludes that the "gap between developed and underdeveloped areas within countries may become similar to the gap between the developed and developing countries of the world", p. 68.

O   "A permanent unemployment problem is being created without alleviation of the rural predicament. The growth of towns is, in the main, out of gear with balanced growth in the economy at large; urban development is increasingly unhinged from rural development. An altogether excessive share of development resources goes into towns without bringing in its train any marked improvement in the living conditions of the masses there." L. Barnes, *African Renaissance,* London, Victor Gollancz, 1969, p. 108.

P Levels of urbanization in the Arab countries are higher than 40 per cent, whereas rates of industrialization are dismally low. Thus, according to the U.N. 1970 Report (p. 80), the manufacturing sector accounts for between 3 and 13 per cent of national income in the Arab countries as compared to 16.8 per cent in India, which is a developing country much poorer than the Arab countries and with a much lower level of urbanization. The comparative figures for Chile and Colombia are 17.5 and 17.7.

Q Thus, according to the U.N. 1970 Report, which goes into the manpower situation in the Arab countries in some detail, in Iraq 25 per cent of agricultural workers are regularly unemployed or underemployed. The figure rises to 75 per cent in off-peak seasons. p. 82.

R Ivan Illich, "Outwitting the 'Developed' countries", *New York Review of Books,* November 6, 1969, reprinted in *People's Action,* New Delhi, September 1972.

S I have discussed this whole issue in the context of the new centre-periphery conditions created by the impact of the present model of modernization in my "State Building in the Third World: Alternative Strategies", *Economic and Political Weekly,* Annual Number, 7 (5–7), February 1972.

T We have discussed the problem of employment and "marginality" more fully in Chapter IV, as it has great relevance to the issae of violence according to our analysis.

U There is increasing evidence to suggest that a technology based on small farms is not only feasible but also more productive (not just more egalitarian), apart from the fact that it is the only course open to poor societies with fast-rising populations. For a good summary and documentation on this, see Edgar Owens and Robert Shaw, *Development Reconsidered: Bridging the Gap Between Government and People,* New Delhi, Oxford & IBH Publishing Co., 1972.

V A good summary of data and hypotheses in these respects and an econometric analysis of the same will be found in Y. Sabolo, "Sectoral Employment Growth: The Outlook for 1980" *International Labour Review,* 100(5), November 1969.

W For important documentation of the decline of urban occupations and life in India under the impact of British colonialism, see B.N. Ganguli's study of Dadabhai Naoroji's drain theory quoted in note 1. See also Gandhi's discussion of the "drain" in which he marshalls evidence to show how exports under colonial rule undermined India's economy and led to exploitation. "Fallacy of Favourable Balances", *Young India,* March 28, 1929. Later he linked the growth of the new commercial class in the cities with the "drain" (in the style of *compradore* capitalists). "The greatest obstacle in the path of non-violence is the presence in our midst of the indigenous interests that have sprung up from British rule, the interests of monied men, speculators, scrip holders, land-holders, factory owners and the like." "Some Implications", *Young India,* February 6, 1930.

X Thus, in India it has been found that the cost of providing one year of undergraduate training in a liberal arts subject (supposed to be the cheapest in college education) can provide primary education for 22 children for one year while the ratio of costs for a master's degree in science to primary education is 1 to 89. For a perceptive analysis of this issue in the context of India, see K. N. Raj, Sardar Patel Memorial Lecture, *Crisis in Higher Education,* New Delhi, Government of India, Ministry of Information and Broadcasting, 1970.

Y The studies carried out at the Centre for the Study of Developing Societies point to such a conclusion. See especially the paper by D. L. Sheth and Bashiruddin Ahmed, "Organizational Affiliation, Education and Political Behaviour", Delhi, CSDS, 1973, *mimeographed.*

Z In India, according to the estimates of a government-appointed commission, the average waiting period between completing education and entering employment for graduates was 92 weeks in 1961–62; by 1975–76 it is estimated to rise to 137 weeks.

AA Ivan D. Illich, *Deschooling Society,* Harmondsworth, Middlesex, England, Penguin Books Ltd., 1973; Everett Reimer, *School is Dead,* Harmondsworth, Middlesex, England, Penguin Books Ltd., 1972.

BB Thus, to illustrate once again from India, according to the relatively modest proposals presented by V. M. Dandekar and Nilakantha Rath in their now famous study, *Poverty in India,* Poona, Indian School of Political Economy, 1971, if the 30 per cent living below the minimum necessary income were to reach the minimum (the so-called poverty line defined as Rs. 324 or $45), consumption would have to be brought down not only for the top 5 per cent of the population with a per capita annual expenditure of Rs. 1544.6 ($214.50) in rural areas and of Rs. 2263.4 ($314.40) in urban areas but also for the next 5 per cent, i.e., those with an average annual consumer expenditure of Rs. 875 ($121.50) in rural areas and of Rs. 1344 ($186.70) in urban areas. The cuts necessary for this stratum (the second 5 per cent from the top) whose incomes are by no means extravagant is of the order of 7.5 per cent of their expenditure in 1968–69.

CC Pitambar Pant, "Population, Economic Development and Food", a paper read at the Southern Regional Conference for Population Policy and Programmes, April 15–29, 1970, *mimeographed,* p. 2. (The paper is available at the Centre for the Study of Developing Societies, Delhi.)

4

ON VIOLENCE

The fundamental human predicament that has haunted philosophers, namely the construction of an *order* that would enable man to realize his *freedom*, has continued to elude modern man despite his claim to have subdued the forces of nature and to have increased his understanding of the causes of war, exploitation, and misery. Throughout the ages, in various lands, men have sought to evolve institutions that would increase their freedom. At various times they thought they had succeeded. But each time the institutions that were created proved either too fragile or too overpowering to maintain the freedom that they were supposed to serve.[1]

Never was this predicament more real than it is today. On the one hand, thanks to the advances in science and technology, man is in a position to put an end to the age-old afflictions of poverty, disease, and ignorance. On the other hand, these very advances have let loose forces that threaten the world with the most elementary problem of its survival. Similarly, precisely at a time when the *values* of justice and participation are acquiring a pervasive appeal for contemporary man, the institutional *structures* through which he has to operate are resulting in growing disparities and concentration of power. Thus both at the elementary level of physical survival—the necessary condition of everything else—and at the level of values and civilizational processes, contemporary man faces a fundamental duality and ambivalence in the prospects available in the future. In what follows, we first provide a diagnosis of the most likely developments if present trends continue, then present an examination of certain countertendencies that are slowly emerging, and finally

---

1. Examples are the Brahminic conception of an ordered hierarchy managed by a learned elite, the Confucian notion of a responsible aristocracy, the Greek idea of direct democracy based on city-states, the Roman conception of enlightened despotism, the idea of representative government in modern European thought, and the communist conception of the dictatorship of the proletariat. There are, of course, more extreme forms of both tyranny and anarchy, found in both the Orient and the Occident, that are not included in this list.

state our own perspective on how to move toward a more peaceful world in which the forces of violence are subdued and conditions are created for man's autonomy and a just social order.

The Violence System

The basic threats to man's freedom and self-realization lies in

1. An increasing role of violence in conflict situations.
2. The operational use of this violence—or of its threat—for perpetuating the prevailing stratification of power and prosperity in the world.
3. The close dependence on access to both the substance and the symbols of violence for effecting any change in this stratification.
4. The linkage between patterns of dominance within and between nations and their respective elites brought about by the prevailing distribution of the instruments of violence and the sinews of modern technology.
5. The consequent centralization and militarization of major societies—the United States, the U.S.S.R., China[2]—irrespective of their different political systems.
6. The deliberate attempt to maintain and reinforce the gaps that exist between these powers and others (symbolized by the use of the veto in the Security Council, the Limited Test Ban Treaty, and the Nuclear Non-Proliferation Treaty).
7. The growing sense of insecurity among these others who have found it necessary to increase their military strength.
8. The development of a major arms industry in the highly industrialized societies and a worldwide supply of these arms that foster 'localized' conflicts and wars.

These various indicators of threat and violence have led to an increasing allocation of world resources to means of coercion for both external security and against internal movements of dissent and subversion, for both of which it is easier to raise support than for programmes of welfare and social justice. Violence is thus fast becoming a major consumer of

2. We believe that China does not enjoy being a militarist power (for a thousand years now it has not exhibited any expansionist designs and until recently its conception of the People's Liberation Army was not militarist). It has been forced into this position by a series of threats—first by the long Japanese aggression, then (after liberation) by American encirclement, more recently by the Soviet Union. There is an important precedent of the same process in recent history—the militarization of the Soviet Union itself following its encirclement after the 1917 revolution by hostile forces from the West.

human productivity and scientific advance in our times and has become the most dynamic element in the preservation of the prevailing world order. The indicators listed above are the interrelated components of such a world order.

ARMS RACE

Central to the violence system is the arms race between nations. It is, of course, an unequal race. Whereas global military expenditures accounted for about $200 billion in 1970 (which was more than 6 per cent of the gross product of the world and the same amount as was spent on both health and education by all the governments of the world), the United States and the Soviet Union alone accounted for close to $120 billion in the same year. Even this is an understatement, for it ignores the fact that these two countries are the leaders of two powerful military blocs that are obliging other rich nations to allocate a large quantum of resources to military expenditure. In 1970 these two blocs accounted for $157 billion ($107 billion by NATO and $50 billion by the Warsaw Pact countries) of military expenditure, that is, more than 80 per cent of the entire world spending [A].

The conclusion is inescapable that the richer and less populous nations of the world intend to maintain their superiority over the poorer and more populous nations, and as the latter begin to challenge this superiority, the former are likely to try their utmost to preserve their hegemony—individually within their respective spheres of influence and jointly over the world as a whole. Thus, while rivalry *among* the more powerful nations (especially between the two giants) may be an important factor in the growing militarization of the world, these rivals seem to have a common interest in *together* maintaining superiority over the rest of the world in a bid to continue their dominance over the international system and their expropriation of a large proportion of the raw materials and other resources of the world. (According to the one estimate [B], the United States alone, which accounts for 6 per cent of the world population, uses up almost 60 per cent of the world's resources.) This and the continuous ravaging of land and life by wars and aggressions let loose by the rich countries are the most glaring instances of ecological destruction, far more menacing than the much-talked-of "pollution" by ordinary people.

Meanwhile, the challengers of this *status quo* (China being the foremost among them), others (such as Japan) who are feeling insecure at the changing world balance, and still others (such as India, Pakistan, Egypt, and the Indochinese countries) who have been victims of great-power politics, have all been stepping up their military expenditures. The sum total of all this is the growing arms race in which, according to the United States Arms Control and Disarmament Agency, whereas till the beginning of this century approximately $4,000 billion was spent on wars and armaments, the same amount is likely to be spent in a span of only ten years, that is, between 1967 and 1977. Whereas in the period before the World War I a little over 3 per cent of the world gross product went to military spending, now it is more than double that percentage of a vastly increased world output; during the last fifty years military outlays have increased twenty-fold. In the five years between 1962 and 1967 alone, there was a 50 per cent increase in world military expenditure, from $120 billion in 1962 to $182 billion in 1967. The annual expenditure on military budgets in the world far exceeds the entire GNP produced by the continents of Latin America and Africa (excluding South Africa but including the Middle East). Whereas all the medical research in the world consumes about $4 billion, military R & D [research and development] accounts for $25 billion.

WEAPONS TECHNOLOGY

Associated with the accelerating arms race and the tendency to maintain the prevailing stratification of world-power groupings is the increasing sophistication of the weapons of destruction that continue to be built despite SALT (Strategic Arms Limitation Talks) and summitry. A great deal of technological and scientific ingenuity and material resources are being constantly channelled into the development of ever more destructive weapons. The race for security is slowly enlarging the number of powers armed with nuclear weapons—the United States, the Soviet Union, the United Kingdom and France, now joined subsequently and with great determination by Communist China. While the first two seem to have reached almost parity in regard to nuclear warheads and missile delivery systems, two of the other three (France and China) are determined to develop an independent capability for nuclear deterrence. In fact, China has already made rapid strides in this direction. Still more pertinent questions are being asked: Will the first or second generation of nuclear weapons, or low-yield tactical ones, be put up for sale in international armament markets for political or economic reasons? Given its inherently inequitable nature and hence its outright rejection (or non-ratification despite formal acceptance) by a number of countries, is it at all likely that the Nuclear Non-Proliferation Treaty (NPT) will be effective in preventing poliferation [C].

This last issue was dramatically brought home by the news of the Indian underground nuclear test in May 1974. The Indian government has announced in unambiguous terms its commitment not to produce nuclear armamants and to use nuclear energy solely for research and development aims. (This itself added a new category of "nuclear power".) Even so—and in a sense because of such a declaration—the Indian success in eroding the oligopolistic control over nuclear energy and technology that had so far been taken for granted has produced a new situation. "Proliferation" is now on the move (in fact there are some countries, such as Japan, whose nuclear programme is far ahead of India's) and cannot be stopped unless the whole issue of disarmament is attacked on a global basis and the "great powers" themselves agree to modify their stand so far, namely, that the threat to human survival posed by modern weapons technology can be handled by tying it up in a few hands. The challenge posed by the Indian test, therefore, goes far beyond the mere emergence of one more nuclear power; it goes to the very basis of the present structure of world power and its reliance on a mad race for armaments. What Jawaharlal Nehru unsuccessfully tried to convince world leaders through-out the fifties (when his own country was a small power) that it is only by putting an end to the arms race that world peace can be secured may perhaps go home better now (with his country having decided not to remain a second rate power). Such is the logic of the world we live in.

Such rethinking, if it takes place, will involve many agonizing steps for the great powers who are so used to think of peace in military terms. It is difficult to predict at this stage what these steps will be. Meanwhile, the arms build-up continues to grow in a number of directions. Outside nuclear armaments proper, tremendous developments continue to be made in weaponry systems. Among the carrier systems, we have the supersonic medium and long-range bombers and bomberfighters, the ICRMS, IRBMS, MRBMS, MIRVS, ROBS, SLBMS, guided missile cruisers and destroyers and nuclear-powered submarines. Missile launching platforms in outer space and on the ocean floor are within the range of technological possibility. Radar systems have been developed to provide early warning of attack, to locate the source of it, and to direct counterat-tack to the enemy positions. Chemical and biological means of destruction have also been developed to a high level of efficacy. These and other major advances in space, communications, and fusion technology and in informa-tion surveillance through the use of satellites ensure both an increasing allocation of world resources to weapons and ancillary technology and an oligopolistic control over it, essentially by the two giants, with the United States still in the lead and the Soviet Union trying to catch up with its rival ally in world dominance.

TRADE IN VIOLENCE

There is at the same time a growing trade in the weapons of

violence. Annual sales to developing countries in 1971 of major arms alone were of the order of $1.8 billion, of which the United States accounted for $610 million, the U.S.S.R. for $620 million, Great Britain for $210 million, and France for $160 million. Between 1950 and 1972 exports of major arms from these four countries alone were valued at $17 billion, of which $7 billion were from the United States and $5 billion from the U.S.S.R. [D].

The logic of such sales and purchases is obvious. The sellers have the economic motivation to dispose of surplus equipment, to sustain the arms industry, to help national balance of payments, and to gain political influence. Many a time, rich returns are obtained by disposing of obsolescent technology and hardware. Supply of arms to a country creates in the course of time a state of dependence on the part of the receiver on the supplier for the former's military needs. The receivers buy in order to remain in competition with neighbouring powers and to meet the challenges of internal rebellions and breakdowns. The acquisition by one country sets its neighbours into an arms race with it. These conditions have led to a fanning of trouble in the underdeveloped regions and an escalating of the resources allocated to military spending.

"BALANCE OF POWER"

All this has been going on in the name of maintaining security and order in the world in which the balance between the great powers and their respective alliance systems and spheres of influence provides the general impetus. Now, with a change from the neat bipolar balance to a more complex balancing operation with the co-optation of China in the system and the emergence of a few other big powers on the horizon, there is likely to be not a muted but an accentuated sense of insecurity among the smaller and intermediate powers, leading to a further step-up in military expenditures, unless there starts a process of basic reconsideration of the whole approach to armaments by everyone concerned. Failing the latter type of change, given the fact that technological capability and national output of almost all nations are likely to grow in the next two or three decades, their war potential may also be expected to increase. This may lead to conditions in which regional tensions, the insecurity of regimes, and sudden eruption of border disputes may spark off extensive destruction of life and the productive process. While the development of nuclear and rocket technology and its gradual proliferation are likely to bring about a shift in the approach of the two giants, from encircling the world with military bases with a view to deter each other to one of cooperative countercheck, and while this may relax external pressure on a number of small countries, this very shift in great power strategy may increase regional tensions and arms build-up.

Sociopolitical Structure of Violence

While powerful forces in world politics are at work maintaining the *status quo* through the "balance of power" and strategic adjustments in it, vast transformations have at the same time been taking place in the relationship between human beings and their natural environment, in the stratification of societies under the impetus of a world sharply divided between the rich and the poor, and in the management of particular societies faced by internal discontent. These transformations have increased the scope of violence in human affairs and threatened the survival of man.

MAN AND NATURE

There has been a phenomenal growth in human numbers that is likely to seriously affect the balance between man and nature. Whereas in the 300 years between 1650 and 1950 human population had grown from 500 million to 2.5 billion, in the next 20 years alone it had shot up to more than 3.5 billion and in another 30 years it is expected to almost double this number. According to current and expected trends, every decade registers a net addition to the population of roughly 700 million, which is more than the entire population of the world up to the year 1650. And the rate of growth is continuously on the increase, with the decade 1970 to 1980 expected to record the fastest addition to human numbers in the history of man. If the expected rates continue—and even these estimates may turn out to be conservative given the fact that the benefits of modern medicine and the consequent decline in death rates that have provided the main spur to population growth are yet to realize their full potential in more than half the world—the carrying capacity of earth and of major sources of life sustenance will run short of man's needs in the next fifty years or so,[3] unless massive starvation or destruction will have already decimated the human race before then.

---

3. There are many aspects of this threat. The availability of both drinkable water and clean air is likely to run into serious shortages, especially in the urban areas. Changes in the biosphere include absolute increase in heat while the actions of human agencies threaten a rapid increase in radiation. Again, while agricultural technology provides a large field for research on increasing productivity (for both large and small farms), the same changes may cause severe stresses in the ecological balance. Also, man's continuous ravaging of the planet threatens depletion of various species, which is likely to precipitate a crisis in genetic variability and flexibility, which are crucial to such balance. Again, while food technologists are counting on an increasing possibility of using the ocean beds to produce food,

The population problem, however, has to be understood in its proper perspective, which has on the whole been lacking in the current search for technological panaceas and blanket prescriptions about family planning. First, the problem is not Malthusian in its classical form—of food supply running short of the increase in population—but is one of a more fundamental relationship between man and nature. It appears that major advances in agricultural technology and other likely developments such as ocean farming will break the back of the problem posed by Malthus. The issue that now confronts man concerns his increasing ravaging of space, ecology, and crucial natural resources for an uninhibited gratification of his ever increasing needs. The result is that whereas food supply may not pose a serious problem for population growth, the fact that the dominant conception of progress entails an exponential rate of human encroachment on nature—on space, on territory occupied by other species, on vegetation, on water resources, on nonreplaceable fossil fuels and raw materials, on fresh air—can produce results not very different from those predicted by Malthus.

POPULATION AND ECOLOGY

This is one reason why population growth and baby booms in richer countries—in fact of the rich anywhere—pose far greater threats to nature and its capacity to sustain life than an increase in the ranks of the poor. According to one estimate, the ecological equivalent of one additional birth in the U.S.A. (especially its well-to-do sections) is twenty-five births in India. This means that the ecological pressure of the present United States population is more than that of five billion Indians, or at least four billion if one makes allowances for a reduced multiplier in the case of the relatively poorer section of the United States population. If we project further on the basis of present trends, the United States rate of population growth of 1 per cent per year, when translated into ecological terms, turns out to be 25 per cent yearly (or 20 per cent if allowance is made for disparities in living standards within the United States), which is almost ten times that of the present growth rate in India [E]. The need to control population (as with the need to control growth of high technology)

there are indications from large parts of the world that the life giving properties of the oceans are being destroyed by radiation just as the cloud cover of the earth is being contaminated by poisonous gases. In a number of regions fish catches have reached a state of saturation, in fact have started declining. Thus, over a wide area of man's interaction with the rest of nature, the indiscriminate use of "science power" is producing crises that the coming generations may find difficult to meet—for in the meanwhile technology also (which still offers choices) will have become a closed book.

is, therefore, far greater in the richer countries than in the poorer countries, though this should not lead to any complacency among the latter, for growth of numbers among them poses more pressing and immediate problems of increasing poverty and unemployment, given the present structure of distribution of the world's resources.

The other reason why the rich are more responsible for the undesirable consequences of population growth concerns precisely this dimension of distribution of world resources. There are many levels of this problem. There is the simplest question of food reaching the hungry, both within and between countries. At present there are many countries where food supply is deliberately not allowed to grow. The point is well known in the case of hitherto surplus countries such as the United States, Canada, Australia, and New Zealand. Although these surpluses will soon be exhausted thanks to the growing demand for them from the highly populated regions like China, India and Soviet Central Asia, it does not seem likely that the rich granaries of the world will agree to put more land under the plough. Even in less-affluent countries where increased agricultural productivity is making them self-sufficient (or even "surplus" according to official claims), there are serious pressures from the well-to-do farmers for keeping the selling price of food high and, in case these pressures fail, of restricting production either voluntarily or with active government support. Argentina is reported to have taken measures similar to those taken earlier in the United States, namely, withdrawal of land under crops thereby restricting output.

Actually, these surpluses are artificial when considered from a world perspective. A large majority of the population in poorer countries still suffer from acute undernourishment and malnutrition and the diseases and mental incapacities that go with them, largely because these millions do not have the money to buy more food. In short, quite aside from the problem of not fully utilizing productive capacities in agriculture where these exist, there is the even more acute problem of lack of purchasing power on the part of the really hungry and undernourished—irrespective of the availability of food. Hence the paradox of world food surpluses combined with hunger and acute undernourishment, largely corresponding with the division between affluent and poor nations, but to an extent also reflected within the surplus countries themselves.

The technological revolution in agriculture based on mechanization that was first put into effect in the rich nations but has now spread to some of the poorer countries as well—thanks in part to aid policies and transfer of wholly inappropriate technology—has contributed further to this situation by diminishing the number of men engaged in food production and by hustling them off the land, in effect making them unemployed and denying them the means to benefit from the vast increases in the supply of food and other nutrients produced by the new technology. Even the more recent green revolution that consists of a different kind of technological package meant specially for poor agricultural societies threatens to lead to a similar result and for precisely the same basic reason—namely, it concentrates on the aggregate supply of food rather than on simultaneously undertaking structural reforms that would ensure that more men and women can stay on land and benefit from the increased supply. Left to itself, the new technology is forcing more and more people to migrate to already overcrowded cities, live in misery and disease, and die much earlier than they would have otherwise done.

PROBLEM OF SURVIVAL

It is in the context of such an inequitous economic structure, even concerning access to elementary suppliants of life, that the problem of population growth acquires a tragic dimension. This growth will be concentrated in the poorer countries, which will account for an expected increase of roughly 3.5 billion by the end of the century, almost the same as the entire world population today and about six times that of the richer countries during the same period. Given the present distribution of land and density and of access to other resources, this will accentuate conditions of mass poverty, malnutrition, physical disease, and mental incapacity, will cause still greater gaps and disparities between men and nations, and will acutely strain the resources and staying power of political regimes. As these populations encroach upon limited natural resources—constantly being depleted by the demands of international trade, by the high-speed technology brought to these lands by foreign collaborative ventures, and, above all, by the pressing domestic need of the industrially advanced countries—the prospect of physical survival of these populations will take on the character of a major crisis in the next few decades. As the present differences in death rates between various continents narrow, as the age structures of more and more poor countries move in favour of the young as compared to the old and the middle-aged, and as the declining capacity of land to sustain growing numbers of people leads to a much faster rate of growth of large cities than has hitherto been the case (according to a report of the World Bank, the urban population in the developing countries is expected to increase by one billion by the end of the century), the political consequences of population growth may become increasingly violent [F]. The desperation born out of felt deprivation, the presence of an alienated and angry youth, and the agitational ethos and psychic turbulence fostered by city cultures will provide precisely the combination that has often provoked—and, in turn, legitimized—military repression and fascist dictatorship.

To sum up, it is the combination of two parallel consequences of expected population growth in the coming decades that sets the stage for an impending crisis. On the one hand, the growth of numbers among the rich (expected to rise by 600 million before the end of the century) and their continuously rising material demands will appropriate larger and larger proportions of the earth's resources. On the other hand, a much larger growth in the populations of poorer regions and the fact that more than 42 per cent of this population will be comprised of children and young people below 15 years of age [G] will press on ever shrinking natural resources, ravaging them for sheer physical survival and running short of them very fast. What makes these two trends (which superficially appear divergent) converge into a common crisis pattern is the present structure of economic and ecological distribution in the world, the hiatus between supply of basic necessities and effective demand for them, and the adoption of a technoeconomic model the world over that has badly upset the balance between man and nature. The doctrine of family planning preached to the poorer countries—which, again, is based mainly on propagating certain techniques and coercing poor people into adopting them instead of instilling a change in expectations and behaviour patterns based on real improvement in their material condition and increasing outlays on such important concomitants such as education, health, and nutrition—is likely to prove too simple-minded in tackling what is basically a problem in political and social engineering.

TECHNOLOGY AND MAN

The dangers inherent in a growing pressure of population on natural resources are made more serious by a technoeconomic model whose increasing sophistication and speed threatens to reduce the importance of man in the civilization process. We do not intend to go into the details of the vast strides made by modern science and technology in altering the nature of biological evolution, in the revolutionary transformation of the chemical content of man's material culture and the manufacture of new life forms, in the use of mathematical language in reconstructing the basic elements of life, in the conquest of space enabling man to reach out to the mysterious heavens, and, above all, in organizational technology through the increasing scale of information-processing and the growing capability for control and management of human systems. We are aware of these great exponential changes, most of which are irreversible components of human evolution and which simultaneously afford man the capability to master the perennial threats to his survival—hunger, disease, natural calamities—and to undermine these very achievements through a Frankensteinian nemesis. But for the purpose of this chapter our interest in technology as an aspect of human evolution is more specific—in the manner in which it affects *man in society* and its impact on patterns of violence and nonviolence.

Now there is nothing necessarily foreclosed in the social consequences of science and technology. By itself, technology can be assumed to be neutral, though in actual reality it tends to generate its own values, which in course of time may become overwhelming, at least for certain kinds of cultures. Be that as it may, any realistic assessment of technology at a given threshold of historical development consists in identifying the directions that it is in fact taking and considering these from the perspective of one's values.

Seen in this way, present trends suggest an increasing probability of an inverse correlation between advances in technology and the value of man as a producer and a creative agent. For a time the relationship took the form of simple mechanization, in part relieving man's drudgery and in part displacing him in productive operations. Up to a point, both kinds proved beneficial to man, even the labour-saving kind, generating employment and incomes through a general process of economic expansion. However, more recent trends in technology take the form not so much of ordinary expansion of machine-based capacity but of processes that are replacing both men and machines, turning stepwise operations and routines into process systems and continuous flows. Automation and computerization of a whole series of manual and mental processes provide the key to this development. The resulting modernization and rationalization of industry have given rise to a productive system that relies more on equipment than on man [H].

The magnitudes of the change brought about by this high technology are far-reaching. According to United Nations estimates, over 80 per cent of the increase in the world's gross product is today contributed by technological progress and capital. In the United States and Sweden, the two countries with the highest average wages for labour, the contribution of technology to GNP is 90 per cent and that of labour 10 per cent. The story is not very different in Japan, the United Kingdom, Germany, and almost all the countries of the E.E.C. (European Economic Community). And as these pioneers set the pace for technological progress everywhere (now with the Soviet Union and other communist countries anxious to catch up with them), one may expect similar trends elsewhere.

REDUNDANCY OF MAN

There are many portents of the new technology all of which point to a declining nexus between man and work and a gradual redundancy of all but the highly skilled. Generation of surplus value will depend more on modernization of techniques and hence reduction of per unit costs than on raising output by augmenting capacity or intensively utilizing existing capacity. R & D expenditure will become more concentrated on industries that are science based and involve high inputs of technology and innovation than on those that are oriented to production and employment. "Already 65% of the West's total capital investment is for greater technological efficiency or labour displacement and only 35% for augmenting capacity upon which employment and living standards ultimately depend" [I].

No wonder that all over the world unemployment and underemployment are on the increase, including in several of the most affluent countries. And as the basic character of this nonutilization of human capacity is structural, its main brunt seems to fall on the less privileged strata everywhere—the semiskilled and the unskilled low status groups and underdeveloped regions, and, above all, the poorer countries of the world [J] that, in their effort to modernize and catch up with the others, are becoming a breeding ground for millions of surplus men for whom society has no use. The growing penetration of these countries by the multinational corporation equipped with high technology and that elusive quantity called know-how, the far greater emphasis placed by their governments on export promotion than on expanding domestic markets by increasing the purchasing power of ordinary people, and the general model of technoeconomic growth on which most of these countries are sold are leading to a rapid growth of national GNPs and a still more rapid decline in employment and well-being.

Both in industrialized and industrializing countries, then, there is likely to be a surfeit of human beings who will be of no use to society, a burden to their families, and an object of self-pity and moral guilt to themselves. That they will be a little better provided for in the richer countries, thanks to doles of mercy handed out from the national exchequer, does not change the basic picture very much. (The poorer countries, with their far greater burden of unemployment are, of course, much worse placed in this respect.) Meanwhile, the new technology, being, as it were, condemned to be constantly dynamic, will contribute quite substantially to the growth of megalopolitan structures and habits of life and, hence, to the deterioration of man's natural environment. There will be not

4. In the words of the M.I.T. physicist Philip Morrison, man will have to recognize three new forms of life (in addition to human, plant, and animal life on earth) in the foreseeable future: the life forms created in the test tube by biologists using off-the-shelf chemicals, the living organisms on other planets, and a form of "machine life" that will evolve out of today's computer science. Morrison presented this view at the symposium held at the Institute for Advance Study in Princeton to honour Von Neumann, the designer of the first fully modern electronic computer 25 years ago.

only a growing marginality of man as a producer; he will also be forced to live under conditions of stress, overcrowding, and despair.

It appears, then, that both modern technology and modern population trends point to the same basic malaise. The chief characteristic of this malaise is obsolescence of man himself. In fact, it is worse than obsolescence. In the years and decades to come man will be looked upon as something undesirable, as a burden on both society and nature, straining the management capacities of the former and the life-sustaining resources of the latter. (Some of the present discussions on family planning already display such a view.) It is, of course, true that science and technology are man's own creation and their only *raison d'être* is to enable man to deal with his problems. However, the fact remains that anything able to concentrate power and energy in large doses, even if it be an inanimate quantity, acquires a life and momentum of its own. This is what has happened to technology in our time. The result is that instead of dealing with the reality of a growing population, with the fact that a very large percentage of this population is born in poverty and misery, and with the further fact of a fast-deteriorating nexus between man and nature, technology is generating forces that deny opportunities for a meaningful life to large numbers of human beings and condemns them to a state of dependence and indignity. It is true that if there were not as many people on the planet as there are today, things would have been better. But it is even more true that if it were not for the present type of technology spreading all over the planet, things would have been better. Indeed, if there were not this technology, there would not have been this surfeit of human beings either. To continue to talk of population control without controlling this technology indicates how little have people thought about this problem.

Yet the principal solution (conceived almost as a panacea) on which national and international technocrats seem to be concentrating their efforts is that of propagating birth control to poorer countries without regard to the reasons for persisting attitudes toward family size on their part. That population control is part of a larger process of wellbeing and enlightenment, brought about through a widespread of health and education among the people, seems to be overlooked in this approach. Meanwhile, the highly distorted pattern of higher education in thse countries [K], in their effort to emulate richer countries, leads to the phenomenon of educated unemployment among the urbanized youth (including among highly qualified persons) while the convergence of poverty and illiteracy among large sections of a fast-growing population produces a class of subproletariat that flocks to the cities and adds to the numbers of slum and pavement-dwellers, squatters, beggars, urchins, and merceneries that join "militant" causes for purely pecuniary reasons. The result is a demographic and economic picture that is becoming explosive both at the top and at the bottom of the social structure.

DESPAIR OF THE YOUTH

The question of a "rebellious youth" has been raised time and again in history. It is equally potent today and will be more so in the years to come, if only for the fact of the growing number and visibility of the young, which in turn will affect the overall balance of the social structure and its mores and customs, and provide to this stratum the character of a major political force. By the end of the century in South and Southeast Asia alone there will be more than 2.50 billion people under the age of twenty-five (which will be two-thirds of the total estimated population of 4 billion). In most Latin American countries (with the exception of Argentina, Cuba, and Uruguay), the percentage of this age group has already crossed the 60 per cent mark, whereas in Africa, due to the late effect of health measures, its already large proportion is likely to rise even more sharply over the next three decades. A large proportion of this age group is expected to live in urban areas, acquire some education and skill, but, given present trends, be unable to find jobs. These are staggering magnitudes. Their potential for violence is as great as their potential for creative fulfilment, provided that society has use for its young and aspiring members. The two great majorities of India, in the words of Prime Minister Indira Gandhi, are its young and its poor.

Given the present technological and economic trends in the world, unless imaginative countervailing strategies are adopted, the outlook for the future is alarming, at any rate for the poorer regions of the world. There will be many more young people in those regions than old or middle-aged, their proportions will be still larger in urban areas, they will be more formally educated and socialized in "modern" and "cosmopolitan" ways of thought and living than the others, they will be more mobile and restless and less tolerant of inequities, there will be much greater unemployment among them ten or twenty years from now than is the case today, and their generation will be less attached to their diverse traditions and thus more open to the trends and fashions set by the metropolitan centres of the world. The upshot of these various coverging trends is likely to be seething discontent, a certain rootlessness, and a widespread feeling of futility and rejection among millions of men and women who are fondled and indulged as children and then thrown mercilessly on to the streets. As this happens, the very carriers of a cosmopolitan culture may become prone to the appeals of national chauvinism and racial prejudice, play into the hands of mobilization regimes and army juntas, and support wars that escalate from localized conflicts for liberation and justice—the sheer pressure of numbers and growing barriers to international migration can lead to a legitimate demand for more *lebensraum*—to much larger hostilities the precise scope of which it is difficult to predict with any certainty [L].

Countervailing Trends

We have described at some length the danger signals in current and expected developments. Our analysis points to a situation in which growing *magnitudes* will be increasingly difficult to control on the basis of prevailing *structures*. These structures have not only become impervious to the threats posed by the magnitudes (the arms build-up by the great powers, growing unemployment and disparities, a restive youth, increasing concentration of political and economic power); they have also lost their autonomy before the onslaught of a new and dynamic species of life, namely, the machine. This simultaneous incidence of *lack of justice* in world social and economic structures and *loss of autonomy* by man and the institutions that he has devised in the face of larger and larger concentrations of power and technology provides the contemporary setting to the predicament of man and threatens him with a growing scale of violence in the coming decades.

It is clear that the control of magnitudes depends on the reform of structures. The latter, in turn, depends on determined political initiative along a more realistic paradigm of action than the one provided by the technoeconomic model of rapid industrialization. Now, there are already a number of countervailing trends in the world that can, if systematically identified and strengthened, provide the basis of hope and reconstruction. In what follows, some of these trends may be briefly mentioned.

REGIONAL ACCORDS

There is a growing perception of the dangers inherent in operating through a political structure based on the assumption of a world dominated by super powers when, in fact, new centres of power are emerging and nations are beginning to value their autonomy and peace in their regions that had so far been compromised in their search for external protection. This is leading on the one hand to important modification of attitudes and strategies within the great power nexus and on the other hand to a realization in the medium and smaller powers that they must put an end to historic animosities the persistence of which account for the dominance of the big powers. It was not a mere coincidence that just when Richard Nixon, Leonid Brezhnev, and Chou En-Lai were laying the basis of a new balance between the big powers, Willy Brandt and Indira Gandhi were striving to achieve a durable peace in Europe and the Indian subcontinent, respectively. Indeed, it is worth noting that in calling upon Indian and Pakistani opinion for a lasting solution to twenty-five years of strife among them, Mrs. Gandhi pointedly referred to how the European countries were seeking to achieve peace and cohesion despite a long history of conflict and enmity. About the same time as the Indo-Pakistani summit agreement of Simla was made public came the news of the move for reunification of Korea. In both cases, the parties involved pledged to resolve outstanding issues bilaterally and to keep all others out. Although in neither case has this resolve been fully carried out, there have been important developments that hold out a promise of stable peace in the respective regions.

Soon after these events came the dramatic developments in the Middle East where, after a long period of waiting for the big powers to work out a solution for them, the Arabs took the initiative to force a settlement that was at once in keeping with their self-respect and sensitive to the realities of the region. The Middle Eastern situation is, of course, full of ambivalence, and the countries involved will not find it easy to shake off foreign interference; indeed, this may become more difficult given the *détente* between the two giants and the high politics of securing oil supplies. The prominent role played by the United States in securing peace after the 1973 war underlined the continuing role of the big powers in the region (which has been a scene of big power rivalry for over a century now). And yet there is no doubt that a major step toward breaking the deadlock that outside powers had imposed on the region for a quarter century has been taken by the Arabs. It is likely to have far-reaching consequences, with implications that go beyond the Middle East, shaking the cohesiveness of the much publicized "five power formula" as well as the stability of the present framework of dominance (although this may not be immediately evident). In the Middle East itself it will strengthen the long-standing peace movement within Israel and the general desire among thinking Arabs to work out an honourable way of putting an end to the state of siege in their regions, just as the war in Bangla Desh hastened the process of national and regional autonomy in South Asia. On the whole there is evidence of growing prospects for peace in the strife-torn regions of the world based on efforts from within those regions, though outsiders may still think they are the ones who have brought peace.

STRUGGLE FOR AUTONOMY

While the big powers still think in terms of controlling international violence through oligopolistic means of control and dominance, there is

also taking place a wide diffusion of the desire to put an end to the state
of dependence that the existing structure of the world entails and to secure
autonomy and self-reliance for national political communities. The following are all indications of the preference for autonomy and dignity
among nations of the world: the long and heroic struggle of the Vietnamese
people in the face of the world's mightiest military machine and the mobilization of opinion around the world in support of the struggle; the
establishment of an independent Bangla Desh despite the cynical support
given by important world powers to one of history's worst genocides;
the emergence of new centres of power in China, in India, in the Middle
East with its new found sense of power, in Iran which has shown an amaz-
ing capacity to recognize the new wind that is blowing over the world and
take advantage of it, and even in parts of Eastern Europe and Latin America, which have long been regarded as backyards of the two giants; and the
desire for regional integration among the countries of East and West Africa,
Latin America, and Indochina with a view to achieving political and economic self-sufficiency. This is in sharp contrast to the earlier atmosphere
of trading off national independence for a few crumbs of "aid" or for a promise of security against one's own neighbours—and often against one's
own people. There is a strong wind of creative nationalism blowing over
the Third World (as well as in parts of the other two worlds, including in
such citadels of the erstwhile bipolar system as France and Canada in
the West and Czechoslovakia and Rumania in the East). In the mood
that is spreading over these nations, progress toward world peace and a
stable world order is closely linked to the struggle for national autonomy
and equality among states.

SEARCH FOR A NEW MODEL

In part reflecting the desire for national autonomy and in part responding to the inequitous consequences of the modernization model,
there is also emerging a new social perspective among some of the elites
and intellectuals of the poor and underdeveloped countries. It is slowly
dawning on them that the prevailing model of technology may prove to
be more a curse than a boon for countries where a rapidly rising population
and growing numbers of poor and unemployed call for a different technological package. Similarly, the kind of urbanization, higher education,
and mass communications that has come in the wake of Western technology
has resulted in a high degree of centralization and led to a wide chasm between the elite and the people. The need, instead, is to evolve new forms of
social and economic policies and new structures to sustain them, leading
to a wider diffusion of capacities and a greater measure of autonomy and
self-sufficiency among both human beings and human communities. These

values and emphases are leading to a critical evaluation of prevailing models and a vague realization of the need for institutional reconstruction.

SENSE OF CRISIS

Providing strong support to such concerns and a questioning mood is a growing sense of world crisis felt by literally thousands of people living round the world. Some of these occupy fairly influential positions in various societies and include outstanding scientists, intellectuals, administrators, and men of affairs. These men and women are not just visionaries; they *know* that a crisis of major proportions is brewing right in their midst and that it calls for concerted action at various levels [M]. Such a sense of crisis is not simply a result of an objective understanding of the dangers of war, overcrowding, and ecological breakdown that lie ahead several decades from now; to a considerable extent it owes itself to the mood and behaviour of thousands of men and women belonging to the younger generation in the richer countries. Full of despair and a sense of futility, alienated from their own societies, and craving new values and a sense of significance for themselves, these young men and women have raised a different kind of protest than ever before, in the process shaking Occidental civilization from its complacency and arrogance.

By now, many of these youth movements are on the decline in the West, thanks to the enormous staying power and both open repression and institutionalized coercion of the existing structures.[5] Repelled by the "system" and its decadence, many among the young and the idealists have started working at a micro level, seeking to set up new kinds of communities and novel experiments in social and political engineering. But both the earlier movements of dissent and the more recent trend toward withdrawal, in sheer despair, from the mainstream of society have served to sensitize the thinking strata of the world to the inadequacies of the present system and the values underlying it. It is this convergence of a general sense of crisis among the more mature thinkers of the world and a widespread questioning about assumptions taken for granted for so long that provides the setting for the new mood of skepticism. It

---

5. Looking back, it seems that Charles A. Reich's *The Greening of America*, New York, Random House, 1970, was a noble thought that was not put to work. The "mini-revolution" that got up some steam at the convention of the Democratic Party held at Chicago in 1968 and travelled from there to Woodstock in 1969, seems to have faded out. The youth cult, symbolized by the Beatles and the hippies and long hair and drugs, suffered from the anarchic model of hedonism as found in the non-literate among the Hindu *sadhus* with their gay abandon and thorough self-centredness. It was bound to misfire. But it did play a certain clinical role in America by disturbing its smugness and complacency.

also provides the background of the recent spurt of interest in different parts of the world in Gandhi, his work, and his message.

Towards Nonviolence

One can build on the trends identified above in moving toward a just and nonviolent world. We have already looked at the issues involved from the viewpoint of justice. We may now do the same from the perspective of nonviolence. In undertaking such an analysis, we shall draw substantially upon the views of Gandhi and his model for a nonviolent society and, no doubt, adapt them to the needs of our time and the future that lies ahead of us. The message of Gandhi, who brought an exceptionally fresh and original mind to bear upon the issues of modern times, is even more relevant to the last third of the twentieth century as it unfolds before us than it was when he lived. The various trends noted above contributing to the desire for a better world can be made to converge into a durable pattern only by reference to a grasp of the totality of the present crisis and the way out of it, just as Gandhi sought to give a comprehensive meaning to *swaraj* (independence) in the midst of his day to day struggle against imperialism. Gandhi's grasp of the conditions that led to violence in civil society was, of course, much better than his understanding of the cognitive content of a new worldview needed by contemporary man. One must, in any exercise like the present one, build on the insights of such men and move beyond, producing a conception that is at once sensitive to enduring themes and suited to the new reality as one comprehends it.

The causes of violence in the contemporary world are to be found in the relationship between increasing inequality in human society, the techno-economic structures that sustain such inequality, and the impingement of these structures on nature and its life-giving properties. These conditions are likely to continue and possibly deteriorate in the next few decades. Gandhi was quite unrealistic in his belief in the inevitability of *ahimsa* (nonviolence),[6] just as Marx was unrealistic in his belief in the inevitability of a humane and classless society. If anything, present trends indicate a likely increase in violence. What is needed is an identification of the specific causes of violence and their deliberate and determined reversal.

---

6. "If we turn our eyes to the time of which history has any record down to our own time, we shall find that man has been steadily progressing towards *ahimsa*. If we believe that mankind has steadily progressed towards *ahimsa*, it follows that it has to progress towards it still further. Nothing in this world is static, everything is kinetic. If there is no progression, then there is inevitable retrogression" (M.K. Gandhi, *Harijan*, August 11, 1940). It is necessary to remember that in Indian thought there is no great distinction between a law of development (which is in-

TWO DIMENSIONS

There are two broad dimensions along which, if present trends continue, violence is likely to increase. They also provide broad parameters for action in the reverse direction. One of these is *degradation in the condition of man* as a result of a declining subsistence function expressed in terms of a ratio between nature and man. The other is *accentuation in the degree of dominance* that is the result of a deteriorating distribution function expressed in terms of a ratio of the power of the peripheries and the power of the centres. The two together threaten man's autonomy and possibly his very survival.

SUBSISTENCE FUNCTION

The problem of degradation in the condition of man has been already dealt with by us in the chapter on justice. To a significant extent, the problem is a direct result of technology, of both its benign and its menacing aspects, of the conquest of hunger and disease on the one hand and the displacement of man by machinery on the other. Here we shall confine ourselves to what appears to us to be the single most serious problem facing the human species. At the simplest level, the problem arises out of a exponential growth in the number of human beings for whom society has no or very little use. Gandhi's tirade against the technological civilization for which he has been criticized from all sides (and which is one reason why most modern people have shirked away from him, both in his own country and abroad) can be better understood if it is remembered that he was addressing himself to the economic problem that faced India. He was candid enough to say so (and by implication admit the utility of machines doing the work of men under different circumstances): "Mechanization is good when the hands are too few for the work intended to be accomplished. It is an evil when there are more hands than are required for the work, as is the case in India" [N]. Where technology, the economic system, and the distribution of natural resources systematically displace people and make them obsolescent in their very prime, both absolute degradation in the quality of life and relative degradation

---

evitable) and a preferred course of action (which is desirable). Gandhi's warning against possible "retrogression" belongs precisely to this kind of thinking: if men will not heed the inevitable, something else will follow. This is quite different from the Marxist laws that, as should be expected, bear the stamp of scientific determinism found in the Western thought pattern. B. N. Ganguli, in his *Gandhi's Social Philosophy: Perspective and Relevance*, New Delhi, Vikas Publishing House, 1973, provides the most comprehensive comparision of Gandhi's thought with that of various thinkers in the Western tradition.

in the form of inequality and injustice are bound to follow. In the next thirty years the number of such people is likely to run into hundreds of millions. Unless the source of this massive injustice in the nature and direction of technology is removed, violence and a general loss of self-control in the behaviour of both men and nations are likely to grow. How does one prevent this?

First of all, there is need to restore health to the nature of work and the condition of labour. Both the origin of exploitation and its continued intensity arise out of a view of physical work as being irksome and unpleasant and out of a search for freedom from labour by living on other peoples' labour or, as in the latest version of this view, living on the labour of machines that will "liberate" man from work as such. In reality, work could both be made pleasant and be made a boost to the spirit if it were not work for someone else, if it were not based on exploitation of man by man, and if it were not something that appears obsolete. The latter condition obtains in the affluent countries where more and more human beings work in the tertiary sector that involves little physical or mental work and where there is a growing amount of leisure that is being consumed by joining in shopping queues or tuning in mass media beaming out cheap relaxation or, as in the socialist countries, programmes of mass instruction.[7] Thus, both in economically backward countries where modern technology is producing growing numbers of destitute and unwanted people and in economically affluent countries where it is producing idleness that few know how to use, work has lost its dignity, become a mark of inferiority, and is being looked upon as something to be shirked.

Thinking the matter through, the main issue relates to the present divorce of intellect and work (reflecting the dualism between mind and body) and the need to restore a union between the two. The divorce has led to an alienation of brain workers from the rest of society and an undue

7. The transformation of leisure from a period of rest and relaxation to a full-time occupation seems to have haunted Western "free thinkers" for a long time, epitomized in Spinoza's dictum that all determination—all specific work being that— is negation. Even Marx, who at one time put so much stress on a productive life and the primacy of work, abandoned that view since writing his *German Ideology* and instead went for "free activity", which he later, in the third volume of *Capital*, with his conception of progress as movement from the realm of necessity to the realm of freedom, raised to the status of almost the final aim of life. It is interesting that this aspect of Marx's writings has had the widest appeal among intellectual circles everywhere. For Marx's utopia is funnily bourgeois: one in which men will read, paint, and write poetry and occasionally do some gardening. Since Marx's time the availability of leisure has become a reality for many millions of men and women, thanks largely to machines doing most of the work. The results, as found in mechanized societies, suggest how illusory this search has been.

accent on scientific specialization that has prompted a pertinent student of contemporary affairs to observe that the progress of science has ceased to coincide with the progress of mankind and that it could even spell mankind's end [O]. It is to this condition that Gandhi addressed his call to the urban middle classes of India to identify themselves with the rural people and go and work among them, thus bringing about a "correlation between intellect and labour" and an end to the great divorce between the classes and the masses [P]. A somewhat similar approach was tried out by Mao during the Cultural Revolution in China.

Closely related to the problem of work and alienation and responsible for the growing stratification of the world into an inequitable order, is the basic cleavage of modern times, that between the city and the countryside. The city, the classic stereotype of a cultured and civilized life, has increasingly become a parasite on society, draining the countryside and destroying its sources of self-sustenance, and in turn, ready to be exploited by still larger cities and metropoles, mostly outside the country. The overall outcome is the division of the whole world into a small constellation of cities and a vast periphery, It is this that made Lin Piao (long before he fell from official grace) conceive of the revolutionary struggles of the peoples of Asia, Africa, and Latin America as essentially one of an encirclement of cities by the world's countryside. Gandhi, who was less concerned with a revolutionary capture of power and more concerned with building a fundamental harmony in life, was more constructive. His model of an egalitarian society was conceived in terms of self-reliance at various levels, including a large measure of economic self-sufficiency and self-government at the village level, restoration of the value and dignity of village crafts and arts that had been impoverished in the mad rush for industrialization, and involvement of the urban middle classes, especially the scientists among them, in the building of a reciprocal rather than an exploitative relationship between city and countryside. Today, as we look to the future, the simultaneous exploitation of the world countryside and the displacement of man by machines in the world's cities suggest the need for a major reordering of the relationship between town and country— and, hence, between nature, man, work, and technology. The basis of such a reordering will have to be mutual sustenance between the two, with work providing the cementing link and technology providing new alternatives for fostering such a link. Only thus can the phenomenon of surplus and unwanted men in a world of plenty come to an end.

DISTRIBUTION FUNCTION

The major source of injustice and violence in today's world is to be found in structures of domination and inequality. These structures

provide stability and institutional form to the magnitudes and relationships—more and more human beings impinging on a shrinking nature,
the decline in the value of work and labour in technological society, the
encroachment of cities on rural areas and their sources of sustenance—
discussed above.   As we have already argued in this chapter and generally
in this book, though the magnitudes by themselves pose serious absolute
problems, what makes them both inequitable and impervious to constructive solutions are the prevailing institutional structures.   Gandhi was
quite clear on this theme: the root of violence is to be found in the system
of dominance that characterizes both the nation-state and the international
order; unless the causes that gave rise to such a system are removed, there
is little chance of bringing an end to exploitation of man by man.   Since
Gandhi's time, this system has spread its tentacles still further in both
economic and political spheres, through the control of communications
media and information channels, through the demonstration effect of the
modernization model emanating from a single world centre (the United
States), and through a growing linkage between domestic and international
patterns of dominance thanks to the myopic effect of modern technology
on the one hand and the politics of a thermonuclear world on the other.

There are, no doubt, important reconsiderations under way on the
nature of technological options available to man, and there are some
striking changes taking place in the structure of world power.   There is
also a growing sense of the crisis facing man in the coming decades,
especially among sensitive intellectuals, scientists, and sections of the
youth.   But the precise direction that these changes and considerations
will take is still not clear, and the kinds of solutions that are advanced
leaves one in serious doubt as to whether the true nature of the contemporary predicament of man is at all properly understood.   The total threat
to the survival of the human species is a comparatively recent phenomenon—at first it was the threat of nuclear war and still more recently
of the collapse of the biosphere—and it is not surprising that responses
to it are either erratic or wholly cynical.

Most of these responses involve elimination of the nation-state
and a movement toward a world system of government, economic planning,
population and ecological control and above all arms control and peaceful settlement of disputes.   Now there is little doubt that for an efficient
pursuit of a number of these functions a system of cooperation and mutual
aid among peoples now living within nation-states will be needed.   There
is also no doubt that a new world consciousness based on a conception
of common interests rather than inevitable discord is called for if the
serious magnitudes facing mankind are to be met without recourse to cata-
clysmic events brought about by men maddened by a lust for power.   And
yet if there is any overriding lesson to be learnt from the deleterious effects

of modern technology and management and communications sciences, it is that we should at all costs avoid excessive centralization and bureaucratization of human organization and the contraction of politics that centralization involves. Patterns of dominance are closely correlated with the loci and distribution of centres of authority and decision-making; the more remote the controls the greater the bureaucratization and the less scope there is for participation, choice and autonomy.

It does not, of course, follow that the smaller the size and the shorter the distances, the larger the scope for the exercise of autonomy and choice. It is well known that very small and integrated communities also tend to be highly closed and intolerant of diversity and dissent. They also tend to lack the necessary resources for self-defense and autonomous existence. (Hence our advocacy of larger nation-states or federations.) One has to strike a proper balance between too much centralization and too much fragmentation and enclavism. As a matter of fact, in the present world these opposite tendencies seem to go together and account for the stability and perpetuation of the dominance system. The main point is to ensure as large a measure of autonomy and self-reliance *at different levels* as is conducive to the realization of both justice and nonviolence. A just and nonviolent world order will be possible only on the basis of transforming structures of dominance and dependence into structures of autonomy and self-reliance. This will not be possible by using some simplistic model of world government no matter how devoted to the values of justice and nonviolence the advocates of such a model are. Nor will it suffice to advocate internationalization of the process of resolving conflicts. In the absence of wider political settlements and substantial modifications in the distribution of power in the world, the former step may well accentuate patterns of dominance, whereas the experience of the United Nations suggests that the latter idea tends to freeze power patterns and may well make them more stubborn and insensitive (as indeed happened in the case of both the Bangla Desh and the Middle East crises).

SELF-RELIANCE AND NONVIOLENCE

Our basic difficulty with the advocates of a centralized world structure is that they tend to think about correcting present inadequacies by changes from above rather than from below. Most of them adopt a

---

8. Gandhi did assign a role to cities in his model, first as "clearing houses" of commerce and distribution, and second, as places where the minimum necessary heavy industries and public utilities that were needed for providing the wherewithal for rural development could be located. These industries were, however, to be socially owned so that they would not become a basis of exploitation.

similar approach at home, as the white liberals in the United States or the middle-class radicals in the developing countries. It is an approach that is in essence elitist, condescending and full of do-goodism, although not always out of design and often in spite of their strong humanist and democratic convictions. Moral action is viewed in essentially institutional terms; most of the proposals in currency would create more institutions and mechanisms of control than already exist. What is missed in such an approach is the paramount need to neutralize conditions of dominance by movements from below so that men and women are able to make their own futures on the basis of a pride in themselves and a sense of solidarity and obligation toward those with whom they choose to identify politically. This is the only legitimate road to both autonomy and integration. The point is that without a real measure of self-assertion by those living in a state of individual and collective dependence, the human species will continue to live in two totally different worlds, the world of the great cities and their hinterlands, controlling and using up a large proportion of the available resources of the earth and its stratosphere, and the world of the vast peripheries, shorn of whatever resources they had to begin with and denuded of their human skills and potentialities by making them redundant in the general march toward world progress. These are not the conditions in which violence can be controlled. In the ultimate analysis, control of violence will depend on the availability of men who are willing to exercise a measure of self-control as an expression of their own autonomy and a sense of collective consciousness that is *sui generis,* not imposed from above.

Seen in this manner, the central task in moving toward a world where violence is kept within bounds and increasingly made illegitimate, consists in asserting the identity of the oppressed and exploited peoples and evolving structures that will facilitate this assertion. The process must begin by the peripheries encroaching upon the centres, not by the centres accommodating the peripheries through aid or alliance. Aid and alliance, if anything, prevents a real sense of interdependence based on reciprocity. The humanitarianism of the advocates of more aid and the internationalism of the advocates of peace through a balance of power ignore this basic prerequisite of genuine interdependence. Hence the great significance of de Gaulles, Titos, Nassers, Indira Gandhis, Allendes and Nyereres for moving towards a world based on real inter-dependence (instead of on dependence) [Q]. The struggles launched by these people will need to be continued.

This change from dependence to independence to interdependence will have to be brought about by those living in the Third World. There is little that outsiders can do except, perhaps, if they mean well, refrain from creating further obstacles. If those residing in the centres are willing to do something more positive and identify with those living in the peripheries, let them change the locale of their work and make common cause with the latter, more or less on the lines of Gandhi's imploration to the Indian middle classes to go and work with the rural people in their struggle for self-assertion.[9]

"LEGITIMATE" VIOLENCE

Such a definition of political tasks, with its accent on the struggle for autonomy and self-esteem from the bottom rather than on the creation of a benevolent superstructure from above, also imparts realism and a certain historical sense to the problem of violence. For, at least for some time to come, the effort to disturb the *status quo* may involve a measure of violence. Nonviolence is not something that can be demanded in the abstract. A world based on exploitation and dominance is already a very violent world. Putting an end to these conditions involves a struggle for autonomy on the part of the dependent and the exploited sections of the world. This struggle is crucial to the realization of a world without violence. For, in its essence, violence is a direct result of the *violation* of the dignity of human beings and human collectivities. To the extent that such violation has to be overcome, some violence is likely to follow as a counter response and as an expression of newly released psychic power. For a long time, both the reality of domination and the sense of inferiority that it induces, produce a process of self-denigration and turn aggressive behaviour inward among those who accept their inferiority. This happens within societies, for example among the blacks in America, the untouchable castes in India, and several of the nondominant tribes in Africa, and also between societies, most typically between neighbours within the colonized regions who share the same identity and have, in fact, much in common. It is when the struggle for autonomy based on a newly acquired sense of self-potency—and solidarity with others who are similarly placed—gains momentum that this inward turned aggression is transformed into a confrontation with the oppressor [P].

9. This will involve major adjustments for these people in their consumption standards, their modes and language of communication, their pet models for the poor and the oppressed, and their perceptions of what constitutes development or progress. Gandhi called these "sacrifices", by which he did not mean giving something that belonged to you to others but, rather, meant rendering to others what in fact was theirs and had been expropriated by you and your kind. Gandhi did not suffer from the psychology of condescending do-gooders who abound in our midst today. Most of the latter happen to enjoy all the perquisites of a parastic class and are unwilling to live austere lives that will convince others that they are not phoney.

The confrontation, which may involve violence, needs to be looked upon as a legitimate transition toward a shared sense of values according to which certain forms of dominance and injustice are accepted by all as illegitimate. Paradoxical though it may sound, this violence, born out of a struggle against injustice and oppression, is an important aspect of the world's progress toward nonviolence.

Gandhi himself, though always emphasizing the need to keep his struggle against imperialism nonviolent and constantly stressing the need to follow good means if one is to achieve good ends, admitted the role of legitimate or permissible violence, not quite on the lines argued above, but leading to the same moral position. In fact, Gandhi's conception of nonviolence (which was far more complex than the mere idea of lack of use of force) was one of active resistance to injustice. "No man could be actively nonviolent and not rise against social injustice no matter where it occurred" [S]. And in fighting injustice, it may be necessary to actually use force. He repeatedly placed high value on the defence of one's own and one's country's honour, on combating injustice, and on upholding one's dignity and freedom. "I would rather have India resort to arms in order to defend her honour than that she should, in a cowardly manner, become or remain a helpless witness to her own dishonour" [T]. Gandhi fully accepted the conception of detached self-assertion in the cause of justice and righteousness as preached in the *Gita*.[10] Violence as such is not desirable under any circumstances except when the choice is between preservation and violation of one's autonomy and self-respect—when it is legitimate as a means as well. When the integrity of the self itself is violated, it becomes a duty and an obligation to defend it. A nonviolent world is only possible on the basis of the autonomy and inviolability of the various selves—individuals and communities—that make up the world. (It was quite in keeping with this conception that Vinoba Bhave, the greatest living Gandhian, approved of India's nuclear test.)

10. We do not, however, accept the notion of technical irresponsibility that is inherent in such a concept of detachment as was advocated by Krishna to Arjun in the *Gita*. Krishna was no doubt moved by a deep sense of predicament in the face of the menace held out by the forces of evil, something not very different from what Plato in his time and Hobbes at a later stage contended with. The solution he offered, however (his imploration to Arjun to do his duty without giving thought to the consequences of his action), was in line with the Hindu propensity to look for ultimate causes in impersonal forces. Gandhi, like a great deal of his other reinterpretations of Indian tradition, sought to turn the dictates of Krishna towards secular causes of national autonomy and social injustice. He had to that extent transcended the limitations of the *Gita*. But by doing so—and thus using a language that was so familiar to his countrymen—he unwillingly legitimized the obscurantist philosophy of the *Gita*.

END TO DOMINANCE

The struggle for achieving this autonomy will have to be carried out at various levels. As already argued in this book, the source of the present system of dominance and concentration of power is to be found in the international order. It is necessary to counter this and establish the autonomy of the various states that make up the world. The least autonomous of these states are to be found in the continents of Africa, Asia, and Latin America, though several Eastern European states and even the states in Western Europe have felt a sense of impotency in a world dominated by the superpowers. The process of gaining autonomy and a measure of equality among these states will involve a number of strategies. Important among these are

1. Resolving outstanding disputes among these states with a view to ensure a climate of peace and doing this without any interventionist role of one or more of the big powers or of the United Nations as it is presently constituted.

2. Moving toward structures of regional peace and integration so that the principle of autonomy does not depend on the acquiescence or inertia of the system but reflects a real distribution of territorial and symbolic power.

3. Fighting against violations of justice and autonomy in international forums and institutions and, in the process, making them more representative of and sensitive to the needs and aspirations of the people of the world. (This appears simple-minded but is actually quite effective. It has not been tried in a sustained manner so far.)

4. Improving the position of these states as factors in world politics through internal consolidation, economic development, and political legitimacy.

The aim of all this is, no doubt, to move toward a truly polycentric world (the present claim of polycentrism is more illusion than reality) based on the principles of equality, mutual cooperation, and peaceful settlement of conflicts of interest and ideology. We believe that it is only on the basis of such a structure of cooperation among autonomous units that the present structure of dominance and insecurity can be brought to an end and larger settlements in controlling the terrifying instruments of war and violence be achieved. But in order that such an aim be realized, it is necessary to upset the existing *status quo* in the world. In this, the countries of the Third World, individually and jointly on a regional basis, will have to play a major role.

INNER AND OUTER WORLDS

This *status quo* is based on two related expressions of world dominance: (1) an oligopolistic control of the world and its economic and military resources through alliance systems and spheres of influence on which the hegemonic powers are agreed and (2) immunization of these powers and their allies (the inner world) from the middle and smaller powers of the Third World (the outer world) by deciding to gradually close their ranks in the latter areas and quarantining them so that whatever happens in the outer areas does not disturb the peace and stability of the inner world. The latter approach can be as dangerous as the former; in fact, the two are tactical aspects of the same overall strategy. The former may be described as a maximal approach that was suited to the period of the Russo-American system of dominance; the latter represents a minimal approach that is a response to a world that is becoming less tidy to manage, thanks largely to the emergence of China but also to the slow assertion of autonomy by several other states (India, Vietnam, Yugoslavia, Tanzania, Rumania, the Arab countries, Iran).

The minimal response of the hegemonic powers, however, may not represent any advance over the maximal approach and can lead to a more turbulent world in which violence is systematically confined to— and may even be encouraged in—the "outer" world. The earlier optimistic expectation, expressed by several moderate Third World statesmen, chief among them being Jawaharlal Nehru, that a *rapprochement* between the great powers will reduce the level of hostilities in the world, contain the armaments race, and release world resources for the ends of economic development and social justice has not been borne out by facts. If anything, the level of armaments is on the increase, and the big powers are adopting a highly cynical view on the role of violence in international affairs (reminiscent of the analysis by the partners in the Holy Alliance). They are also motivated by a fundamental social analysis, namely, that the regions of the outer world will be increasingly engulfed by insoluble internal problems and that it is best to leave them alone to stew in their own juices.

The only way to deal with such an apparently adaptive but, in essence, pernicious doctrine of power is for the countries that are being condemned to the outer world to upset the *status quo* and disturb the stability of the inner world, mainly by continuing the process started by China—even if China is no longer willing to cast its lot with the former. There are three (not necessarily mutually exclusive) roads to such change:

1. An increasing proliferation of arms technology (including nuclear power).

2. The emergence of new power centres in the world based on

the assertion of intermediate powers and by smaller powers aligning into regional combinations.

3. A deliberate disturbance of the balance of the inner world by some of these powers, partly by an effective use of sanctions and pressures available to them as done by the Arabs, but mainly by moving from a policy of strict nonalignment to partial understanding with one of the great powers and thus taking advantage of the still persisting conflicts of goals and interests among them.

A successful pursuit of any one or a combination of these strategies, however, will require a bridging of intraregional differences and resolving conflicts among these countries, a great deal of attention to building internal economic strength, and simultaneous attention to attaining internal political cohesion and viability. We shall discuss in the next chapter the steps involved in moving towards such a world and the likely sources and sites from which such initiatives can be mounted. Basic to the whole design, however, is the capacity of a large number of political communities to attain autonomy and make it a fundamental principle of world order at various levels, including in the internal poltical arrangements of the various states.

END TO CENTRALIZATION

Indeed, man's struggle for autonomy is not confined to the structure of relationships between states. It will have to be fought within existing and future state structures as well. Our ultimate value is the dignity and autonomy of the individual. It is in realizing this value that some of the most stubborn features of the system of dominance are to be found. The roots of this system are to be found in perhaps the most universal characteristic of modern technology and organization, namely, a continuous growth of centralization and hence a constant expansion of bureaucratic control and a corresponding shrinkage of political choice and freedom. This is true of almost all societies and irrespective of the differences in dominant ideologies. It is in this context that our point about building from below as a means of combating structures of dominance is to be understood.

Gandhi was ahead of his time when he preached his model of a decentralized socialist democracy based on a series of levels or, rather, in his own words, "ever-widening, never-ascending circles" of self-reliance and mutuality, with a view to providing the necessities of all, in which every man or woman knows what he or she wants, and what is more, knows that no one should want anything that the others cannot have with equal labour, and in which there is no room for machines that would displace human labour and that would concentrate power in a few hands.

Today, with an uncontrolled technology that has taken possession of man, with a growing number of surplus men for whom the world has no use, with still more fundamental forces of alienation and a sense of power-lessness before the system, and with even the revolutionary ideologies losing their messianic appeal, one has to seriously consider the model of democratic decentralization as a means of arresting these tendencies and producing a more wholesome culture and society. Such a model, if accepted in general principle though no doubt interpreted and implemented in great diversity, can lead to a step-by-step end to exploitation, to mini-mization of the element of bureaucracy in human affairs and of the encroachment of monopolistic structures whether private or public, to a taming of technology by bending it to serve human ends rather than the other way around, and to a general increase in individual autonomy and control over one's own future.

Such a reversal of the centralizing tendencies in modern society will require new directions in technological research and human inven-tiveness (it is a folly to import R & D from developed countries), a shift in the location of productive as well as decision-making units with a view to maximize the involvement of the concerned people, and a recognition and validation of the sources of self-reliance of local populations and the diversity of their skills and traditions rather than dismissing these as parochial or particularistic. Indeed, it is the totalistic onslaught of the dominant universalism of today that has done more damage to the world than the self-sustaining quality of local particularisms. Self-reliance, autonomy, and pride in oneself and one's culture need to be cultivated at all levels, for they provide the surest soil from which interdependence, compassion, and humility will grow and lead to a strong sense of "ever widening, never-ascending" circles of identity and integration. To quote Gandhi more fully,

> Life will not be a pyramid with the apex sustained by the bottom. But it will be an oceanic circle whose centre will be the individual always ready to perish for the village, the latter ready to perish for the circle of villages till at last the whole becomes one life composed of individuals, never aggressive in their arrogance, but ever humble, sharing the majesty of the oceanic circle of which they are integral units. Therefore, the outermost circum-ference will not wield power to crush the inner circle, but will give strength to all within and will derive its own strength from it.

If we translate Gandhi's model in terms of our concepts of centre and periphery, a durable world order can be built only by making the autonomous individual the centre (inner circle) and the world institutions the periphery (circumference), with the nation and intermediate structures occupying mediating positions, thus reversing the present structure in which there are a few world centres who alone are autonomous and the large bulk of the people are peripheral and in which most of the national units themselves are peripheral. A nonviolent world order necessitates such a reversal.

APPROPRIATE TECHNOLOGY

Any attempt to reorder society along a similar model in the context of present-day reality and the foreseeable future—a reality that is becoming far more complex than when Gandhi lived—will call for clear thinking on a number of critical issues. Perhaps the most important issue that must be faced in any effort at remodelling a given social order (only partially faced by Gandhi) relates to technology itself. The solutions to the problems created by the dominant technology of our time will, no doubt, have to be primarily political in character. Operationally, however, they will involve a close understanding of technology itself and an ability to bend it toward implementing the political choices. This is the most important challenge before the scientists and the intellectuals of the world—how to harness technology to the new situation that faces man.

In the history of evolution there are certain things that are irreversible. Science and technology are among these evolutionary irreversibles, which cannot be undone except perhaps by a total eclipse of the entire technological civilization. It is no longer possible to go back to a world without technology—if ever there was such a world. It is not even possible to return to a world of simple technology, where there were no cities and no city-based industries and where men lived by cultivating crops without aid of industrial inputs. In some ways this *would* be a regression. For technology, which shares with nature the quality of being at once benign and sinister, has brought many blessings to man. Also, technology and, even more so, pure science (on which major advances in technology depend) are expressions of man's adventure and creativity, quest for truth, and exercises in freedom and self-realization. Any critique of technology must bear this in mind and seek to channel these basic creative urges into constructive directions. The main point is not to allow *things* to take possession of *man,* not to allow them to stimulate baser instincts in him, not to allow relations between men to become relations between things (as Marx pointed out in his theory of reification).

As a matter of fact, the relationship between technology and civilization is by no means a one-way relationship. Technology offers many choices, more so after recent advances in diffusion technology and the important strides made in inventing new and appropriate technologies suited to the needs of diverse societies and their economic potentialities [V]. Also, while it is true that nearly all industrial societies have adopted a technology of accelerating centralization, it is nonetheless also possible to adopt a technology of decentralization in which individuals and communities will be able to attain greater self-sufficiency and in which information systems and organization structures are oriented to expanding the area of political choice rather than contracting it, as has been the case so far. Perhaps the crux of the matter lies in the choice of an appropriate organizational technology and in subjecting all other technologies to it. (So far organizational technology has not been a determinant but, rather, has been an instrument of other branches of knowledge.)

NATURE OF THE STATE

This leads to a few other imperatives. The state and its political organization will have to play an increasing role in disseminating knowledge and information of a scientific and technological kind; ordinary men must understand what science—and what is known as applied science —is all about. Without this, it will be difficult to bring an end to structures of manipulation and dominance, which are the sources of all violence. To rely on either innovative entrepreneurs in private industry or on enlightened technocrats for promoting the values of justice and nonviolence is a most risky game. If politics is to become increasingly an area of choice and participation, science should follow suit and not be hidden away into the interstices of the knowledge establishment. It follows that the scope of politics must expand rather than contract. The notion of the withering away of the state when the governance of men will be replaced by the administration of things advanced by Marx suffered from the intellectual predispositions of classical liberalism to which the best in Marx was heir. These are noble but misleading concepts, for both these philosophies (liberalism and Marxism), despite their common mistrust of the organized state, placed all their faith in the inevitability of progress through a self-generative technology. The result has been twofold: a contraction of the area of choice in modern societies and an increasing gap between state and society, the common reason for both being a submission of critical decisions to a highly centralized technocratic elite.

It has been a false diagnosis that the causes of exploitation and dominance are to be found in the enlargement of the scope and functions of the state (so-called statism). What is missed in this diagnosis is that the cause of these evils lie not in the *scope* of the state but in its *nature;* it lies in the phenomenon of centralization that appears to pervade not just the state but almost all modern institutions. Once you have a decentralized state, the state ceases to be an oppressor, becomes coterminous with society, and indeed becomes the latter's instrument par excellence for the realization of preferred values.

One final and critical question (already briefly discussed in the last chapter) remains. Is it possible to build a just and nonviolent society based on a decentralized polity and a corresponding technology in one's own society while others carry on as before? We have, all along in this book, placed emphasis on the autonomy and self-reliance of nation-states, both as a means to checking and defeating the existing structures of dominance and exploitation in the world and as a necessary condition of the autonomy and self-reliance of the individual. The question is: Will it be possible to undermine the structures of dominance and centralization in one country while world trends work in the opposite direction? Is it not true that the major citadels of economic and political decentralization (for example, in the smaller European democracies) are giving way to technological forces that require an increasing switch to the dominant mode of both production and participation? And what about the great revolutionary states of the U.S.S.R. and China—hasn't the former already decided to catch up with the Americans and won't the Chinese also follow suit? Also, as the various countries and regions in the Third World undertake to upset the *status quo* will they not be forced to acquire the same technological package (both for acquiring some kind of international parity and for developing an industrial base for the same) as is found in the highly centralized states of today?

These are highly pertinent questions that will have to be squarely faced as one thinks of moving towards an alternative model of human arrangements. They point to an issue that is not new but one that has now, with the growing shrinkage of the world, acquired greater relevance. Can any large-scale reform, any basic transformation in human thought and institutions, be effected without, following Leon Trotsky, aiming at a worldwide movement? Gandhi believed that he could convert his countrymen to his view of a nonviolent social and ethical order. But he failed in this mission, partly perhaps because political events that he had not expected—partition of the country and large-scale violence—overtook his country, but largely because the world intellectual and technological trends as well as the structure of world politics had obliged Gandhi's closest followers to discard a large part of his model. Instead, they adopted a model which stabilized patterns of dominance both internally and externally. Since that time there is, no doubt, a greater concern at removing at least the more menacing aspects of the present system of dominance and exploitation—not just in Gandhi's India but in a number of other countries as well.   But there is as yet no evidence that this will necessarily lead to new models of sociopolitical order.   Perhaps a major impediment may lie in the fact that nation-states have to function in an essentially competitive world (which will become more competitive with the growing scramble for world resources) and that unless a good many of them cooperate in removing the worst forms of exploitation and tension, the scope for individual initiative is likely to be limited.

It appears, then, that the struggle for creating a just and non-violent order has both worldwide and regional dimensions.   While the struggle against both internal and external patterns of dominance will need to be carried out at national and regional levels, the battle against overpowering technologies—including military technology—and persisting inequality in man's access to natural resources will necessitate wider cooperation between nations and regions through certain world institutions, as well as the development of powerful worldwide movements of intellectual opinion.   The two aspects are closely interrelated.   It is in the process of translating our design for the future into reality, identifying the most relevant agents of change, and evolving strategies that would incrementally bring about the desired changes that the precise linkages between different levels of world reality will become clear and provide a coherent integral framework for both thought and action.   It is to this final exercise in our argument that we shall now turn.

Notes

A   The figures are taken from the Yearbooks of 1972 and 1973 on *World Armaments and Disarmaments* of the Stockholm International Peace Research Institute (SIPRI), Stockholm, Almqvist & Wiksell, New York, Humanities Press, and London, Paul Elek, 1972 and 1973.

B   Richard A. Falk, *This Endangered Planet: Prospects and Proposals,* New York, 1971.

C   For a good summary of the attitude of different "near-nuclear" countries toward nonproliferation, see the SIPRI study, *The Near-Nuclear Countries and the NPT,* Stockholm, Almqvist & Wiksell, New York, Humanities Press, and London, Paul Elek, 1972. As part of the World Order Models Project, the Indian team undertook an opinion survey of elites and emerging elites in India on policies affecting world-order prospects. For an analysis of the view of the Indian elite on NPT, see Ashis Nandy, "The Bomb, the NPT and Indian Elites", *Economic and Political Weekly,* Special Number, 7(31-33), August 1972.

D Figures are from the SIPRI Yearbook of 1972. It should be noted, however, that exports of major arms from both the United States and the U.S.S.R. have declined of late, though for the United States the long-term trend (as measured by five-year moving averages) is one of increase, and, in any case, total arms exports (as distinct from major arms exports) have been rising. The decline in the U.S.S.R. exports has been caused by a sharp decline in supplies to India and the Middle East. See SIPRI Yearbook, 1973, *op. cit.*

E For a documentation of the relevant studies on which the above estimates are based, and generally on this whole theme, see Richard A. Falk, *op. cit.,* especially pp. 138-145.

F It is, of course, in the industrialized countries that the *level* of urbanization is highest, but it is in the developing countries that the *rate* of urbanization is faster. Thus it is estimated that by the end of the century 62 per cent of the world's urban population will be living in the present developing countries. What is more, a larger proportion of the migration to urban areas is to large cities that are precisely the centres of conspicuous disparities in living standards, growing unemployment among the young and the educated, a virtual breakdown in social services, and political turmoil. See United Nations, 1970 *Report on the World Social Situation,* New York, 1971, pp. vii, 190.

G The corresponding figures for the developed countries will be 28 per cent. See *Ibid.,* p. vii.

H See the illuminating treatment of this whole subject by Charles Levinson in his *Capital, Inflation and the Multi-Nationals,* London, George Allen & Unwin, 1971, especially pp. 40–69.

I *Ibid.,* p. 51.

J According to United Nations estimates (1970 Report, *op. cit.*), unemployment and underemployment are of the order of 30 per cent in many developing countries. Incidentally, as already argued by us in Chapter III, underemployment is an even more grievous problem than overt unemployment.

K We have already discussed this problem at some length in Chapter III.

L See, however, the pessimistic scenarios based on somewhat precise considerations given by Carl F. von Weizacker in his essay, "A Sceptical Contribution", prepared for the World Order Models Project and published in Saul H. Mendlovitz and Ian Baldwin (eds.), *On the Creation of a Just World Order,* New Delhi, Orient Longman,

New York, The Free Press, and Amsterdam, North Holland, 1974.

M Almost all great scientists and humanists of recent times have expressed such an anxiety. Unfortunately, a large number of them are highly superficial in their analysis and indulge in platitudes. To take the best among them, Albert Einstein's *The World As I See It* makes somewhat shallow reading. So does J. Robert Oppenheimer's *The Open Mind*. Examples can be added. And yet there is real pain in these writings and a readiness to devote precious lives to securing a safer future for man. The need is to join forces between such men, analysts who have given sustained thought to the problems of social engineering, and the social engineers themselves. See in this connection the outstanding essay by the Soviet physicist Andrei Sakharov, *Progress, Coexistence and Intellectual Freedom*, London, Andre Deutsch, 1968.

N D. G. Tendulkar, *Mahatama: Life of Mohandas Karamchand Gandhi*, Vol. IV, Bombay, Vithalbhai K. Jhaveri and D. G. Tendulkar, 1952, p. 3.

O Hannah Arendt, *On Violence*, New York, The Viking Press, 1963.

P Tendulkar, *op. cit.*, p. 228.

Q For an excellent analysis of the issue of reciprocity and how in its absence philanthrophy leads to resentment and ultimate revenge in a quest for autonomy and self-esteem, see Wilton S. Dillon, "Anthropological Perspective on Violence" in Gene Usdin (ed.), *Perspectives On Violence*, New York, Brunner/Mazel Publishers, 1972, pp. 69-107. It is interesting to note that this American author characterizes such a backlash against the benevolent hegemony of the United States as "the Gaullist effect".

R For a perceptive treatment of this whole topic, mainly in the context of the American Negro problem but relevant also for the struggles of oppressed peoples elsewhere, see Harvey Wheeler, "A Moral Equivalent for Riots", in Ng. Larry (ed.), *Alternatives to Violence*: *Stimulus To Dialogue*, New York, Time-Life Books, 1968, especially pp. 47–70.

S Nirmal Kumar Bose, (ed.), *Selections from Gandhi*, Ahmedabad, Navjivan Publishing House, 2nd ed., 1957, p. 31.

T *ibid.*, p. 162.

U "Content of Independence", *Harijan*, July 22, 1946.

V E. F. Schumacher has, through his Intermediate Technology Development Group, located in London, done outstanding work in this direction, especially in African countries. Among his various writings, see "An Economics of Permanence" in Ted Dunn (ed.), *Foundations of Peace and Freedom*, London, James Clarks, 1970; "The New Economics", *Resurgence*, September–October 1968; and *Small Is Beautiful: A Treatment of Economics as if People Mattered*, New

York, Harper & Row, 1963. Another outstanding group, who prefer to call their approach "soft technology", is the Biotechnic Research and Development Group, located in London and Paris. This group is led by Robin Clarke, a well-known British writer on science, until recently editor of *Science Journal* and author of *The Science of War and Peace*, New York, Jonathan Cape and McGraw-Hill, 1972. The soft technologists are, like the intermediate technologists, working mainly in the Third World countries. See their *Soft Technology: A Proposal for Alternatives under Conditions of Crisis*, UNESCO (Youth Division), October 1971, *mimeographed*, and Janine and Robin Clarke, "The Biotechnic Research Community", *Futures*, June 1972.

5

FOOTSTEPS

THE basic issue that has engaged us in this book can be stated quite simply: how do we move from a world in which there is a growing divorce between scientific and technological progress and the freedom and well being of human beings to one in which the two are harmonized? We are interested less in projecting scenarios based on known trends and more in designing a future based on certain value premises and an assessment of the emerging reality and in indicating steps by which we can get there. We are interested in prediction only insofar as it prompts men to action. In sum, our central concern is with politics, not prognostics.

Approach to the Future

Such an approach has the danger of being infected by unrestrained romanticism and lack of sensitivity to the historical context in which human actions have to take place. We have, in this book, tried to avoid this pitfall. First, there is no assumption of a *tabula rasa* on which an *a priori* model of a preferred future is sought to be imposed. Not only is there a long history (the past) that any future should take into account; the world around us (the present) also displays certain persisting traits and propensities in and through—and against—which one has to act. Second, anyone who conceives of the future as an enterprise in realizing certain values as against one who is satisfied with accepting (or at best expediting) a predetermined historical sequence must adopt a highly responsible attitude to the future: the consequences that follow are in good part a result of what one does and not of some impersonal laws beyond one's control. It follows from these two stipulations (that one must reckon with the past and feel responsible for his actions in the present) that the nature of action involved in moving towards the future is of necessity stepwise and incremental. For one is not pinning faith on some dramatic happening that is about to take place but is working stepwise towards a progressive realization of values on which a wide degree of consensus is simultaneously being created. In other words, one thinks in terms of footsteps into the future by operating at a number of levels, not catastrophic reversals of existing arrangements that may or may not produce the desired results.

INCREMENTAL REVOLUTION

This does not mean that one does not aim at major changes or does not be bold in conceptualizing alternatives to existing reality. We have, in previous chapters, argued for some major restructuring of prevailing institutional relationships and for basic changes in the attitudes and normative perspectives that inform them. Our preferred changes in existing attitudes and structures call for some rather fundamental reassessments of man's approach to his own destiny and the destiny of his fellow men, to his relationship with other beings and other forms of life, and to his impressive creations in the realm of technology and social organization. The most relevant revolution that needs to be carried out has to be directed against the overpowering *culture*, the dominant worldview, of our time that is driving men and institutions towards the present malaise—revolution in the minds of men as the cliché goes. Without that, no amount of tinkering with institutional structures or particular magnitudes (such as the arms race) will prove effective. Simultaneous efforts at reconstructing prevailing institutional arrangements for the purpose of furthering the values of autonomy, justice, and nonviolence will, of course, be necessary as part of the same action strategy; we do not subscribe to the view that changes in attitudes should *precede* institutional changes; the two are reflections of the same system. Thus while we go along with the structuralists who see the sources of both violence and injustice in structures of exploitation and call for a transformation of those structures in a bid to bring about a peaceful and just world, we go beyond them in stressing the cultural dimensions of any strategy of institutional change.

A MINIMAL UTOPIA

Involved in this recognition of a close interrelationship between cultural and institutional changes is another preference of ours: our aim should be not to create some kind of a perfect world social system that will provide peace and prosperity for all and in which everyone is liberated from the realm of necessity and led to the realm of freedom. We do not believe that freedom is a mere function of socioeconomic structure; all that the structures can accomplish is to provide minimal

conditions necessary for its realization. In the model that we have
proposed in this essay we are concerned with providing these minimum
conditions, leaving a great deal of scope for individual creativity and
cultural diversity.   We are not addicted to the vision of a fully worked-out
model of a utopia, as we believe that such a utopia can soon turn into a
"disutopia."

The basic point, indeed, is not to determine the future along any
one direction, however lofty it might appear, but rather to permit a large
area of *choice* to individuals and collectivities. It is this that has been
undone in the contemporary march of man towards a predetermined
model of progress and its embodiment in a set of institutions. We have
already discussed at length the deterministic character of this model,
its basic *Weltanschauung*, its reification of external   concentrations of
energy and power and a corresponding decline in the value and utility
of man as a creative force, and the consequence of such a model in the
form of a growing duality among men and nations. We have also, in
previous chapters, provided the elements of an alternative model based
on the autonomy and dignity of human beings and of the political communities to which they belong, the diagnosis and thinking that lies behind
such a model, and the policy implications of such a model for moving
towards a more just and less violent world. It is not necessary to repeat
all that here. Rather, the purpose of this chapter is to indicate the manner
in which steps can be taken to implement the model we have in mind.
Having discussed at some length *what* should be done, we should now
address ourselves to *how* to initiate the process of change towards such
a model.

This calls for an identification of strategic points in the technoeconomic structure of the world where early action is called for, actual
actors who are likely to take initiative, and the necessary changes in the
institutional and political structures of the world that will have to
accompany these initiatives. It should be remembered that our exercise
is limited to what can be done in the next twenty-five years or so by
proposing what we consider to be a *feasible utopia*. It still is a utopia,
because the world that it envisages is very different (in certain aspects
fundamentally different) from the world of today and also because such
a world will not come into being if the course of history is left to work
itself out and men of conviction do not intervene in it. For us, a utopia
is not something that is bold and exciting but without much of a chance
of being realized. It is, rather, a picture of a world that is both desirable
and possible and hence something that man should strive to bring about.[1]

1. Methodologically, this implies moving from a *diagnosis* of present trends (according
   to a theoretical paradigm) and a *design* (based on a value paradigm) to a *strategy*
   (a paradigm of action).

Hitherto man has lived by visions of utopia in some distant future without worrying about how to get there; the task now is to take steps towards realizing one in the not too distant future. The situation that faces man and his species has drastically changed. It is necessary that he also changes his way of thinking and of relating thought and action.

Critical Sectors

As we have argued in this book, the basic problem facing contemporary society is the increasing obsolescence of human beings and a correspondingly rising value of nonhuman artifacts and techniques for which there is a rising demand in all countries, including the rich ones. The problem is accentuated by the fact that both these characteristics—surfeit of human beings and scarcity of nonhuman resources—are found in much larger proportions in the developing countries. There are two other related facts. One is that the continuing increase in the expansion in the demand for, and hence the supply of, capital goods and R&D means that expansion in these sectors will be far ahead of expansion in the consumer-goods sector, thus producing inflationary tendencies everywhere. The other is the growing needs of the richer countries for capital resources will mean that the capacity of the developing countries to generate employment through industrialization will be severely limited, at least in the foreseeable future. A structure of international trade that has systematically discriminated against these countries, the increasing concentration of economic power in the hands of multinational corporations, and the myopic effects of high consumption standards propagated by these corporations to the people of these countries point to the same general picture of diminishing opportunities for a fast-increasing population that willbe concentrated in the peripheries of the "outer" world.

Meanwhile, the increasing ecological cost of the populations living in high-consumption societies, the incessant innovation in techniques[2] resulting in unemployment there also, the growing militarization of the nerve centres of that world, and the psychological cost of living under high technology and huge organizations for men who have jobs but not enough work to keep them occupied and hold their interest have all given rise to a loss of balance and a mood of escapism in the "inner" world. Such a combination of drift born out of extremes of affluence in one part of the

---

2. The proposition that you must constantly innovate in order to survive has now become a way of life in the industrially advanced countries, so much so that some entire industries and large parts of all other industries are devoted to this enterprise. No respite for modern man indeed! The "leisure" and "relaxation" for which he strives are based on this incessant search for novelty and constant tension.

world and chaos that is likely to result from extremes of poverty in another, the common factor in both being the growing disutility of man,
presents a picture against which it is necessary to act.

EMPLOYMENT

The elements of an alternative to the present technoeconomic
model that can provide the basis of such action have already been outlined by us earlier in this book. The key to initiating steps toward them
are to be found less in recipes in the *aggregate*, such as diversion of
capital resources from rich to poor countries (or, within the latter,
from defense to development) and more in the direction of creating
opportunities for *specific* human groups so that they are in a position
to work and look after themselves and, on that basis, determine their
own futures. A world that is faced by the impasse of there being less
and less for *men* and more and more for *mankind* calls for a package
that is different from the one based on infinite specialization, high-speed
communications, and glistening shopping centres that may constitute
the dream world of the urban middle classes living on borrowed intelligence but that in fact produces a world that creates wants that have no
relationship to human needs and fails to fulfill those very needs. The new
package has to quite simply and clearly fulfill the minimum needs of
every human being. In concrete terms, it should provide employment
and adequate income to all men so that they can obtain life's necessities
on the basis of their own work and so that the "effective demand" for
goods and services that is generated becomes "need effective", that is, it
gives rise to a structure of production that fulfills basic human needs [A].
Let both national governments and international agencies concentrate
on this one single issue of relating the organization of economic activity
to a conception of human needs. The concentration on the supply side
of the production equation that has produced the phenomenon of more
and more men having less and less, and less and less men having more
and more, must give place to a realization of the most elementary postulate of political economy: the creation of effective demand for basic
necessities among all the people.

EDUCATION

The focus on employment and purchasing power of a growing
population can become the basis of a major transformation of policies
in various sectors of technoeconomic development. It is clear by now
that without acquisition of minimum skills, large segments of the world
population would not find entry into the employment market even if

jobs were available. This calls for imaginative attention to one of the most critical areas of policy initiative: education. We are aware of recent Western studies that show that investment in education does not lead to commensurate returns in economic productivity. Even if we were to avoid the temptation of saying that here is another instance (the other being the limits of growth thesis) of preaching to the underdeveloped the virtues of underdevelopment, the basic point is that what most people mean by education is indeed economically costly, politically counterproductive, and culturally disruptive. In most countries education also has become capital-intensive, with endless years of formal schooling, costly school buildings and equipment, graded qualifications, and teacher-training based on latest methods. This has led to the result that in most of the poor countries there is a high correlation between investment in formal school education and educational underdevelopment.

A totally different approach to education, requiring not only a new outlook but also a new technology, is called for [B]. First, formal education has to be less bookish and more analytical, with the objective of instilling skills and aptitudes that make of men meaningful participants in social and economic life. Second, the technical skills (imparted not by universities but by modest and decentralized training institutes) that are generated should be related to the needs of society: more medical and public health workers with short term diplomas who are willing to work in the villages than highly trained doctors and fancy nurses working in expensive clinics in large cities and administering costly antibiotics, more middle-range technicians than degree holding engineers, a larger supply of plumbers, carpenters, electricians, and truck drivers trained in local polytechnics than irrigation experts, architects, electrical engineers, and pilots with foreign degrees. Third, and perhaps most important, there is need to undertake massive campaigns of adult education for which the large band of social workers that are available in all societies can be mobilized and to make use of recent advances in technology, for example for beaming television programmes on community sets through space satellites. Adult education not only leads to an almost immediate return on investment, both in terms of economic productivity and in terms of expanding general awareness, but also produces a considerable multiplier effect by contributing to the education of the children of the adults as well other adults in the neighbourhood or workplace. The basic task is to awaken the span of consciousness for transforming large human potentials that exist everywhere into skills and capacities that could overcome the basic dilemma of underdevelopment: the growing chasm between aggregate growth and individual deprivation, between community resources and individual opportunities, between productivity and purchasing power.

RESEARCH

The need to define, develop, and implement a series of alternative policies points to the critical importance of scientific research in the countries of the Third World. This is one sector that has been most ignored by a majority of countries who have preferred to borrow ready-made packages from "advanced" countries and have in the process surrendered the possibility of attending to their own problems in their own ways. One of the principal reasons why the United States has achieved and sustained a position of economic superiority and dominance in the world is that it has been able to stay miles ahead of others in research, both scientific and technological. Even more pertinent than this technological dependence, however, is the fact that so long as a majority of countries are happy to simply adopt (at best, adapt) techniques developed elsewhere, there is little scope for them to shape their futures independently. There is urgent need for these countries, especially those that face totally different situations and also wish to evolve a different model of human society, to undertake comprehensive research programmes of their own, devoted in the main to evolving new alternatives to the existing package of methods and techniques without, of course, denying the validity of historical experience in this as in any other area of human enterprise.

The principal rationale of such research is that one is dealing with a situation that for a long time to come will be scarce in the supply of capital goods (that would be necessary if the bulk of the population were to be involved in machine industry) but abundant in men, the richness of tradition, and the vast social potential that can be mobilized if there is the will to do so. The idea of following the familiar course provided by the aggressive salesmanship of the world's technological establishment is both impossible—the money needed to multiply the United States all over the world will not be available even in a hundred years—and undesirable if the world is to survive and preserve its sanity. In any case, if autonomy of men and nations, and justice and nonviolence among them, are values we seek to realize, the need for independent research is self-evident.

Catalysts of Change

There is a wider context in which an alternative design for the future will have to be worked out. It will depend on major changes in the power structure of the world and, what is still more important, in the attitudes and values that sustain it—in the culture of world politics. To undertake these larger changes is not an easy task, as it calls for some very hard considerations. The main point is: from where will these initiatives come, from which areas of the world, from which social strata, and through what combination of use of formal political power and movements of ideas and protest?

BALANCE OF POWER

There are at present three theories of intervention in this regard that have wide currency among different thinkers. The first of these is the so-called realist view of international relations shared by an influential section of the academic profession, quite a few political leaders spread over many countries belonging to different ideological camps, and a large group of international civil servants and technocrats. According to this view, a stable balance among the great powers and a containment of the arms race can lead to a significant transfer of capital and technological resources of the world from supporting war machines to promoting economic development of the poor countries, can eradicate misery and deprivation from the world, and, in turn, can control international violence except in sporadic localized forms (the latter are supposed to act as safety valves that would prevent larger eruptions). It seems to us that such a gospel of stable peace and world prosperity based on a combination of balance of power in the inner world and economic development of the outer world through aid and expansion from the present industrial centres is both unrealistic and unacceptable. It is unrealistic because it extends the neat and simple model of a bipolar world to a far more complex relationship among the great powers that is based less on positive multi-lateralism and more on checking and balancing a set of bilaterial competitions (among the United States, the Soviet Union, China, Western Europe, and Japan) with important new powers on the horizon. The balance that is proposed is, therefore, inherently unstable and precarious. It is unacceptable because both the international political system based on the dominance of a few powers and the international economic system based on the worldwide penetration of the Western industrial machine on which the balance of power system depends will forever condemn large parts of the world population to a condition of dependence.

INTERNATIONALISM

The second theory of intervention (sometimes described as "idealist" as opposed to the first realist school) is based on a conception of internationalism in which the sovereignty of nation-states should be surrendered to a centralized world authority that will eschew violence from human affairs, treat all human beings equally, and utilize scientific knowledge for the betterment of mankind.   Again, the recipe is both unrealistic because it ignores the crucial dimensions of power politics and exhibits an uncritical faith in technology, and unacceptable because it is bound to lead to a vast bureaucratic straitjacket that will undermine human autonomy and the cultural diversity that is the essence of freedom and dignity.   It is also a rather quiescent perspective that is at once naive and pretentious.   It is no accident that it comes essentially from either daydreaming philosophers found everywhere in the world or comfortable peace researchers found mainly in the richer countries.

REVOLUTION

The third theory of intervention—whose proponents also share the internationalism of the second school of thought—is based on the call for a revolution made by exasperated intellectuals from the West who are convinced that nothing short of total change will improve the present state of affairs.   Repelled by the decadence of Western industrial society and the wretchedness of the poor in the Third World countries, they are found to lead protest movements in the former and preach revolution in the latter.   There are many versions of the revolutionary path based on crude combinations of Sorellian, Marxist, Maoist, and Gandhian perspectives.   In a peculiar way, however, the deeper psychological predispositions of many of the revolutionary internationalists are not different from those of the advocates of globalism based on a neocolonial balance of power: they both see chaos in the miserable underdeveloped world and seek to check it through a condescending evangelism.   Whereas one seeks to enlighten them through the gospel of modernity, the other seeks to save them by extolling to them the virtues of a revolution.   Neither places high value on the autonomy of individuals or nations, and they have little confidence that people can work out their own solutions.   Deep in both is the spectre of anarchy that is going to be let loose from the poor, fast-multiplying, and inert peripheries of the world.   The difference between them is that whereas the balancers of the world want to quarantine the peripheries, the revolutionaries wish to use the peripheries for mounting an assault on their own establishments against whom they otherwise feel powerless.

The revolutionary theorists have a large horde of followers in the Third World countries also.   The latter share the totalistic perspective of the former and wish to transform the societies they live in by a revolutionary capture of power.   Not a little of the confusion and chaos in the Third World countries owes to the activities of these radicals who draw their inspiration from models of revolution manufactured elsewhere (almost in the same way as the establishment elites draw their inspiration from models of growth manufactured in the same intellectual centres).

REVOLUTION AT THE CENTRE

There is an opposite variant of the revolutionary theory on which the radicals of both the rich and the poor countries are often found to bank. This is based on the assumption that the post-industrial world is going to collapse under its own weight, as a result of ethnic violence, youth unrest, urban dislocations, industrial pollution, and so forth, and that at long last, as Marx had predicted, a revolutionary situation will arise in these countries and from there will spread to the rest of the world. It seems to us that this is an exercise in self-delusion and is based on a naive optimism regarding the prospects of change in these countries. The indications are to the contrary: the youth revolt is in utter confusion, problems of ethnic minorities and environmental pollution have been accepted as urgent agenda by the ruling elites who alone can find the capital needed for solving them, the United States is going strong, Western Europe has put itself in good shape and acquired for itself protective tariffs at home and expanding markets abroad as well as a new basis of relationship with their former colonies, Japan is going to use its economic might to ensure stability for itself despite some severe strains, and hitherto antagonistic powers such as the Soviet Union and China have been successfully contained. If anything, the inner world has fortified itself against difficulties and it is the outer world, ridden as it is likely to be with an increasing pile of problems, that is going to be left to stew in its own juice.[3]

As things are currently shaping, it appears that the inner and the outer worlds are likely to drift further apart into two totally different universes: one controlling the centre and the other left lurching in the periphery; one suffering from satiation, the other from scarcity; one showing a declining salience of politics in managing society, the other highly politicized and tension ridden; one perfecting the instruments of a centralized and basically authoritarian state disposing of petty liberties, the other oscillating between totalitarian repression and democratic revolts. It would be quite unrealistic to expect a breakdown in the former. And it is self-delusion to hope that transformation in one region—be it

---

3. On the basis of this scenario it might appear that we too share the judgment of the globalists that the Third World countries are incapable of looking after themselves. We do not share that view, as should be clear from the book as a whole and will become more clear in this chapter. What we have presented above is a picture of the world that the dominant powers are trying to create.

technological or political—will lead to a worldwide change in some automatic way.[4]

ROLE OF THE THIRD WORLD

The initiative for improving their state of affairs will have to come from the Third World countries themselves. They face a different set of problems from what the industrialized countries faced, they will have to show a capacity for independent thinking if they are to solve these problems, and in any case nothing short of their political independence and dignity is at stake. There are two courses open to these countries: accept the present world *status quo* and a long period of colonial status under the tutelage of the metropolitan centres of the world or work for their independence both politically and by intellectually responding to the domestic and regional challenges they face. If they succeed in evolving an alternative model of responding to fundamental human problems, it is possible that they may contribute to the thinking in other parts of the world also. (The latter are not without problems, some of a rather fundamental kind.)

The broad features of an alternative model needed to both tackle an unprecedented mix of problems and avoid the pitfalls and aberrations of the already industrialized nations have been outlined by us in this book. The tasks involved in realizing such a model are basically political. But in order to undertake them with confidence and in the face of the overpowering appeal of the prevailing paradigms, these tasks will need to be backed by a major intellectual effort. The mobilization of political will and economic resources requires a persuasive theoretical rationale.

INTELLECTUAL TASK

This is a task in which the intellectuals, scientists, and social scientists of the Third World have to join forces with politicians and administrators. It is a role that has not been adequately performed until now. Almost everywhere intellectuals and scientists are being co-opted and absorbed by national and international establishments most of which are unable to think beyond the prevailing theory of modernization. The

4. The diffusion theory seems to be the common assumption underlying the three prevailing theories of intervention that we have examined: in the first case export of resources and technology, in the second case export of the Christian ideal of brotherhood and unity of all men, and in the third case export of revolution. Also common to all three is a reliance on outdated and typically European solutions, lack of sensitivity to the fact that we face a wholly different world reality, and a tendency to still draw upon past experience instead of anticipating what the future holds in store and work out a design for it.

intellectuals of most of the developing countries have been especially lacking in performing their roles as interpreters of tradition and catalysts of change. Perhaps the new trend towards professionalization is responsible for this. Or perhaps it is the exaggerated ego of intellectuals subtly inflated by their counterparts abroad. And yet no society can hope to bring about basic changes in ruling paradigms without the active involvement of scholars and intellectuals. Most of the major advances of recent times that have changed the nature of the world we live in, the collection and dissemination of useful information on society, and construction of new organizational models and policy alternatives have been the work of scientists, social scientists, journalists, literary men, and other intellectuals, mainly in the Western countries, the Soviet Union and Japan all of whom place a high value on intellectual activity. In a number of newly independent countries, too, intellectuals played a considerable role in creating new values and launching new movements of ideas, as well as in the growth of scientific knowledge. And yet when any of these achievements is either undermined or misused or simply ignored (as in the case of empirical research and policy proposals based on it), the same intellectuals are unable to make themselves felt. Many of them prefer to be on the right side of the establishment while others choose to contract out of the system as a price for their autonomy.

This situation needs to be changed. Scientists and intellectuals have to learn the value of power in human affairs, something that they have either despised or feared. They have to become autonomous participants in the processes of decision-making without, however, arrogating to themselves any superior status by virtue of their learning or specialized knowledge. The basic point is that a divorce between intellect and power is as undesirable as the concept that only philosphers should be kings. It is through the intellectuals' involvement in the larger processes of political change that the ability of governments and oppositions to accept and implement new choices based on a new vision (as well as to avoid short-term temptations based on expediency) will become possible. The basic postulate of our model, that men must intervene in the process of history and not be passive spectators of some predetermined course, necessitates the primacy of politics and an active role of men of ideas in it.[5]

5. We have often in this book criticized the manner in which the middle class intelligentsia have, through their imitation of imported models and their lust for consumption items, undermined the autonomy of their societies. Nonetheless, it is also true that the initiative for change of a basic kind, which is based on fundamental questioning, comes from this very stratum that has the capacity of rising above their class interest and shaping human destiny along new paths. This is what Lenin meant when he argued that the lower classes cannot develop a

In carrying out this role there will be very substantial scope for international cooperation. Whereas the thinkers and politicians of the Third World will have to perform the main task in solving the problems of the Third World, there is also the need to mobilize intellectual opinion in the affluent countries, both for exposing the sources of dominance and for policies that perpetrate exploitation and discrimination against poorer countries and suppressed races. This role will have to be performed less by permanent dissenters and prophets of doom who have given up all hope and are advocating catastrophic action here and now and more by men of science, literature, philosophy, and the arts who are possessed by a deep sense of world crisis and are able to perceive the limited perspective on which their civilization has been built without, however, being bewitched by the new breed of charlatans from the mysterious East or seeking a return to their own biblical past [C].

The basis of cooperation between such men from the affluent countries and the intellectuals and political leaders of the Third World will have to be quite different from the one-way traffic that both sides seem to have accepted as natural until recently. It is not merely that this will have to be a relationship of equality; that is assumed in any civilized interaction. It is, rather, that the intellectuals and scientists from the affluent world will have to carry the struggle for values in their own societies, not by merely evolving solutions for others.[6] For it is from their societies that the danger to human liberty and survival in recent times has come.

Much more is, of course, called for. It is not enough to undertake a struggle against the forces of reaction. It is also necessary to devise new modes of attending to the affairs of society based on a philosophy of life that is at once relevant to contemporary reality and based on an understanding of history, evolution, and the perennial dilemmas of human life. It is in this task—and its translation into a set of action proposals without which the new alternative will remain confined to books like this one—that intellectuals from different parts of the world will have to work together and become effective agents

revolutionary consciousness on their own. It is in the intellectuals that such consciousness develops and is then turned into organizational effort. ("The Indispensability of the Intellectuals", *Selected Works*, Vol. I, pp. 148-9).

6. Some concrete examples are resistance against monopolizing the world's raw materials for meeting the ever rising consumption demands of overdeveloped societies, against arms supplies to militarist regimes in tension ridden areas of the Third World, against nuclear tests in the Southern Hemisphere, against discriminatory and unduly restrictive immigration policies, against support to blatantly fascist and racist colonialism. M. Malraux offered to go to fight for the liberation of Bangla Desh. Let committed intellectuals like him join their black counterparts in active resistance against what is going on in South Africa and Rhodesia.

of historical change. There are not many such people to be found in individual countries; indeed, there are not many the world over. The case for pooling their efforts as a means of influencing opinion in national and international settings is very strong indeed. One of the real weaknesses of intellectuals is their inability to organize themselves collectively. It is necessary to cross this barrier without loss of time.

We do want to think of intellectual effort in global terms. Thus the Western worldview that we have subjected to critical scrutiny in this book is now part of the human civilizational process as a whole, and so are the philosophies of the East, though this is being felt only gradually. There is a bond that unites these different worlds despite the duality between them caused by modern technoeconomic structures. It is necessary to give new life to this bond through intelligence, courage, and a perspective on human history and, above all, through mutual empathy and common commitment to common values. As the future unfolds itself, the problems of the developing world will become staggering and call for enormous political *and* intellectual effort. A titanic struggle has been going on for the minds of men on a world scale—between the militarists and the multi-nationals on the one hand and a small section of humanity commited to a different model of the world on the other. Such a struggle necessitates an alliance between thinking strata everywhere who have nothing to lose but their hopeless encirclement by archaic institutions controlled by new professional classes—nothing to lose but their chains [D].

OTHER MOVEMENTS

Beyond the involvement of the scientific estate of the world in moving towards an alternative model of social and political arrangements instead of towards the one that the world seems to be heading, there is need to mobilize various other cross-sections of professional and activist groups. On the whole, most of these movements have produced somewhat ambivalent results and are at the moment in bad shape. The much publicized youth movement, the inspiration for which came from alienated strata in the industrialized countries, has made little headway. This is largely due to the fact that it is a movement without a theory, the leaders of the movement having failed to construct an alternative model to the one that dominates the world today and basing their action strategies on it. It is only lately, with frustration in launching and sustaining a confrontation with the establishment, that the more committed and resilient elements in this movement have withdrawn from the battle royal, and are devoting themselves to creating alternative life styles and community organizations within their own societies.

Similarly, there seems to be little prospect that the workers of the world will unite; if anything, with some exceptions,[7] the organized working classes have turned out to be one of the main defenders of the *status quo* (political, economic, even racial).   The people for whom neither most of the angry young men nor most of the labour movements seem to care are precisely the millions throughout the world who have been rendered surplus and hence useless by the inexorable march of modernity.   Even the more committed among the educated youth in most countries seem largely to be at a loss when the interests of the unionized and employed working class come in conflict with the interests of the unemployed and the vagrant. These antagonisms become sharpest at the international level, with the establishment in the labour unions being the most dogged opponents of immigrant labour from abroad and the youth movements caring little for them, and with the labouring classes making common cause with the ruling elites in the rich countries against the interests of the proletariat in the poor countries.   But the situation is not very different within individual countries where organized labour, with its constant demands for wage increases, stands in the way of the unorganized and the unemployed.

The need is to provide these sectors as well as certain other lower-middle-class groups (for example, school and college teachers that in several countries provide the elements of a massive organization) with a new perspective for their activities that takes them beyond agitating for higher wages and a shorter working day.   They can be involved in programmes of political education, in the shift of professional manpower into rural areas, in organizing agitations against ostentatious consumption by the privileged strata (which, of course, necessitates that they themselves do not hanker after a similar life), and in efforts to enable the unemployed and the very poorly employed—the true proletariat of the world—to find entry into job markets by participating in adult-education

---

7. An interesting exception is Cesar Chavez's United Farm Workers Union in the United States. We have already discussed the general point in Chapter II and have said there that though certain labour movements, such as the British and the Scandinavian, played a progressive historical role, trade unionism has by and large become a force for conservatism and even reaction (as in their stand against poor immigrant labour).   Faith in proletarian revolution still persists, however.   Attention is often drawn to the role of the unions in the massive student revolt in France in 1968. There are some who believe that as the multinational corporation spreads and displaces labour everywhere with its high technology, a worldwide labour resistance joined by the ranks of the unemployed will follow.   It is also possible that as the struggle for autonomy in the regions of the Third World gains in power and these regions become conscious of their advantages, as shown by the Arabs in 1973, the labouring classes in these regions find common cause across local boundaries.

programmes and imparting requisite skills to them. Starting within individual countries, these activities as they acquire momentum can become regional and international in scope and can press for vital changes towards progressive equalization of opportunities, for example by relaxation of immigration policies to allow for a more optimal distribution of a fast-rising world population. These are only illustrations of possible activities, the main point being that unless the various movements in different parts of the world are directed along constructive action programmes and informed by a clear perspective, they are unlikely to make any meaningful contribution to the solution of pressing world problems. The same applies to more anomic but highly significant movements within the post-industrial world such as the hippy, the women's lib, and the yoga cults, all of which seem to be somewhat self-centred and indifferent to the more serious problems facing the world we live in. Any redirection of their energy depends on an adequate theoretical understanding among these various groups of the precise nature of the crisis of our time and its implications for action.

One other drawback of all these movements is that each is a fragment by itself and that there is little effort to relate to one another or to other actors in the process of change, namely the political leaders of the Third World countries, the scientists and intellectuals who are trying to mobilize world opinion, and the more committed among the international civil servants working in various agencies who are trying hard to improve the lot of the undernourished, the illiterate, the unemployed, and the diseased. There is need to join forces, to engage the leaders of the underdeveloped regions and the leaders of intellectual and other movements everywhere in a continuous dialogue, and to undertake coordinated thinking and effort at both national and international levels for realizing human dignity and well-being in all parts of the world. There is at present little organized effort in this direction.

Structural Changes

That brings us to the last and most important phase in our argument. In order to make a start toward the design outlined by us in this book it is necessary to initiate important structural changes in the distribution of power and resources in the world. There is need to translate an intellectual model of a preferred world into a practical design for political action. The present economic, territorial, political, and military structure of the world provides a powerful institutional framework for continuing both the general duality of the world between inner centres and outer peripheries and the specific patterns of domination and dependence on which that duality is based. Unless a sustained and united effort is made to alter this framework and restructure world politics on the basis of greater autonomy for and equality between states there is little chance of a better future for man.

SOLIDARITY

Two broad strategies are called for. First, there is need for the nations of the Third World to reaffirm their solidarity by finding a new and more effective instrument than was formulated at Bandung and Belgrade. These earlier efforts had to be given up in part because of wide differences in approach among these countries and in part because of the permeation of great-power rivalries into the regions of the Third World. Since then there has been greater appreciation of the need to prevent the latter but there seems to be still little chance of evolving a full-fledged tri-continental association covering all African, Asian, and Latin American states as an instrument of world change. There is, however, a greater chance of moving along the following directions.

1. There is need for close consultations among the non-aligned countries in these continents for influencing world politics and the world economy—on a more systematic basis than has been the case until now. The Algiers conference symbolized an important step in this direction but it was no more than a beginning. The inequitous burden following the steep rise in oil prices by the Arab countries in their just struggle against Western dominance and exploitation, badly affecting a majority of the Third World countries, brought home to the leaders of the non-aligned world the need to do more than engage in mere rhetoric of solidarity. The fuel crisis has brought out fully the distortions in the world economy with the result that legitimate reversals of prior policies undertaken in one part of the Third World hurt other parts of that world more than they hurt any of the Western countries against whom those policies were presumably aimed. It has underlined the need to meet such situations by meaningful consultations among the former and by providing necessary correctives in keeping with norms of justice and fair play on the one hand and larger political considerations on the other. There is need for greater coherence in the Third World, a readiness to give up looking for short term advantages for individual states (in reality they have little to lose individually), and a step-by-step movement towards a conception of a collective interest with a view to designing a better world.

2. It follows that the socioeconomic aspect of solidarity among the Third World countries should be made durable and properly institutionalized, starting perhaps with the present (now expanding) "Group of Seventy-Seven" within UNCTAD, the main aim being not political

trade unionism but an exertion of economic pressure in international forums.[8]

3. There is need for a greater coordination of policies among the Third World states in the United Nations and various international agencies for influencing economic and social policies, fighting for human rights in the remaining vestiges of imperialism such as South Africa, Rhodesia, the Portuguese colonies, and Indochina, pressing for internationalization of new resources such as sea beds and outer space in which the great powers are seeking to extend their control, and mobilizing opinion for structural reforms of the United Nations and for adequate representation of the populous but poor continents of the world in United Nations bodies.

4. There is also need to press upon and mobilize international civil servants and technocrats for the objectives and values of the developing regions and turn them into silent but effective instruments of change.

REGIONALISM

Second, there is need for much greater regional cooperation among the various small and weak countries of the world, pooling their economic, political and military resources, entering the world power structure on that basis, and ultimately upsetting the system through which a handful of states are able to dominate the world. Such regional cooperation, on which many of the nationalist leaders in the Third World countries had pinned their faith at one time, has met with serious problems so far arising from the region based policies of the great powers, the mutual fears and conflicts of interest among states located in the different regions, and the fact that many of these countries have had stronger ties with imperial centres of the world than with others in the region. But the most

8. Success in this will depend on how far there is real content to this solidarity. There is an aspect of Third World reality that has so far, in the preoccupation with the dichotomy between "developed" and "developing" countries, received scant attention. This is the fact that the Third World itself is economically highly stratified, with considerable scope for the better-off in it assisting the worse-off in it and thereby consolidating their overall bargaining power with the metropolitan centres. That despite the immense wealth of the rulers of oil-rich countries the populations of those countries have remained backward is a major indictment of such rulers; that while the problem of how these rulers should dispose of their massive reserves of hard currency is being discussed in the financial centres of the world a large number of their own neighbours are still languishing in poverty is no less an indictment. Similar situations prevail in other parts of the world—in Latin America, in Southeast Asia, in parts of Africa. Inherent to the struggle of Third World countries with a world economic order based on exploitation is the need to deal with inequalities within each of these countries and between them.

important impediment to regional consolidation has been the successful penetration of the great powers in the various regions in the form of military alliances, economic aid, and political corruption. Gradually, an awareness is spreading among these states that their co-optation into big-power politics in this way has only turned them into client states, pitched them into a position of unnecessary rivalry against their own neighbours with whom they have so much in common, and exposed them to a state of perpetual tension with consequent neglect of real tasks at home. This awareness is likely to spread as the regimes propped up artificially by outside powers are brought down and new elites who are closer to the people and in tune with the culture of their lands come to power. These new elites are likely to value regional co-operation as a means of consolidating their individual independence and promoting the autonomy of the region.

There is need to galvanize such action through a series of institutional moves, starting with general political settlements providing for mutual consultation and affirming the need to resolve regional disputes regionally and without the need for big-power mediation, moving toward comprehensive trade and cultural agreements and, then, by stages, toward economic unions, loose political confederations in which certain functions such as communications, defence, and international trade are delegated to a centre, and finally moving toward a genuinely federal state incorporating the various regional units into a single juridical entity (that can still retain considerable internal dispersal of power).[9]

We have already outlined our model of a smaller number of larger states as a means of abridging the present wide gaps in power and resources and countering the prevailing patterns of dominance and inequality in the world. We are convinced that without such a territorial restructuring of the world, the ability of human collectivities to attain autonomy and dignity for themselves and their citizens will be limited to a few large states—if that.[10] The alternatives that face the large number of small states of the world are either to accept a neo-Hobbesian solution in which

9. It is possible to argue that such a step-by-step approach may in fact misfire, as the adjustment process will be more painful that way, and that it would be better to accept integration at one stroke. We find it difficult to accept this as a general proposition, especially in the light of some rather abortive (or stillborn) moves in the Middle East, but we can see that in some regions it may be necessary to skip some of the stages mentioned above. In any case what is suggested here are hypothetical stages. The actual sequence that takes place may be quite different and is likely to differ from case to case.

10. A state may have a dominant position in the world but it does not follow that individuals living in it enjoy autonomy and dignity. The very instruments of power that such a state wields may make its citizens less free. Even if it is a "democracy."

they surrender their autonomy to a great power—or a concert of great powers—who in turn will ensure security to all and provide resources for their development from a centralized system, or to attain self-reliance and autonomy on the basis of political associations of adequate strength on the one hand and participation in world politics on the basis of such consolidated power on the other.

If the choice is the latter—as far as the values of our preferred model goes, that must be the choice—these states should strive to their utmost to resolve internal differences and jealousies based on historical animosities that are no longer relevant and to move toward political integration that, while respecting cultural plurality, derives strength from the need to forge a sense of regional nationalism and common destiny. At the present time, only the stronger states in the world have shown initiative in forging such solidarities as found in the economic integration of Western European states and in the alliances represented by NATO and COMECON treaties that have over time become more than mere military arrangements. The need for such integration is much greater among the states of Southeast Asia, South Asia, Latin America, the Middle East, Eastern and Western Africa, and the West Indies if they are ever to acquire a sense of autonomy and undertake a concerted plan for the well-being of their peoples. Many of these regions include units with different levels of development and resource endowments thus providing scope for a pooling of complementarities in economic, technological, administrative, and other spheres and thus bringing an end to independence on the metropolitan centres of the world whose technological and institutional models are not really relevant for the poorer regions.

Although the various units differ in their levels of development (as indeed is the case with units within individual countries), most of these regions have a great deal in common—shared history and cultural traditions, trade routes and community relations that are often centuries old, frequently a common language and religion. There is a substantial potential for unity in many of these regions—in Latin America, in East and West Africa, in the Arab region, in South and Southeast Asia, in the Carribeans—which has been undermined by the imposition of artificial boundaries by the colonial powers. The regional model proposed by us should not be viewed as a mechanical development of a territorial type but rather as growth that is *sui generis*, based on a sense of common historical roots, common stake in the present, and common destiny in the future. It should be looked upon as a consequence of a political movement, not just of economic or administrative convenience. For without a felt need based in a consciousness that is *national* in the best tradition of that term, without determination of finding a way out of common bondage and humiliation, and without a strong sense of community of interest, the kind of steps towards territorial reconstruction proposed by us as a means of putting an end to the present structure of dominance will not be possible, or even if possible at one time will not be enduring.

These steps will not be easy to take in many of the world's regions. One main reason for this will be the fear that the larger and more cohesive units among these regions—India in South Asia, Indonesia in Southeast Asia, Egypt in the Middle East, Iran in the Persian Gulf, Brazil and Argentina in South America, Nigeria in West Africa, Tanzania in East Africa—will dominate the regional federations. It will be necessary to deal with this fear in two ways, first by showing that such dominance is easier to deal with than dominance by a big power that has global considerations and has little regard or sensitivity for local aspirations; second by arguing that the larger units will dominate more when the various entities are separate and divided than when they are part of an organic union; and third by admitting into the regional federations a considerable scope for internal decentralization and diversity in socio-economic and cultural policies. The point is that the alternative to this kind of an arrangement is a permanent state of economic and political dependence on remote centres of power that will become increasingly indifferent to the plight of the world's peripheries—indeed, cynical and contemptuous toward them. The model of territorial reconstruction that we have proposed, therefore, provides a crucial component of the overall model of a world order based on the values of autonomy, justice, and nonviolence.

WORLD INSTITUTIONS

The note that follows this chapter outlines the general rationale and a suggestive outline for such reconstruction. It will be seen that such region-based federations also provide a step towards the ultimate emergence of world federal institutions to which certain functions can be devolved by the constituent political units. We are not interested in moving towards a centralized world system of government, as we are convinced that it will result in a violation of our basic values. We do, however, visualize a further development of institutional structures beyond regional federations with the express objective of promoting justice and a fair distribution of resources, restraining powerful states and adventurist regimes from violating the freedom and rights of human beings, and ensuring the preservation of nature and its life-sustaining qualities against undue encroachment by human agencies. We have already, in Chapter I, indicated the categories under which such institutional development should take place. In this Chapter, which deals with strategies of moving towards the proposed model and not the model as such, we may consider how to build on existing structures and make them serve the ends we have in mind.

1. The present Economic and Social Council (ECOSOC) appears to us to provide a good nucleus for becoming the principal executive organ of the United Nations. Until the world territorial map is restructured into twenty or twenty-five states along the lines suggested by us, the present ECOSOC, which has approximately double that strength (54), may be treated as the authoritative organ for decision-making at the world level. It should continue to be an organ of the General Assembly but should function with considerable autonomy based on the simple fact that it is in the area of development that a truly global effort needs to be mounted. The ECOSOC should be entrusted with substantial resources for carrying out its functions of social and economic development and reduction of world disparities. Apart from receiving contributions from member states according to their respective GNPs, it should be entrusted with collecting taxes from users of international facilities such as merchant ships and civilian aircraft calling at foreign ports and airports as well as commercial satellites and space vehicles, expatriated profits of foreign business corporations and incomes of multinational corporations and royalties from new sources of wealth that are not under the domain of any state such as ocean beds and outer space. In regard to taking on new functions, the ECOSOC should plan and undertake economic enterprises of a multinational kind in the developing regions, subject to the agreement of the states concerned, counter monopolistic tendencies let loose by the multinational corporations in that way, and take on substantial roles in resource planning, development of new energy sources, migration and ecological policies, and food conservation for assisting scarcity ridden areas anywhere in the world, all of these being functions whose scope extends beyond existing states.

2. The General Assembly may continue to be the world body that represents national governments (as distinct from national legislatures or the people) and to which ECOSOC reports its decisions with the additional provision that any matter decided by a majority in both ECOSOC and the General Assembly should be considered obligatory for all other organs of the United Nations and for all member states.

3. As a step towards greater federalization of world political processes, a World Parliamentary Assembly may be constituted. Its main function should be to act as a forum for discussing various issues facing different regions as well as the world as a whole, articulating legitimate demands of different regional and cross-regional social groups, and generally promoting greater understanding of diverse points of view. Whereas the General Assembly consists of representatives of national governments, the Parliamentary Assembly should consist of representatives from various national legislatures (or their equivalents). While we do not stipulate proportional representation for sending delegates to the WPA,[11] a convention may be gradually promoted that each national delegation should include members belonging to opposition parties (or, in single-party states, other nongovernmental groups).

The Parliamentary Assembly can recommend measures to ECOSOC and the General Assembly for action. In the beginning, we do not envisage any decision-making role for this body, whose main function is to sensitize representative political groups from different regions to the problems and viewpoints of each other. We also do not stipulate that the General Assembly or any other executive organ of the United Nations should be held accountable to the Assembly. We do not think such a jump in institutional restructuring is yet called for. As the world territorial system gets restructured into larger units, as greater equality in power and political status is achieved, and as the present climate of fear and distrust gives place to greater confidence in world bodies, it should be possible to endow the Parliamentary Assembly with more powers. In the absence of these conditions, such a step is likely to prove abortive.

4. ECOSOC should be assisted by a number of agencies that can furnish requisite information, administration expertise, and specialized action. We propose the establishment of technical commissions for such subjects as interregional planning and economic development, human rights, world population and immigration, science and technology, and human environment and ecology. Each commission should be provided with an adequate staff and resources for undertaking studies, formulating targets, and recommending actions to ECOSOC and its subcommittees. Similarly, a World Food Bank should be set up to serve as a world buffer stock from where food can be rushed to drought ridden areas.

5. The various specialized agencies that are currently rendering considerable services should be continued and strengthened. Examples are ILO, PAO, ICAO, WHO, IMCO, ITU, UNESCO and UNDP. Regionally based commissions should also be strengthened and gradually their efforts coordinated with the efforts of various governments in regional cooperation and federalization. Similarly, the present institutional structure for dispensation of justice may be strengthened by the setting up of a high-powered World Court of Justice, which should have the power to intervene in cases of genocide and gross violation of human rights on the recommendation of a Council of World Jurists and the Commission

---

11. We do not wish to insist upon this for the simple reason that if it is made into a formal requirement it may become a tool in the hands of outside powers for interference in the domestic affairs of states.

on Human Rights, which should both be institutionalized as regular parts of the organization of justice at the world level.

6. In the area of minimizing interstate violence and containing the arms race, we suggest two steps. First, there should be at the disposal of the world body an armed force that should be small in size in normal times but expandable when serious violence breaks out by calling upon countries that have a proven record of peace and neutrality to contribute to it. Second, there should be set up a high-powered Commission on Disarmament to initiate and supervise negotiations between states on various aspects of disarmament. The function of this Commission, which should consist of outstanding scientists and international civil servants, cannot be anything more than that of a catalyst. For we do not believe that much progress in disarmament is possible as long as the big powers continue to "balance" each other and themselves together against the rest of the world. Indeed, the chances are that as long as wide gaps in political and strategic power exist, the arms race will continue; there will also be greater proliferation of nuclear armaments, the non-proliferation treaty notwithstanding. (India has already shown the way; its breaking of big power monopoly of nuclear technology was welcomed in large parts of the Third World.) On the other hand, once the world territorial order is restructured on the lines suggested in our model, considerable progress towards disarmament will be possible. Until then, one can only hope that the growing convergence of viewpoints between the two world giants will make for some progress towards arms restraint and that the emergence of new power centres and the possibility of further nuclear proliferation will force the two giants to come forward before world bodies with a satisfactory plan for disarmament.

7. The same argument holds for the Security Council, whose present composition defies the principle of equality between states to which the United Nation is committed. We do not believe any reform in its composition is possible—the most "revolutionary" of all states is now part of the system—until the effective distribution of power in the world changes. This will depend on the success of the federalization process envisaged in our territorial model, or of a workable alternative to it.

Disturbing the Status Quo

Indeed, even the prospects of the relatively modest and only "transitional" institutional arrangements proposed above will depend crucially on changes in the structure of world politics. The countries of the Third World—or, rather, those among them that value their autonomy—have to take the initiative in this regard. For it is up to them to unsettle the existing system of world power. It is not only compromising their integrity as states through a highly institutionalized system of political stratification; it is doing so essentially by relegating them to a position of marginality in the technoeconomy of the world; and this, in turn, is resulting in concentration of poverty and social tension in their lands and resulting in the political instability that goes with it.

The international *status quo* that is the source of such a linkage pattern extending into domestic political systems is once again, after a period of disturbance caused by the emergence of China, getting stabilized. The much-talked-of trend toward multipolarity is likely to turn out to be another co-opting and balancing operation, with the development of a complex system of limited adversity among pairs of big powers in the inner world and joint hegemony of the same powers over the rest of the world, and a single country (the United States) lording over the whole system thanks to its tremendous technological and economic superiority. For a quarter century now the United States has been the core of the international *status quo*. What it has been trying to achieve since 1971 is a rehabilitation of this core which had been successfully challenged by a series of encroachments—starting with the Soviet challenge in the fifties and continuing ever since with some dramatic setbacks in recent years thanks to Vietnam, Bangla Desh and the Arab resurgence. Behind the formula of the five power concert is a clever move to restore the hegemony of the United States. While the other four powers—the Soviet Union, China, Japan, Western Europe—understand this, they have at least for the time being decided to cooperate with the United States. The prospects for the rest of the world appear bleak if it continues to play proxy to this elaborate balancing game. It is only by cooperating among themselves to acquire sufficient strength that those in the outer world have any chance of challenging the dominance of the centre powers. That such an approach is necessary for both the political integrity of these states and the dignity and well-being of their peoples is obvious.

Let us make it clear that we have neither any illusion that the entire Third World can stand solidly against the present establishment of the world—it is too mixed a group with many conflicting interests and not a few among them who would rather hang on to one of the great powers—nor do we consider it necessary or desirable for the peace and sanity of the world to mount an all-out confrontation against anyone. What we have in mind is at once more modest and feasible and in the long run more effective for moving towards a world based on the principles of autonomy and equality of states. The need is, on the one hand, for several small and medium-sized states located in the same region to close their ranks and create integrated political and economic structures and policies and, on the other hand, for them to evolve institutionalized means of consultation and cooperation across regions, in world bodies, and in international agencies dealing with economic and social matters. It is within this latter, tricontinental, framework of the need for co-operation among the myriad nations of the "outer" world, relying as far as possible on their own strength and mutual complementarities[12], that regional consolidations and acquisition of self-reliance on that basis become meaningful. At the same time it is also clear that without the latter type of consolidation and self-reliance the more comprehensive framework of cooperation will become difficult to evolve: small and atomized states, each riven by internal problems, will find it difficult to assert themselves in world bodies in any unified manner.

ROLE OF CHINA AND THE SOVIET UNION

In working out such a strategy, those in the outer world who care to assert their autonomy and keep big-power politics from intruding in their regions will also find that the "inner" world is not that homogeneous an entity and that there are enough conflicts of interest and ideology in that world to work on. It should be remembered that in the disturbance of the bipolar structure China played a crucial role. Even if China has for the moment agreed to act in concert with other big powers, it will still be possible—given its own past and its assessment of the future—to turn it into a crucial link between the inner and the outer worlds and to make the balance in the former a precarious one. With all its recent tactical compromises, China (which has been closely associated for long with the nonaligned world) is "different", and it is not too much to hope

---

12. We do not believe in the maxim that there is little to co-operate among "paupers" (the so-called "beggars can't be choosers"). For even economically the countries of the Third World are not all that vulnerable. And the situation is fast changing in their favour. Some of the most important resources of the world are to be found in these countries—industrial raw materials, energy sources and metals. The so-called oil crisis has dramatized this fact. But even in respect of other primary commodities—jute, copper, zinc, iron ore—it is the industrial countries that are dependent on the nonindustrial countries, not the other way round. Now, with overall shortage of fuel, and cost of producing synthetics going up steeply, the terms of trade can be reversed in a big way and the producing countries can use this as a major political lever. Similarly, the fact that some major breakthroughs in technology (electronics, pharmaceuticals, industrial chemicals, diffusion technology) are labour intensive and the fact that labour costs in the industrialized countries are rising steeply give to the highly populated and poor regions of the world a major opportunity—if they know how to use it. With all this a more rational system of international economic relationships can be worked out and the hitherto exploiting parties made to see that they cannot any longer cash on structural inequalities in the world.

that it will see virtue in continuing to be so.[13]   The Soviet Union also, still working on the strategy of making bipolarity (which is not yet dead, at least in the sphere of military and strategic relationships) more advantageous to itself than to the United States and deeply fearful as it is of the future Chinese colossus, can be counted upon to provide entry points for disturbing the balance of the inner world.

In some respects the Soviet Union is even more available to Third World regions seeking autonomy from Western domination than is China,[14] in part because it is still wedded to an anti-imperialist position in world politics (so is China but it has had to make a number of tactical compromises because of its deep suspicion of the Soviet Union), and in part because the Soviet Union knows that its standing in the major regions of the world depends more on political than on economic linkages. Its role in the European *détente* and its approach to the South Asian and Middle Eastern crises have established it as a highly flexible actor in world politics which is willing to subject the big power system to pressures from other centres of power, while still continuing to play a major role in that system. It is necessary to realize that the presence of the Soviet Union and its successful ascendancy in world politics have greatly facilitated the movements for national autonomy in large parts of the world.   Unlike the hostile attitude of the Western powers, the Soviet approach to these movements has been consistently friendly. Despite its accommodation with the bipolar nexus and later the five power formula at the world level and despite its overall commitment to the stratification of the world as enshrined in the United Nations and its Security Council, the Soviet Union has on the whole gone along with the principle of equality of states and the growth of a multi-centred world.   Taking a long look, it seems that the two major turning points of the twentieth century are the October revolution after the First World War and the liberation of ex-colonial countries after the Second World War.   The two have converged to produce a world wholly different from the nineteenth century. The role of the Soviet Union in bringing about this massive shift in world politics has been very great indeed.   It is most unfortunate, of course, that in

13. Personally, I think it was a great tragedy that the earlier attempt towards building Third World solidarity (then expressed in terms of Afro-Asia) proved abortive and that China and India, on whose cooperation the whole enterprise depended, could not work together towards a common goal and against a common adversary, namely the world power structure dominated by the industrialized giants on the North. The result has been a continued domination by the latter powers, which have lost no opportunity of exploiting differences within the Third World countries. A cooperative relationship between China and India was crucial to meet this threat.
14. The Chinese emergence as a centre of power was itself facilitated by the presence of the Soviet Union and its powerful position in the post-1945 world (unlike the far more hostile situation faced by the Soviet Union itself after 1917).

playing this role it has found it necessary to suppress the autonomy of countries in its own orbit and subject some of its own finest scientists and intellectuals to inhuman treatment.

There are other important points in the industrialized world from which considerable cooperation and understanding can be expected —Yugoslavia, which is the only European country that has for long identified itself with the nonaligned world; Sweden, which has shown a remarkable record of cooperation with the developing nations; Norway, which had the courage to decline membership in the EEC; Australia, whose location and recent capacity to think for itself instead of continuing to be an outpost of the Anglo-Saxon world has made it revise its policies towards Asia; Canada, which is itself going through a deep sense of being dominated by its giant neighbour and is, on the other hand, beginning to play an important role in the Commonwealth;[15] even France which itself symbolized, under Charles de Gaulle, the search for autonomy within the Atlantic world (just as Yugoslavia did within Eastern Europe) and which is willing to support similar aspirations in other parts of the world. It would be shortsighted to lump the whole of the developed world as if it belonged to one camp.

NEW POWERS

Finally, new powers are emerging that by the end of the century will be quite strong and whose very emergence is based on asserting their autonomy and bringing to an end big-power intrusion in their regions. The most important among these is India, but there are others on the horizon—Indochina, which may well become a single state, Indonesia, Argentina, Iran, Nigeria, perhaps a more united Arab community. But Japan also, as it asserts its independence vis-a-vis the United States and provided it uses its economic might with imagination (this might is not based on very stable foundations), can provide a suitable link with the inner world, at least for the Asian nations. The issue in

15. We have, in this essay, argued at length in favour of regional territorial associations. However, there is also scope for a number of associations of noncontiguous member states. The Commonwealth of Nations, composed of those among former British colonies and dependencies (except a few) who decided to continue as an informal forum of opinion, is a case in point. The Commonwealth is interesting as an association in at least three respects: it brings together countries from Asia and Africa as well as from other areas; it has increasingly been used as a point of pressure against—and not by—the United Kingdom and its allies in South Africa and Southern Rhodesia and in Europe; and it includes countries such as Canada and Australia, which, for their own reasons, may be willing to work with Third World countries without compromising their autonomy.

the case of countries like India and the Arab countries on the one hand and Japan and China on the other is the choice they will make: between being tempted to join the big-power club and underwrite the *status quo* and becoming catalysts of major structural changes in world politics; between political opportunism and an enlightened use of political opportunity. (The offer made by the Indian Prime Minister to share India's know-how in the application of nuclear technology with its neighbours and other friendly countries conveys the latter kind of spirit.) Much will depend on what is done in the next decade or so through economic cooperation and political consolidation in different regions and simultaneous consultations of a tricontinental type designed to reconstruct the political structure of the world.

To a significant degree, the answer to these questions will depend on the ability of the Third World countries to attend to their internal problems, to move rapidly toward economic policies that will raise levels of satisfaction, to develop durable political structures that can integrate the many fragments of language, tribe, and religion in which their populations are divided, and to contain turbulent elements by evolving appropriate structures of participation. There is a close linkage between success on these fronts internally and success in achieving autonomy externally.[16] In making this linkage work, the leaders and intellectuals of these countries will have to think for themselves and evolve solutions that will work in their situations, which are quite different from those faced by the industrialized countries when they were developing. We have, in this essay, developed at some length an alternative model that can provide a basis for these solutions.

EVER WIDENING CIRCLES

Common to our consideration of the steps needed in meeting an

---

16. This fact is of particular relevance to Latin America. The concept of *dependencia* in explaining the present plight of the developing countries has been a major contribution of Latin American intellectuals. Though such an analysis is more pertinent to the Latin American situation than elsewhere, it is becoming increasingly relevant to other regions of the Third World as well. But it is necessary not to overstretch this perspective. There is a serious danger of its being used as a total explanation of all one s ills, and made into an alibi for inaction. Such an attitude is widely prevalent among Third World intellectuals who are prone to pass the responsibility for improving things to the metropolitan centres, and do nothing themselves. In a deep sense this is a survival of the colonial psychology. For the fact of the matter is that "they" can do little for improving the lot of the people in the Third World. The issue of autonomy cannot be resolved that way. It calls for positive self-assertion, internal improvements in these countries based on fresh thinking, integration between similarly placed countries, and only on the basis of all this, struggle with external sources of dominance and exploitation.

unprecedented social situation that the human race faces and the equally unprecedented concentration of technological and military power in the world is the need to provide man with the necessary means to realize his autonomy and dignity in the framework of states that are able to embody the same values. (Whether the world as a whole will embody these values or not is something that, at the present stage, is hard to predict. We have argued in this book that this will depend very much on what happnes inside and between the existing states.) Our end is to create not a highly structured and determined world in which everyone is provided for but few are really free but, rather, one in which minimal structures are built with care and consideration with a view to enable human beings to work out their own destinies—and the destinies of the collectivities with which they identify according to their heritage and their wisdom. It is our assumption that, over time, the definition of these collectivities will change toward wider and wider circles (to use Gandhi's architectonic phrase). But this will not happen by merely jumping the intermediate circles that, according to our analysis, are vital for a world organized around the twin principles of autonomy and integration.

Such a utopia—modest though it may appear—will not come about by sheer expansion of knowledge and intelligence; there is nothing certain in the historical process except what men make of it. That, at any rate, is our conception of *politics:* active intervention in the flow of time. Even if the end is (as it was with Marx and Gandhi) to allow each man the freedom to pursue what he deems proper without encumbrance of a state or of politics (a conception that we find to be unrealistic in the light of what we know about the human predicament), the fact remains that while most men may not be interested in politics, it is those who are interested in it that shape the world. This makes it incumbent upon the thinking and sensitive strata of the world to actively define goals and the means to achieve them, and to ensure that the professional politicians do not lose sight of the true ends of politics. It is for such men, in active association with the political leaders of the world, to take the necessary first steps in the direction of their preferred world. This will require not merely vision and imagination but also patience, sound judgment, and an ability to steer through the maze of institutional inertia, human frailties and, above all, the unexpected consequences of their own actions. There is no short cut to a good life. But a good life is possible even in this elusive world.

Notes

A For a theoretical discussion of the relationship between the economist's concept of effective demand and our concept of need effectiveness, see Chapter III.

B We have already discussed at some length the various theoretical dimensions of the problem of education and its relationship with other policy areas in Chapter III. Here we confine ourselves to certain policy measures arising from that analysis.

C A leading example of the former is Rene Guenon, *The Crisis of the Modern World,* London, Luzac, 1962 and *Reign of Quantity and The Signs of the Times,* London, Luzac, 1953 (written by the author in French, in this order). The latter position is well represented in Jacques Maritain, *The Range of Reason,* New York, Scribner's, 1942. As we have argued in Chapter II, while we find it difficult to accept certain postulates of the modernist worldview as developed in the West and while we do want to capture certain attitudes and values of enduring value from the East and even from religious teaching, we cannot accept any of these philosophies as providing relevant guidelines for contemporary man who must move beyond both the traditional East and the modern West.

D Although Marx and Engels used this phrase in *The Communist Manifesto* for the struggle to be waged by the working classes of the world, both they and later Lenin put the responsibility of this initiating struggle on the intelligentsia.

APPENDIX

Further Notes on the Regional Model

The purpose of this book is somewhat comprehensive: designing a future world based on certain preferred values and suggesting ways of implementing such a design. These notes are concerned with a consideration of a more limited question that follows from *one* of the proposals made in the book, namely, a territorial restructuring of existing nation-states with a view to combining the values of autonomy and self-respect of individual states with the values of justice among men and nonviolence within and between states. The following questions are relevant:

1. What institutional model should be adopted to bring about a functioning federation at various levels of world reality? What should be the nature of its territorial organization?
2. How and on what basis should such a process of territorial reorganization be initiated?
3. How many and of what size should the constituent units of the world association of nations be?

Steps towards Federation

Because autonomy and diversity are the fundamental values we want to preserve in any design for the future, it seems inescapable that a world political structure composed of autonomous nation-states is accepted not only as a reality that cannot simply be wished away but as a *preferred* reality that should be made more real than is the case in today's world of super, intermediate and marginal states. At the same time there is need to admit that both the size and nature of political and economic problems facing these states and the vast technological changes and demographic problems that will overtake the world in the next few decades call for institutional arrangements that go beyond the nation-state, at any rate for certain kinds of functions. There are three aspects of the present political reality of the world. First, with differing degrees of intensity and historical memory, the states of today have developed a set of identities—political, cultural, economic—among their people. Second, faced by the political situation of a world dominated by a handful of powers there is slowly emerging a sociopolitical milieu in which a large number of regionally identified communities, while strongly attached to their own individual lands and cultures, are also developing different kinds of interlinkage with one another. There are also strong economic reasons for this. Third, through a still very slow process of multifarious interactions in diverse spheres, these different states are becoming conscious of a larger world community within which, in their individual as well as collective interests, they want to see some operative machinery of maintaining peace and order and achieving justice and development. (That the desire for some sort of effective world organization exists is quite clear from the existence and proliferation over the last twenty-five years of the United Nations and its agencies, the wide hopes that were at one time pinned in the U.N. by ex-colonial states seeking to redress their individual weaknesses in economic and military spheres and their continuing faith in it despite great frustration in its functioning, and the aspiration on the part of even such "revolutionary" states as the People's Republic of China to obtain a seat in it.) Overall, there exists a strong desire to protect national autonomy, an emerging sense of regional identity, and a slowly developing desire for a meaningful world organization for the preservation of peace and the expediting of the development process. It appears that some kind of federal or confederal situation already obtains at the psychological level, because the essence of a federal situation is the existence of the sentiment for local autonomy alongside an urge for overall unity.

That the evolving world political pattern lends itself to some sort of a vertical multifederal situation appears to be the case if one looks at the secular trend in the development of both international cooperation and international conflict. As to the former development the movement from the League of Nations to the United Nations and its various constituent and affiliated agencies dealing with a wide range of activities is a portent of far more extensive international effort at consultation, lobbying, and crystallization of competing interests. That this has so far been mainly limited to the problems of socioeconomic development and racial discrimination is, of course, true. At the political level, barring a few small events, the United Nations has been a miserable failure; indeed, it has only reflected and at times reinforced prevailing patterns of dominance and discrimination. This has led to a growing realization of the need to develop concerted group efforts if the United Nations is to become an effective vehicle of a world order based on the principles it is committed to.

A similar trend in thinking informs the area of settlement of inter-state conflicts. The prevailing pattern of conflicts and their pacification has taken the form of exacerbating regional tensions that are often manu-factured at the instance of one or more of the big powers. More recently, awareness is growing among some of the affected countries that this pattern of conflicts and external intervention should be brought to an end and efforts made to establish regions of peace, and to stop playing the role of secondary or tertiary partners in great-power conflicts that was imposed on them during the period of the cold war. Meanwhile, political and technological developments have forced the big powers themselves to adapt their global strategies by recognizing in their scheme of thinking the new craving for autonomy among medium and small powers. Some of these powers have discovered that they too are "dependent" on the smaller states for some of their most basic needs.

Time, therefore, seems opportune for evolving an effective strategy of world organization that makes it possible to move from a system based on fear and manipulation on all sides to one based on the recognition of political autonomy of constituent units, and hence to a relaxation of fear and tensions. Such a world system and its organizational structure will have the makings of a genuine federation the constituent units of which are not sovereign but autonomous. What should be the nature of the territorial organization of such a future world order? What should be its different tiers of authority; what and how many should be its constituent territorial units?

At this point two fundamental features of federalism should be borne in mind. First, a federal system, as against a unitary one, has three tiers of authority—local, regional, and central. Second, federalism is a gradual development and seldom a sudden growth. The way to federalism has always been through a gradual rise of a sense of larger identity: from local units to the region and from the region to the more inclusive nation. In this progression the logical next step in a world order context would be from the nation to the region. For most of the existing units of the world, a single supreme federation of nations looks too distant, too impersonal, and devoid of any great meaning. Therefore, it seems necessary that in order that what is called the world becomes a more organized system and a functioning whole. some mechanism for developing larger yet not-too-distant identities among the existing nation-states is evolved. While we reject the concept of a centralized world authority—even in the distant future—we do admit, indeed prefer, the evolution of such intermediate linkages through an upward-moving structure of federations, eventually extending to the world level.

The Middle Tier

For taking the necessary first steps towards such a system, it is necessary to first evolve a middle tier of world organization that should be fashioned in such a way that the national constituents of each region are easily attracted to attach their loyalties to it. The choice of criteria for delimiting these world regions is, of course, far more difficult than in the case of nation-states. The reasons for this are obvious. At the level of the nation-state, diverse factors, such as history, tradition, language, culture, and economic interdependence, appear relevant and helpful. Even at this level it has not always been easy, as we know from the experience of the changing political and ethnic geography of Africa. When one thinks of world regions, on whatever basis they are defined, one has necessarily to start with states and nations of not necessarily complementary cultural and historical traditions. More often than not, these differences and antagonisms have been the source of their independent nationhoods, for example after a larger state was divided after a civil war. In thinking of regional consolidations as a way of mitigating present states of dependence and inequality in the world, one has to always keep in mind these hard realities, as it will help in clarifying concepts or propositions. Thus it would seem that any talk of cultural regions would not take us very far given the fact that outside Europe (and even there wide differences in legal, political, and social systems prevail) the growth of homogenoeus cultural regions will have to *depend on, rather than be a cause of*, political choices in the direction of regional associations. It is true, as we have already argued in Chapter V, that many of these regions are characterized by long historical bonds and common roots. But overlaid on these bonds are many divisions caused by internecine warfare before the colonial period and the boundaries imposed during that period. Rediscovery of common cultural roots is thus to be seen *as part of a new political process* based on a striving for autonomy, and not as something that is just available. Similarly, the political geographers' age-old preoccupation with carving out geostrategic and geopolitical regions based largely on military and strategic characteristics that are supposed to give rise to single feature regions is also irrelevant for our purpose because we are not planning for a division of the world for military or strategic ends.

For any programme of regionalization to succeed, then, it needs to be grounded in the most salient pattern of linkages that can be evolved within the contemporary structure of nation-state reality, on the assumption that political and economic interests spread beyond the juridical boundaries of individual states. The emerging incongruence between closed national political space and economic and technological forces that operate across political boundaries provides the basis of this linkage pattern. In the words of a noted geographer, "A new iconography, based upon wider concepts of regionality and internationalism, is in many ways as strong as national iconography and tends to neutralize the barriers which the latter produces" [A]. Of course, it is only as the new iconography gets rooted in either already existing or new structures of loyalty or awareness of interdependence that a firm basis for durable multicore regions will be laid.

Economic Integration

Historical experience of federations suggests that in situations where long traditions of united political existence are absent or where cultural, historical, and social factors are not particularly strong forces for unity, a sound base for initiating a fruitful relationship can often be found in economic interdependence. This holds particularly well in situations in which external threat is not a factor of great and continuing importance. The Pakistani example amply demonstrates that superficial external threat or a temporary sense of unity born from cultural factors, such as allegiance to a common religious faith, does not provide a durable factor for national cohesion. (The Nigerian example provides the opposite case of a strong sense of nationhood cutting across deeply felt but transient ethnic identities.) The essence of a durable federal relationship is that the constituents of the union should find themselves better within than without the union. For this it is necessary that the federation should help the constituent units to better realize their economic and other interests, which they are not able to do in isolation. The case of Jamaica vis-a-vis the West Indies Federation also illustrates this point.

A review of the history of interstate organizations would be interesting in this regard. There have been diverse types of groupings, some largely military and strategic (NATO, SEATO, CENTO, ANZUS, Warsaw Pact), some culturally and politically oriented (OAS, COMECON, the Andean Pact, Arab League, OAU), some based on historical association (the Commonwealth), and some based primarily on a perception of common economic interests (European Economic Community, EFTA, IAFTA, the East African Common Services Organization, the so-called Entente in West Africa). A comparative view of the diverse military-strategic pacts on the one hand and the economic unions on the other makes rewarding study. Despite all the pomp and show and the huge funds that have been spent, the military pacts have served the interests of a predominant power and have never progressed beyond the stage of loose alliances. This is apparent from the attitudes of France in NATO and of Pakistan in SEATO. In sharp contrast stands the example of Benelux. It began as a small economic union of two tiny states (Belgium and Luxemburg), with Netherlands coming into the fold a little later, but soon developed into a considerable economic force in Western Europe. Building on the success of the Benelux experiment the movement for a much larger union was initiated and resulted in the present-day EEC.

A number of suggestions have been made for the creation of similar regional economic unions elsewhere. Some have already made a start while others have had to contend with inhibiting factors mentioned above. The case of India and Pakistan is a glaring example of how historic animosities and great-power politics have inhibited the development of regional cooperation. It should be possible now to overcome these factors and develop much closer cooperation, though it would be difficult and, according to us, undesirable to seek to annul the partition of the subcontinent. The whole of the subcontinent had developed for a long period as a single economic system. Today also, judging from the present stage of their agro-industrial development and communications network, the states comprising the South Asian region provide a ripe case for a regional economic community: not just Bangla Desh, India, Nepal, Bhutan, and Sikkim, which have economic relations—though still only bilaterally with India—but also Pakistan, Afghanistan, Ceylon, and the Maldives (and perhaps also including rice-surplus Burma).

Similarly, a common market arrangement in the South Pacific may prove of great advantage to the islands as well as to New Zealand and Australia, both of which are at present faced with difficult economic prospects as a result of the British entry into the EEC. In Southeast Asia there is already a case for a common market arrangement between Malaysia, Singapore, the Philippines, Indonesia, and perhaps Thailand, and some moves have already been initiated in this direction by the formation of the Association of South East Asian Nations (ASEAN). The emergence of a single Indochinese nation-state is also now within the range of the possible. And it is not difficult to conceive that in the course of time all these subregional arrangements will come together into a single Southern Asian community. (It would be best for Australia and New Zealand to give up the concept of being a separate continent.)

As for the other great land masses, the prospects for a regional economic union of some kind between Brazil and the Plate River region (Argentina, Uruguay, and Paraguay) also seem bright. In Africa encouraging signs are present—despite recent setbacks—in the East African Common Services Organization and the French West African Entente with which perhaps the former British West African territories could be associated with advantage. Similarly, the Central African Federation as it then existed was, no doubt, a political monstrosity, but there perhaps always was a case for some kind of a limited economic union in the area.

It will be such unions, starting primarily through a recognition of mutual interests (and only indirectly through a larger sense of belonging) that will provide the requisite start for the rise of regionally based federations. If we employ the triad used by Kenneth Boulding to describe the organizing principles of all social systems, the task that the world political system faces is to move from operating on the basis of *threats* to operating on the basis of *exchange,* so that ultimately a structure of *integration* comes into being. At present, attention has been mainly given to the first and the third principles (the war machine on the one hand and world organization on the other), though the world invests enormously more in the organization of threats (approximately $200 billion a year, which is roughly equivalent to the total income of the poorer half of the world's population) than in the integration system (less than $500 million). It will be by investing around the second principle, namely, exchange, that a complex series of mutually antagonistic relationships will be subjected to preceptions of complimentarities in various settings, in the process both reducing the role of threats and gradually moving towards the principle of integration. Mere moralistic appeal based on humanitarian motivations for one world will not succeed in taking the world any closer to it, largely because such an appeal fails to base itself on a realistic perception of mutual give-and-take among actors. Hence the crucial importance of regional economic cooperation in the general progress of the federal political process.

Political Compulsions

Once the problem is conceived in this manner, it will be seen that the idea of regional economic cooperation is not merely an economic idea; it has far-reaching political implications as well. This is especially the case with the economically and politically weaker regions of the world as compared, for instance, to the EEC countries. The latter are at a stage when they can sharply differentiate between promoting economic association and preserving separate political existence over a long period of time; the former must of necessity move from one form of association to another in a rather short span of time, and cultivate the will and the self-confidence to begin the process.

Indeed, the political factor underlying regionalism must enter into the exchange relationship underlying regional economic cooperation. This is not simply because the economic problem dominates and will increasingly dominate the future of political relationships among states. It is also because, for the large number of small states in the poor regions of the world, the reality of external domination and threat and the strategy necessary to counter them are at once economic and political. If these states wish to preserve their independence and dignity vis-a-vis the larger powers, their principal instrument will have to be regional cooperation—economic to begin with and political soon after.

The enormous gap between rich and poor nations that everyone talks about is not just economic; it is compounded by being at the same time a gap in size and resources and is still more compounded by being a gap in *power*—technological, military, political, and strategic. The need for regional consolidation is real not so much for the world as a whole but for the two-thirds of it that is poor and divided. The other one-third is well organized and can any time mobilize both economically and politically, despite power conflicts and historical antagonisms. It is for the Third World countries—the vast periphery of the human race—that a region-based process of cooperation and integration is necessary if they are to survive as states and preserve their integrity and as a means thereto become economically self-reliant. For them, economic and political factors are closely intertwined.

Size and Numbers

There remains the question of size and number of regional units. The point can hardly be disputed that the number of political units constituting the world should neither be too large (as the present-day 170) nor too small (as the 5 or 6 continental units proposed in some quarters). A study of experiments with federalism even within the nation-state framework shows that if the constituent units are too small in number, an element of built-in instability is introduced because this provides scope for both direct conflict among one or two powerful rivals and their domination over the rest; in other words, the classic situation of unstable balance of power would evolve [B]. The point is best illustrated by the example of Nigeria before the Civil War, when the federal structure with a three-way territorial dispersal of political authority permitted and indeed encouraged two regions to combine and pit themselves against the third in the struggle for power. The strain on the federal relationship in Nigeria was further aggravated because of the numerical preponderance and hence political domination of one of the units (the North). On the other hand, Pakistan broke up because of both its inability to forge a genuine federal union and the fact of its two major constituents being too evenly balanced.

So far federalism (at the level of nation-states) has never been faced with the problem of too large a number of constituent units. In the United States, where this number is the largest, hardly any problem has arisen on this account. But it is not difficult for anyone with some idea of the functioning of federalism to anticipate the difficulties that would arise if the number of constituent units were to run into the hundreds, more so if the units were to remain as disparate in effective size and power potential as the members of the United Nations at present are. The existence of a large number of small units alongside four or five very large units in today's world system has already miiitated against the realization of the values of autonomy, justice and nonviolence. Any further increase in numbers—and there is little chance of the present "giants" breaking up—will only worsen the situation.[1]

Though we reject the model of a large number of units of very uneven size, we wish to make it clear that we do not think that the constituent "regions" can or even should be of uniform size or potential. Territorial size is often an irrelevant factor because size by itself means little. Population and productive potential undoubtedly are relevant, but they are factors on the basis of which it may be almost impossible to carve out any meaningful functioning regions. Productive potential is often so complex in nature that it cannot easily be quantified. The difficulty springs mainly from the fact that the resource potential of different areas of the settled world and the technologies they will adopt are yet not adequately known quantities while production possibilities vitally depend on these factors. Similarly, though population is a very important factor, it is impossible to make it the sole (or even the main) criterion in the delimitation of politicoeconomic regions. Because the distribution of population density in the inhabited part of the planet is so uneven, no comparable regions can be evolved on this basis alone.

It seems to us that there are two main criteria for moving along the process of regionalization. The first is complementarity of resources and economies so that there can be a continuous give-and-take among the different components of each region, in course of time producing an integrated economy and also having considerable spillover effects. Second, whatever type of region is carved out, it must consist of geographically contiguous areas. Contiguity, whether over land or by sea, helps to bind areas into regions—in spite of obvious points of tension and conflict. Despite all the technological advances in transportation and

1. Another intermediate position that may be argued is for a 10- to 12-state system instead of the 20 to 25 we have suggested (e.g., the United States, Brazil, the Andean countries, EEC, USSR, the Arab World, Sub-Saharan Africa, South Asia, Southeast Asia, Japan, and China). We cannot agree to this for two reasons. One is that just on the basis of facts of political geography this scheme leaves out a number of countries, and when these are brought in the number will shoot up to more than 20 without having the balanced strength of our proposal. The other is that a world of 10 to 12 regions will produce only a slightly extended "balance of power" structure, will call for a much bigger sacrifice of national autonomy than is involved in the 20 to 25 proposal, and will not permit flexibility in the relationships *within* the regions.

communication, proximity continues to be of fundamental importance in the process of political and economic cohesion.

While each of these different factors—population, productive potential, complementarity of economies and resources, and physical proximity—should be taken care of, it is also essential that the region that is proposed constitutes, at least potentially, what may be called a natural political region that in course of time can act as a single autonomous politico-economic entity. It should, in other words, have the potentiality of becoming a new national (or nation-like) configuration.

Some Other Issues

This brings us to the age-old question of the role of cultural, religious, and ethnic factors in forging regional federations. The cultural-ethnic factors have both a *positive* value in promoting the rise of a regional entity, and a *negative* value, sometimes of potentially explosive character, in inhibiting such a development. Wherever possible, these factors should be harnessed in such a way that the chances of these conflicts are minimized. For example, even if all considerations of economic and locational factors were to call for including Israel in the same region as the Arab states, cultural considerations alone will for a long time to come forbid this arrangement. (Perhaps this situation will change with the rise of new generations of leadership and with the decline in interference by the big powers. We hope it does.) Similarly, care should be taken not to indiscriminately lump together former subject and colonial nations; historical memories may still persist and, consciously or otherwise, vitiate the relationship from acquiring confidence and trust. Wherever this type of multinational region becomes a feasible proposition, some statutory precautions on the lines of the Swiss practice of dividing single cantons into two or three autonomous subunits could be adopted at a stage when economic unions begin to assume a political character. Such a device may well be necessary if after detailed investigation and negotiation it is found useful to join the South Pacific islands along with Australia and New Zealand into a single politico-economic region.

One final issue remains. If the Third World countries are to take a lead in initiating the process of regional consolidation and on that basis acquiring a status of greater equality vis-a-vis the countries in the rest of the world, it will be necessary that the factors making for inequality *within* the Third World are somehow contained. The world is not simply divided between large, rich, and powerful countries on the one hand and small, poor, and powerless countries on the other. There is the very crucial middle stratum too—of states intermediate in size, economic development, and political-military power. A number of these intermediate states are located in the Third World. One thing that has inhibited the process of regionalization in the Third World is precisely the fear of the larger neighbours in the eyes of the smaller neighbours, a fact that has been cleverly utilized by outside powers until now [C]. It seems that for the regional movement to make any progress, much would depend on the stance adopted by the intermediate powers: will they go all along with their smaller neighbours in a genuine regional partnership, involving necessary costs in the transitional period as part of the attempt to change the structure of regional and world politics, or will they exploit their superior status in their region and *thus* gain an entry into the world power establishment? We have already discussed the role of China in this connection in our chapter on strategy. But the answer to the question posed here will also depend upon how India, Japan, Indonesia, Brazil, Argentina, Mexico, Yugoslavia, Iran, Algeria, Egypt, and Nigeria behave in the coming decades in the context of the emerging structure of world politics.

A Tentative Proposal

The exact delimitation of possible regional federations will require a detailed inventory of resources, economies, communications, social structures, and political attitudes that was clearly not possible to undertake for this limited exercise. Nonetheless, we offer below a very rough and tentative sketch that appeals to the eye as one looks at the world map in the light of our model. The regions proposed are by no means comparable on any single criterion or group of criteria. But they broadly satisfy the condition of having the chance to develop into viable economic communities whose functioning would in time give rise to regional identities and solidarities that may lead to some form of federal political arrangements. Care has also been taken to see that even though all the regions cannot be made comparable in power and status, there are nevertheless a sufficient number of large units of comparable size and status to prevent both the domination of the world by a handful of giants and the likelihood of direct conflict between two or more such giants.

ROUGH SKETCH OF POSSIBLE REGIONS OF THE WORLD

1. The Russian Region: U.S.S.R., Byelorussia, Ukraine, and Mongolia.
2. Northern Europe: Norway, Sweden, Finland, and Iceland.
3. East Central Europe: The German Democratic Republic, Poland, Czechoslovakia, Hungary, Rumania, and Bulgaria.
4. The Mediterranean Region: Yugoslavia, Albania, Greece, Turkey, Cyprus, Lebanon, and possibly Israel.

5. The EEC Region: The German Federal Republic, France, Belgium, Denmark, Netherlands, Luxemburg, Italy, Ireland, United Kingdom, and the very small but sovereign states of Malta, Andorra, Monaco, San Marino, Liechtenstein and Vatican City State, with the possible future membership of Switzerland and Austria, and still later of Spain and Portugal.

6. The Persian Gulf Region: Iran, Kuwait, Saudi Arabia, the two Yemens, Oman, and the Persian Gulf States including Bahrain, Qatar, and the Trucial States.

7. The Arab World: Iraq, Jordan, Syria, Egypt, Sudan, Libya, Tunisia, Algeria, and Morocco.

8. West Africa with possibly two subunits: (i) French-speaking West Africa: Liberia, Ivory Coast, Upper Volta, Mali, Guinea, and Guinea-Bissau (though the latter is Portuguese-speaking), Senegal, Mauritania, Togo, Dahomey, Niger, and Spanish Sahara (Spanish-speaking); (ii) English-speaking West Africa: Gambia, Sierra Leone, Ghana, and Nigeria.

9. East Africa: Uganda, Kenya, Tanzania, Rwanda, Burundi, and Mozambique, perhaps along with Ethiopia and Somalia.

10. Central Africa: Central African Republic, Cameroon, Gabon, Congo (Brazzaville), Zaire (Kinshasa), Zambia, Malawi, Angola, Chad, and Equatorial Guinea.

11. South Africa: Zimbabwe, Namibia, Bostwana, Lesotho, Swaziland, Malagasy Republic, Mauritius, and South Africa.

12. South Asia: India, Pakistan, Afghanistan, Sri Lanka, Bangla Desh, the Himalayan kingdoms of Nepal, Bhutan and Sikkim, and Maldive Islands.

13. Southeast Asia: Burma, Thailand, Malaysia, Singapore, Philippines, and Indonesia (including West Irian).

14. Indochina: Laos, North and South Vietnam, Khmer (Cambodia), and Brunei.

15. China including Taiwan, Tibet, Hong Kong, and Macao.

16. Northeast Asia: North and South Korea and Japan.

17. North America: Canada and Greenland.

18. United States of America.

19. Middle America: Mexico, Guatemala, Honduras, El Salvador, Nicaragua, Costa Rica, and Panama.

20. The Carribean Region: Cuba, Jamaica, Haiti, Dominican Republic, Puerto Rico, Barbados, Grenada, Trinidad and Tobago, Guyana, and the few "territories" and the many small island groups of the area of which only the Bahamas are fully independent.

21. Brazil.

22. Plate River Region: Argentina, Paraguay, and Uruguay.
23. The Andean South America: Venezuela, Colombia, Ecuador, Peru, Bolivia, and Chile, along with the three Guyanas.
24. South Pacific: Australia, New Zealand, Fiji, Tonga, Gilbert and Ellice Islands, New Caledonia, New Hebrides, Solomon Islands, Nauru, Papua New Guinea, and the many small islands in the region.

What is outlined above is highly tentative and speculative, given the present stage of our knowledge of the conditions in the various regions. We are aware that any such attempt at concretizing a proposal exposes one to controversy and even ridicule. For it can be said with good reason that some of the inclusions in one region or exclusions from another as proposed here may not work. The only reason why we have made bold to undertake such an exercise (instead of simply depicting broad regions) is to provide a heuristic basis for discussion and criticism. It is not intended as a blueprint in any way.[2] We are aware of the serious problems in moving toward such regional arrangements—political, psychological, historical. Thus, for Albania and Yugoslavia to cooperate within an otherwise non-Communist region will require important modifications in doctrinal positions; the inclusion of Greece, Turkey, and Cyprus in the same region will call for a mature approach to the future that transcends past animosities; the same with the inclusion of Israel along with Lebanon; the South Asian region will require careful handling, given the intractable problem of Hindu-Muslim amity and the bitter memory of the Bangla Desh episode in 1971 as well as the strained relationship between Afghanistan and Pakistan over the Pakhtoon issue; even the most logical union of East African states will have to face the changing fortunes of internal regimes within the constituent states. These are examples of the kinds of issues that will need to be candidly faced and resolved.

It may be stated that we do not envisage the restructuring of the entire world into regional units at one stroke, nor do we think that the precise organizational structure need be the same for the different regions; both of these would be unrealistic expectations. On the other hand, such a development cannot be left merely to the pressure of local factors; there

2. While care has been taken to include all existing states as well as some that are potential states, our listing leaves out a few small entities (islands, dependencies, etc.). Our assumption is that as the various regions configurate, these will be drawn toward them. We also do not wish to provide a total scheme. There should be enough room left for flexibility and negotiation. There should also be scope for some of the smaller entities (even islands) to continue unintegrated in larger regions if they so desire.

is need to think of such structures in general terms and to spread the idea as desirble for all. The development of several such regional groupings where the prospects for such arrangements are already good (for example South Asia, West Africa, the South Pacific, Southeast Asia, or one of the Latin American regions) may perhaps start off a chain sequence, and in the not-too-distant future bring about a quite differently structured world than is the case today.

Unity in Diversity

Finally, we may restate the point already made more than once in the book: such a change in political structure is only a part—and not the most important part—of our model for the future. It is itself seen as an instrument of the struggle for man's autonomy and dignity, the realization of which involves a number of other strategies outlined in the book. It is a basic tenet of our more complete model (of which the territorial model is only a part) that it should not be too complete, too structured, too institutionalized. To do so would be to violate the very values it is designed to serve. It is only with a view to provide greater freedom and autonomy to men, and hence to states, that we have found it necessary to advance the idea of territorial reconstruction. But it is conceived as no more than a preferred instrument for realising basic values.

Also, such territorial consolidation is not proposed on any assumption of benefits of largeness, though it may appear so. We have no grand design in mind, no overarching institutional utopia. As indicated by the institutional part of the model presented in the book, we want to provide considerable scope for diversity and decentralization within functioning polities (each of which we would prefer to be federal in form as well as spirit), a high degree of economic self-reliance at lower levels (as is involved in our conception of bridging the wide gaps that exist between centres of production and consumption), and indeed a measure of dispersed autarchy and self-sufficiency at various levels or, rather, along ever widening, never ascending circles, to quote again the words used by Gandhi in his famous model of world reconstruction.

It is this combination of on the one hand large federal structures able to fend for their autonomy and leading to a more equal distribution of political power in the world, and on the other hand considerable scope for individual and local self-reliance, that provides the key to our general model for the future. It is, to use an old phrase, the model of unity in diversity. Diversity, not unity, is our norm. The larger unities that we propose are needed to preserve the integrity and self-confidence of the diverse entities, not to engulf them. Hence our preference for 20 to 25 instead of 5 or 500 constituents of the future world order.

Notes

A S. B. Cohen, "The Contemporary Geo-Political Setting: A Proposal for Global Geo-Political Equilibrium", in C. A. Fisher (ed.), *Essays in Political Geography*, London, Methuen, 1968, pp. 61–72.

B R. D. Dikshit, *The Political Geography of Federalism: An Inquiry into Origins and Stability*, London and Delhi, Collier-Macmillan, forthcoming.

C We have dealt with this fear and shown why it should not prevent regionalization in Chapter V.

INDEX